σ|ω

The Which? Guide to Divorce

About the author

After qualifying as a solicitor, Helen Howard (formerly Garlick) specialised in family law and became the matrimonial partner of a central London practice. Now practising as a mediator and family lawyer in Oxford and London, she is also a visiting lecturer in Family Law at the Oxford Institute of Legal Practice. She teaches and writes about mediation and other family law issues, and speaks regularly about divorce issues on television and radio. She is the editor of *Family Law Practitioner*. Helen Howard is married, with two children.

Acknowledgements

The author and publishers would like to thank all those who have contributed towards this book over the years. For this new edition, thanks are due to Alastair Logan, chair of the British Association of Lawyer Mediators, for his help with revisions to Chapter 4, and Suzanne Kingston, a solicitor with wide experience on domestic violence issues, for guidance on Chapter 12. David Nichols wrote the chapter on Scotland and William Cross the chapter on Northern Ireland.

The Which? Guide to Divorce

Helen Howard

CONSUMERS' ASSOCIATION

Which? Books are commissioned and researched by
Consumers' Association and published by
Which? Ltd, 2 Marylebone Road, London NW1 4DF
Email address: books@which.net

Distributed by The Penguin Group:
Penguin Books Ltd, 27 Wrights Lane, London W8 5TZ

First edition August 1992
Second edition August 1994
Third edition January 1996
Fourth edition May 1997
Fifth edition July 1998

British Library Cataloguing in Publication Data
A catalogue record for this book is available from the British Library

ISBN 0 85202 720 6

For a full list of *Which?* books, please write to Which? Books, Castlemead,
Gascoyne Way, Hertford X, SG14 1LH or access our web site at
http://www.which.net

Cover and text design by Kyzen Creative Consultants

Photoset by Paston Press Ltd, Loddon, Norfolk
Printed and bound in Great Britain by Clays Ltd, Bungay, Suffolk

Contents

Introduction

At current estimates, two in every five marriages end in divorce. Experts argue over what factors are most likely to lead to marriage breakdown; second or subsequent marriages, marriages begun when both partners were very young, marriages under strain because of work demands and emotional unavailability and marriages involving people with particularly stressful jobs have all been identified as vulnerable. Whatever the individual experience leading a couple to contemplate divorce, everyone in this painful situation has to weather and overcome the legal, financial and practical processes involved.

The costs of divorce can be crippling. One factor that all separating or divorcing couples have in common is that they will have two households, not one, to maintain in future. *The Which? Guide to Divorce* focuses on helping couples to minimise the costs of the divorce process itself in order to free up as much money as possible for the family. This itself can reduce the stress of the situation, before, during and after the divorce. The guide establishes how to find a good lawyer – one who knows what he or she is talking about and who will adopt a conciliatory approach in legal proceedings, rather than getting too readily into the boxing ring of litigation and building up high costs. You will need to use your lawyer to your best advantage (not as an expensive emotional prop or a source of basic information, for example), and knowing how the system operates will put you in a better position to do this.

The law on divorce is in the throes of massive change and the issues surrounding divorce are probably more complex now than they ever have been before. The new Family Law Act 1996, if fully implemented in 1999 as expected, will change forever the landscape of divorce. In the new millennium, the way in which people experience divorce will be almost unrecognisable to anyone who went through the process in, say, the 1980s. Some developments – such as new law on domestic violence, the Child Support Acts, the 'earmarking' of pensions, the procedure for dealing with financial matters, and increases in court costs – have already come into effect. Other changes – pension-sharing (the new term for pension-splitting), divorce information meetings, establishing mediation and marriage counselling as part of the divorce process – are yet to come. This new edition of the guide has been updated to cover all the effects of the Act, including those yet to be implemented.

The Act is being phased in in parts – Part IV was introduced on 1 October 1997, sweeping away a host of old laws on domestic violence and introducing in their place a new all-encompassing law to cover domestic violence cases.

The key changes on divorce, marking a radical departure from what the media have described as 'quickie' divorce, are likely to be implemented at some time in 1999. Around 26 per cent of all divorces in 1995 were based on adultery and 44 per cent on unreasonable behaviour. Under the new law, the concept of whose fault it was that the marriage broke down will be side-stepped. Whilst the sole ground for divorce will remain the same – that the marriage has irretrievably broken down – the way that people will have to prove that their marriage has broken down is to show that they have lived separate and apart for a period of time: in other words, we will have time-based instead of fault-based divorce.

The most marked difference under the new law will be how long it takes to get a divorce. Under the current law, seven months is about average for ending a marriage, with many divorces being completed within three to four months. Working out financial matters can take much longer; indeed, these often remain unresolved long after the decree absolute. Under the new law, it will take at least 12 months to get a divorce (18 months where there are children under 16). That year (or 18 months) must be set aside for 'consideration and reflection' about the ending of the marriage and for working out and putting into place new arrangements for the family's finances and for the children: the courts will no longer finalise a divorce until these arrangements are in place. As people contemplating divorce realise how much longer it will take them to get out of their marriage under the new system, it is likely that there will be a rush to get divorces through under the old system. After implementation of this part of the Family Law Act, there will be a two-year transitional period during which a couple can choose whether to divorce under the old or the new law, but by the year 2001 or 2002 the new law is likely to apply to all new divorces.

Many of the most significant features of the Act – divorce information sessions, free marriage guidance (for those who are financially eligible for legal aid) and increased impetus towards mediation – are currently being tested in pilot schemes at a number of centres throughout England and Wales. The guide helps you assess whether mediation could help you and your spouse resolve your disputes. Mediation offers a potentially faster and more cost-effective route through the divorce process, avoiding costly and time-consuming litigation, and allows you to create tailor-made settlements according to your individual and family needs. Its family-oriented approach reduces conflict and improves communication, so is much better for the children too.

Further significant changes have occurred over pensions. For divorce petitions filed since July 1996, parties have been able to apply for an 'earmarking' order so that a spouse without any pension can get a court order giving her or him the right to a share of the spouse's pension on retirement. Earmarking orders still have their drawbacks: the ex-spouse will receive full benefits only if the pension scheme member survives until retirement, receiving the same or a higher salary than when married, stays in good health, and (ideally) does not remarry. How to value the pension has also proved problematic. But the chief drawbacks for many will be that a divorcing couple can no longer achieve a clean financial break from each other if a pension is earmarked, and the spouse who has a share of the pension earmarked for her (or him) will lose those rights on remarriage. Pension-sharing – where the concept is that the pension-holder's pension is divided up on divorce and the spouse gets a pension nest egg at that time to invest as she or he chooses – will probably be a much more popular option than earmarking, but political and technological problems are delaying its introduction.

People getting divorced in the late 1990s will find that the Child Support Agency, rather than the courts, will most likely be dealing with child support payments wherever there is a dispute. The Agency, set up with the laudable aim of improving the system of child maintenance, has failed to live up to its promise, largely because of the Byzantine complexity of the system. Since December 1996 a new 'departure system' has introduced a little flexibility into the formula to take account of payments which the Agency had to ignore before, such as debts built up while the family was together and child care costs. This is providing a very little relief, but until the Agency really improves its own poor record on delay and inaccuracy it will continue to be unpopular. In mid-1997 an independent audit showed that 85 per cent of its assessments were still inaccurate.

Changes brought into the system by the Children Act 1989 have by and large improved the way that children are treated when their parents divorce. Parents are now encouraged to make their own arrangements for their children following divorce or separation, rather than look to the courts to do this for them. Where conflicts do arise, simpler and more specific court orders can be sought in order to resolve them; moreover, couples do not have to wait until they start the divorce process before applying for a court order about their children. Grandparents can make court applications to see their grandchildren, and the new, more flexible system means that other family members, or even other interested parties, can seek the courts' remedies over children (there is a filtering process to make sure that this will really be in the children's interests). Most important, children's voices are better heard within the system, as it ensures that their wishes and feelings are taken into account where possible along with a range of other factors affecting their welfare.

On a point of terminology, although throughout the book the term 'he or she' is used when referring to a spouse, in certain chapters (e.g. those on money in divorce, and domestic violence) one or other gender is specifically referred to. This reflects what happens in the majority of cases: for example, it is rare for an ex-wife to pay maintenance to her ex-husband, so the pronoun 'he' is used to refer to the payer.

Throughout the book you will find the names of helpful organisations marked with an asterisk(*). Their contact details can be found in the address section at the back of this book.

Divorce is never easy – but this guide endeavours to help you through the maze. Good luck.

Chapter 1

The costs of divorce

> **LEGAL HEALTH WARNING**
> This could be the most important chapter of the book for you:
> please do not be tempted to skip it

Starting off a book about divorce with the issue of costs may seem a little odd, but for many people the problem of finding the money to pay for a divorce presents one of the biggest headaches of all. It is all too easy to 'forget' about the question of costs until your divorce and financial problems are resolved, but then the total sum of legal costs that has built up can come as an unexpected shock and can severely limit your and your spouse's ability to adapt to your future lives apart. This chapter throws light on the complex issue of costs and looks at what steps you can take to keep them low – a constant theme throughout the book.

The issue of costs can create particularly severe problems in a divorce in which one party is determined to mount an expensive legal campaign against the other. Whenever there is a legally fought dispute over the children, or over spousal maintenance or property, both sides will generally have to instruct solicitors (and perhaps barristers too). There will therefore be two bills to pay at the end of the case.

Since January 1997, when a new court fee structure was introduced, the costs involved in court proceedings have gone up dramatically – the court fee for petitioning (starting) a divorce, for example, has risen from £80 to £150 (it was only £40 in 1995). Fee exemptions are still available, following a valiant and successful endeavour by an applicant on income support to challenge the Lord Chancellor of the previous government, who had introduced fees for everyone. However, the fee exemptions are limited to those for example on income support, on family credit or receiving legal advice and assistance under the legal aid 'green form' (see below). Everyone else will usually have to pay the full whack. For many this may mean that the cost of going to court to sort out their legal family problems will be prohibitive.

It is sometimes possible to get an order for costs (which would include court fees) made against a spouse who 'loses' a case, but courts can be reluctant to do so. This issue is explored later in the book. In any event, irrespective of who 'wins' or who gets an order for costs against whom, the two sets of legal fees will still have to be paid out of the same source – the couple's joint assets. The more the lawyers get, the less the family will be able to share between them. This is especially true in the stressful financial times we are still in, when the assets and the individuals' earning power may be considerably restricted.

This does not mean that it is necessary to cave in to a spouse who is demanding too much. A good solicitor (see Chapter 3 on where to get legal help) will be able to negotiate strongly on your behalf and can in most cases work out a reasonable settlement with your spouse's solicitor without the added expenses of a full-blown court battle. You may well be able to negotiate a settlement with your spouse either by yourself (see Chapter 2) or with the aid of a mediator (see Chapter 4 for a full explanation of what mediation is, how it works and where to find a mediator), thus saving considerably on legal costs. Using the Child Support Agency (CSA)* to work out the amount of child support and collect it from your ex-partner can cut down on legal costs too (see the end of this chapter and Chapter 5). But gaining a good understanding of the complex system of legal costs is likely to be very helpful.

In the following pages you will find an explanation of how legal aid works, how costs in the proceedings are worked out and how solicitors charge. We also explode the myth about legal aid meaning *free* legal help: this is only rarely the case.

Legal advice and assistance, and legal aid

At your first interview with the solicitor, it is worth asking if you qualify for legal advice and assistance and/or for legal aid. The solicitor should tell you about this even if you do not ask. Whether you are eligible will depend on your circumstances.

What is commonly referred to as 'legal aid' in matrimonial cases is two different things. The first is 'legal advice and assistance', under which a solicitor can advise you and deal with correspondence for you but cannot appear in court on your behalf. This is commonly known as the 'green form scheme' because of the colour of the application form. 'Assistance by way of representation' (ABWOR) is in effect an extension of the green form scheme to cover representation in, for example, the family proceedings court on an application for spousal maintenance or residence/contact outside divorce proceedings.

Second, there is full civil legal aid, for which you can apply to cover representation in what lawyers term 'ancillary' matters – for example, disputes about the children or financial proceedings.

Whether you qualify for any form of legal advice and assistance depends on your financial circumstances and, in the case of full legal aid, on the merits of your case. The limits for financial eligibility for legal advice and legal aid are reviewed by the government each year and change in April.

Not all solicitors are willing to take on legal aid cases because their remuneration for these is lower than for private work. Your local Citizens Advice Bureau (CAB) should be able to give you names of solicitors willing to take on legal aid work.

The Legal Aid Board* has administered the legal aid fund since April 1989. (This is a separate body from the Law Society, which is more like a trade union for solicitors.) The Legal Aid Board has set up a franchising scheme, under which solicitors' firms can apply for a franchise if they meet certain management and quality control standards. You can ask a firm which offers legal aid whether or not it has obtained a franchise. In the future it is likely that only firms which have been franchised will be able to undertake legal aid cases. For now, the only difference that you may notice is that franchised firms can make their own decisions about certain legal aid matters, for example whether or not to grant an emergency certificate. Moreover, they will be paid (by the Legal Aid Board) a slightly higher hourly rate for legal aid fees and may be more efficiently run than those that are not franchised.

More legal aid changes?
In 1995, the previous government announced plans to shake up the legal aid system. These changes are still some way off, but you may

read about them in the press and they are worth knowing about, especially as it looks as if the present government will not only follow through on its predecessor's plans but may restrict legal aid yet further. In essence the plans were that legal aid cases could be taken on only by solicitors' firms and other bodies (like Law Centres and CABx) which obtain a contract with the Legal Aid Board. A contract to provide legal aid services is something separate from a franchise, although it is likely that contracts will be given only to franchised firms.

One option being considered by the previous government was that a contracted CAB or a solicitor in a contracted firm – rather than the Legal Aid Board as at present – would assess whether or not a case should be handled on the basis of its legal merits. The main effect of these changes on potential clients would be that a contracted firm could perhaps take on only a certain number of legal aid cases. Once that ceiling is reached a client would have to wait until the firm could take on the case or go to another contracted firm and see if it had space to take on a new case.

In October 1997 the new government announced further radical proposals to restrict the legal aid system. A consultation period on the proposals was to run until about April 1998, during which time the legal profession expected lobbyists to highlight the worst aspects of the proposals, but the outcome is not known as we go to press.

The slightly better news was that the poorest may in one area be better protected than they would have been under the previous government. Plans to make recipients of income support contribute £5 or £10 to their legal aid bills are to be scrapped.

The green form scheme

The basic idea behind the legal advice and assistance scheme, known as the green form scheme, is to give the opportunity of obtaining legal advice to people who would not otherwise be able to afford it.

In May 1996 the Legal Aid Board issued guidance notes on what constitutes 'reasonable' limits for work carried out under the green form scheme. According to the Board, an initial interview in matrimonial cases should last only up to an hour. For dealing with a case involving divorce proceedings, child maintenance and welfare benefits advice, 4½ hours is deemed reasonable, with a possible extension of an hour for urgent financial matters. If a case is more complex, permission may first need to be sought to exceed the guidance limit, which may slow the case down.

The solicitor's hourly rate for preparing a case under the green form scheme is fixed at £45.50 (in London £48.25) for franchised firms, and £44 (in London £46.50) for non-franchised firms (April 1997 rates). If your income (less certain allowances) is under £77 per week (April 1997 figure) you should qualify for getting green form advice as long as your capital is within certain limits. If you receive non-contributory jobseeker's allowance, income support, family credit or disability working allowance, you will automatically qualify on income but you also have to come within capital limits.

Work the solicitor may do under the green form advice and assistance scheme relevant to money and divorce includes:

- general advice on whether there are grounds for divorce or judicial separation
- advice on questions of domicile; proving the validity of a foreign marriage
- advice on the procedure for getting a divorce
- the drafting of the petition and documents to accompany it
- advice on defending a divorce and the implications of doing so
- help with an application for full legal aid
- advice on obtaining an injunction
- registration of 'matrimonial home rights' (formerly called 'rights of occupation')
- advice about who will look after the children, about 'parental responsibility', 'residence' and 'contact' orders, and other orders under the Children Act 1989
- advice about spousal maintenance, and arrangements concerning the family home
- guidance on pensions – whether a claim might be made under the new law which provides for pensions to be 'earmarked'
- limited correspondence or discussions with solicitors acting for the other spouse to try to negotiate a settlement.

However, as the CSA now normally deals with child maintenance, green form advice is not usually available for child support unless the problem concerns a question of law.

The green form scheme is appropriate for simple undefended

divorces or for negotiating straightforward settlements. When the initial 'reasonable' time guidance is used up, the solicitor can apply to the Legal Aid Board for an extension (although you will have to wait for it to be granted before actually being able to get further legal advice). One extension is usually granted without too much difficulty if the solicitor can show that the extra work proposed is merited.

You are entitled to only one green form covering all matters 'arising from proceedings or judicial separation' – the divorce itself, spousal maintenance, issues concerning children and injunctions – and all of them are to be covered comprehensively in the 4½ hours allowed under the scheme. If, however, there are other matters arising from the matrimonial situation that are not part of the divorce, these can form the subject of a separate green form application and entitle you to further time. A separate green form could cover, say, correspondence with a building society, hire purchase and finance companies, or public utilities over problems about payments of bills, instalments or other debts following the breakdown of a marriage.

One considerable advantage that you will have if you are financially eligible for the green form is that you will thereby be exempted from court fees. You may also be eligible to receive free mediation sessions if you live in an area where one of the Legal Aid Board's pilot mediation schemes is running (see Chapter 4 for more information).

Eligibility for the green form scheme

The solicitor will carry out the assessment of your financial means while you are there, basing the calculations on the figures provided by you: your savings and other capital, your gross weekly income, your own outgoings and those of any dependants. He or she will enter these details on the green form and can tell you straight away, by use of a 'key card', whether or not you are eligible for the legal advice scheme. The figures given here came into effect in April 1997: the amounts are revised upwards annually, so check with your solicitor or the leaflet *Legal Aid: A Practical Guide to Legal Aid* available free from the Legal Aid Board.

Income

The disposable income limit is £77 in the last seven days. Disposable income is your weekly income after deduction of tax and National

Insurance contributions, and an allowance for any dependants, namely:

- £28 for a spouse or partner
- £16.90 for a child under 11
- £24.75 for a child aged 11 to 15
- £29.60 for a child aged 16 or 17
- £38.90 for a dependant aged 18 or over (for example, a disabled son or daughter).

The income of the spouse or partner is not included where he or she has a contrary interest in the case at issue, as would be the case when a divorce was contemplated. This means that the non-working wife of even a very wealthy man may be eligible for the green form scheme (but see the new rules overleaf about the 'apparently wealthy').

Before April 1993 those on incomes which were only slightly above the basic limit were eligible for green form advice on the basis that they paid a contribution assessed on the amount of their income. But in April 1993 the numbers of those eligible for legal aid were dramatically cut. One of the cuts meant that green forms with a contribution were abolished, so nowadays green form advice is available only to those on low incomes. If your income is higher than the basic limit, you will have to pay your solicitor's fees privately (some solicitors may be willing to be paid in monthly instalments).

If you are eligible, you have to sign the green form confirming that the information given by you is correct and that you accept the terms.

The solicitor has a charge (similar to the 'statutory charge' in civil legal aid cases, see page 26) on money or property 'recovered or preserved' (i.e. gained or retained during legal proceedings), subject to certain exemptions (including maintenance, the client's main or only home and £2,500 recovered in matrimonial cases, but note that there was a proposal from the last government to abolish the £2,500 allowable in matrimonial cases). This means that if your costs are not recovered from the other side they must be met by you out of unexempted money or property recovered or preserved. In certain limited circumstances, the solicitor's charge may be waived but this requires the authority of the Legal Aid Board.

Capital

Your disposable capital (such as shares, savings and so on) must not exceed £1,000 (or £1,335 if you have one dependant, £1,535 if two dependants, for example). The value of the family home and its contents, personal clothing and tools of a trade are not usually counted as part of disposable capital.

However, new rules introduced in June 1996, targeted at the apparently wealthy to restrict them from gaining legal advice or assistance and/or legal aid, mean that, for example, the value of houses worth over £100,000 can be taken into account as capital. This is unlikely to affect most divorce cases because usually the matrimonial home is in dispute. If it does, the value of the home, less whichever is the lower of the mortgage or £100,000, will be taken into account to produce a net equity figure. If this figure exceeds £100,000, the excess over £100,000 is taken into account as capital. There is also a further discretionary power to take into account the assets of other people or bodies if money has been placed in a company or trust, for example, but the Legal Aid Board thinks the applicant still has access to the funds.

Anyone receiving non-contributory jobseeker's allowance, income support, family credit or disability working allowance automatically qualifies on income but must also come within the capital limits. (Note that the capital limits are £2,000 higher for qualifying for ABWOR – see earlier in the chapter – so that an applicant with no dependants can have £3,000 savings, for example. Applicants on income support also automatically qualify for ABWOR on both income and capital.)

Exemptions from fees?
People receiving green form advice or income support, family credit or jobseeker's allowance are exempted from paying full court fees for undefended divorces, if they complete a fee exemption form.

The legal aid scheme

Where there is likely to be any contest, or a hearing in court, the green form scheme will not be adequate, but, at least as at the time of going to press, you can apply for a legal aid certificate. Civil legal aid is available for applications in a divorce court relating to any spousal maintenance orders, property orders, lump sum orders and arrangements for children. (An application is a request to a court for that court to make a particular order.)

Legal aid is not generally available for an undefended divorce; nor is it available for preliminary appeals against CSA assessments (for further information, see Chapter 5).

If a legal aid certificate is issued to you, this means that the services of a solicitor (and of a barrister, where appropriate) will be paid for initially by the legal aid fund. You may have to pay a contribution (usually by instalments), but otherwise no initial payment will be required. Later, however, if assets are recovered or preserved for you within the legal proceedings and the statutory charge applies (see page 26), your legal costs will be deducted from those assets before being paid to you. So beware the myth that legal aid is free: this is by no means always true.

Applying for legal aid

Your solicitor will supply the application forms for legal aid and may assist you to complete them under the green form scheme. You will need to complete an application form (and an emergency application form if appropriate) and a statement of your financial circumstances.

The forms are sent to the local Legal Aid Board office for consideration of the legal merits of your case and then to the legal aid assessment office of the Benefits Agency to assess what contribution (if any) is required. (In some cases, in an emergency, a franchised firm of solicitors may be able to decide straight away whether you can be granted legal aid.)

There are different forms on financial means to be completed depending on whether or not you are receiving welfare benefits or are living outside England and Wales. If you are in work, confirmation of your income must be provided.

Eligibility for legal aid

As with the green form scheme, the criteria are disposable income and the amount of disposable capital, but the limits are higher. The general rule is that if either is above the limit, you will not be eligible for legal aid. In a matrimonial dispute your spouse's income or capital are usually ignored when disposable income and disposable capital are calculated.

The figures given below came into effect in April 1997. Each year these figures are updated: check with your solicitor (or the Legal Aid Board's leaflet *Legal Aid: A Practical Guide to Legal Aid*). Note, however, that the legal aid scheme is increasingly coming under pressure from the government and further restrictions on eligibility for legal aid may yet be introduced.

Income

Disposable income is your annual income net of tax and National Insurance contributions, but including child benefit and any maintenance received under a court order or agreement from your spouse. From this will be deducted:

- expenses incurred in connection with employment (fares to work, trade union membership dues, childminding costs)
- rent or mortgage payments
- council tax
- insurance commitments
- maintenance paid to your spouse
- allowance for dependants: if you and your spouse are living together, £1,460 is deducted from annual income for him or her and £881 to £2,028 for each child dependant, according to age
- allowances may also be made for some other items including outstanding debts.

A contribution towards your legal costs will be required unless your disposable income is less than £2,563 a year. If it is more than £2,563 but less than £7,595 you will be asked to contribute $\frac{1}{36}$ of the 'excess' disposable income above £2,563 until the certificate is discharged (ended). If your disposable income is over £7,595 a year, you will not qualify for legal aid.

Capital

For disposable capital, the following are usually ignored:

- the value of the house you live in
- the value of any other property or money that is 'in dispute' between you and your spouse (for example if your spouse is laying claim to some shares that you own)
- furniture, personal clothing, tools of a trade and, usually, a car.

(If, however, you do not have a dispute over money, but only over, say, the children, the new rules aimed at preventing the 'apparently wealthy' from getting legal aid will apply – see page 18.)

Apart from this, virtually everything that is capable of being valued in money terms will count as disposable capital: not merely cash or deposits or shares but, for example, sums that could be borrowed on the security of insurance policies. Also included are jewellery (other than engagement and wedding rings), antiques and other valuables. There are, however, extra capital items that are exempted for pensioners, assessed on a sliding scale.

Where the capital assets come to between £3,000 and £6,750, you will have to contribute a lump sum equal to the capital above £3,000. This means a maximum contribution of £3,750. This payment is additional to any contribution that has to be made because of your income. There are higher limits for 'capital disregards' for pensioners on particularly low incomes. For example, a pensioner whose income is between £1,571 and £1,870 a year (excluding interest) will be entitled to have £10,000 of capital disregarded.

Waiting for the decision

A disadvantage of applying for legal aid is that you may have to wait for some weeks before knowing whether a legal aid certificate will be issued. The only exception to this is where an emergency certificate is issued, for example to cover injunction proceedings. A solicitor in a franchised firm may be able to decide straight away whether your application should be granted, but otherwise he or she must apply for emergency legal aid either in writing, or over the telephone. The Legal Aid Board's area officer may refuse to grant emergency legal aid over the telephone except in the most extreme cases. Emergency written applications are usually dealt with within a few days.

A legal aid certificate does not normally cover work done before the date the certificate is issued. By that time, the limit of the green form is likely to have been reached, and the Legal Aid Board is unlikely to allow further extensions on a green form except in relation to the divorce itself. This means that your case will in effect come to a halt once an application for legal aid has been made.

On being granted legal aid

If the decision is that your case is approved on legal merits and that you are eligible without a contribution, the legal aid certificate confirming that legal aid has been granted will be sent to your solicitor, with a copy to you.

If a contribution is required, you will be sent an offer setting out details of the amount of contribution required and how you will be expected to pay it. Contributions based on income are ongoing and payable at the rate of $\frac{1}{36}$ of the excess over £2,563 for the life of the legal aid certificate. Any capital sum contribution will have to be paid there and then. If you feel there has been some error in calculating your own financial circumstances, you can ask for a detailed break-down of your assessment. If it is incorrect, you can ask to be reassessed. Once you accept the offer, a legal aid certificate will be issued and there need be no further delay. However, if you do not accept the offer, you will not yet be legally aided so the solicitor will not yet be able to act for you.

The legal aid certificate will not be issued until after you have accepted the offer and have made the first monthly contribution. You will also be obliged to make any lump sum payment required of you.

It is important to keep up monthly payments and to carry out the conditions of the legal aid certificate (such as informing the legal aid office of any changes in your financial situation, perhaps brought about because of maintenance payments).

Normally no work done by the solicitor before the legal aid certifi-cate was issued is covered. The solicitor is entitled to charge you for any pre-certificate work and you will have to pay (unless the work was carried out under the green form scheme).

If your income or capital changes

If your yearly disposable income increases by more than £750 or decreases by more than £300 following the assessment, you must inform the Board's area office. You will then be reassessed and your contribution may be adjusted or the certificate discharged, so that you become responsible for your legal costs from then on (but not retro-spectively).

As far as disposable capital is concerned, you must report increases of £750 or more. You may be called upon to pay another lump sum contribution and/or the certificate may be taken away. If in doubt report any financial changes to the Legal Aid Board.

Revocation or withdrawal of your certificate

If it is found that you have in some way misled the Legal Aid Board about your financial position, your legal aid certificate will be

Financial criteria for legal aid

Disposable income and contributions

If less than £2,563 a year	'Free' legal aid i.e. no contribution (provided capital also within 'free' limit)
If between £2,563 and £7,595	Contribution: $\frac{1}{36}$ of excess over £2,563
£7,595	Upper limit for legal aid for matrimonial cases

Disposable capital and contributions

If less than £3,000	'Free' legal aid i.e. no contribution (provided income also within 'free' limit)
If between £3,000 and £6,750	Contribution: £1 for £1 on excess over £3,000
£6,750	Upper capital limit for legal aid

(April 1997 figures)

revoked. This means that it is treated as though it never existed. Your solicitor will then be entitled to seek to recover from you the full amount of costs he or she would have charged on a private basis rather than the reduced fees under the legal aid certificate.

If you fail to respond to correspondence with the Board, or fail to meet your monthly repayments, your certificate can be discharged although (unlike the situation where a certificate is revoked) this does not make you liable for the full costs assessed on a private client basis.

There is a further penalty in the Legal Aid Act 1988: if any person intentionally fails to comply with regulations about information to be furnished by him or her, or in the furnishing of such information knowingly makes any false statement or false representation, he or she will be liable to a fine, or imprisonment for up to three months.

Legal advice and/or legal aid

	Green form scheme (legal advice and assistance)	Legal aid scheme
Who is financially eligible?	Anyone with disposable income of not more than £77 per week and with disposable capital of not more than £1,000 (with extra allowances for dependants)*	Anyone with disposable income of not more than £7,595 a year and with disposable capital of not more than £6,750
What does it cover?	Advice, and help with documents up to 'reasonable' limits of a solicitor's time except (usually) matters relating to child support	All legal work required within the scope of the certificate, including representation in court by a solicitor and, if necessary, a barrister
How long does it go on?	Until the limits are reached (but extensions can be applied for)	Until case concluded and certificate discharged afterwards
How do I apply?	By giving information to solicitor about income and savings; he or she completes green form if you are eligible	By completing application forms given by solicitor to send to local Legal Aid Board area office with your personal details, grounds for case, and details of your income, expenses and capital
How long does a decision take?	Solicitor decides there and then	Weeks while assessment is being made; solicitor cannot do legal aid work until certificate is issued (emergency certificate granted in urgent cases)

What does it cost me?	'Free' if disposable income under £77 per week; however, where property (other than home) or lump sum over £2,500 is recovered or preserved, solicitor's charge is taken from it	If disposable income between £2,563 and £7,595 a year, contribution payable by monthly instalments, and if disposable capital between £3,000 and £6,750, capital contribution payable when offer of legal aid is accepted. On recovery or preservation of property over £2,500 when statutory charge arises, legal costs of case taken from property recovered or preserved
	Court fees must be paid in full by all applicants, except those who can claim a fee exemption, who must complete Form EX160. Fee exemptions apply only to undefended divorces. Note: the £2,500 exemption may be abolished soon by the goverment	

*For ABWOR, the capital allowance increases to £3,000 plus allowances

Legal fees for someone on legal aid

A person granted legal aid ceases to become personally responsible for his or her own legal fees. A solicitor for a legally aided person is not able to bill the client direct for work within the limits of the legal aid certificate. From the solicitor's point of view the financial limits on legal aid work mean that he or she may not be paid to attend court on your behalf if there is a barrister acting, and so a solicitor's clerk may be sent instead. In practical terms, the personal attendance of your solicitor at this stage would make little difference. You cannot insist on it in such circumstances, even by offering to pay him or her additional costs: such an extra payment is not allowed where you hold a legal aid certificate.

However, if you do get legal aid you may still have to pay some court fees out of your own pocket. Since January 1997, if you decide to defend your divorce for example, the court fee will be £100 – no fee exemptions are available.

The statutory charge

Solicitors should hand to all applicants for legal aid the last page of the application form explaining how the scheme works and should also personally explain to each applicant how the statutory charge may affect him or her.

The statutory charge is intended to recoup some of the taxpayers' money which finances the legal aid fund. Sometimes the contributions paid to the Legal Aid Board might cover the overall legal costs. More usually the legal costs exceed the amount collected by way of contribution from the legally aided person. Even if an order for costs is made by the court it may not meet the legal aid bill in full, so in order to recover what it will have to pay out the Legal Aid Board has a first call on any money or property recovered or preserved either under an order or by an agreed compromise.

This applies to all proceedings for which legal aid is granted, not just those relating to the property recovered or preserved. For example, if a legal aid certificate covered the divorce, a residence application, an injunction and an application for a transfer of property order, the legal fees for all those proceedings would be part of the charge on the property transferred.

'Property' could be a lump sum payment, the value of the house (or a share of it) and any other asset that was transferred or handed over or has been kept. In matrimonial proceedings, the first £2,500 of any property gained or preserved is currently exempt from the statutory charge (although there is a proposal to end this), and the charge does not apply to any maintenance payments made.

Property is held to have been recovered or preserved in the proceedings even if the case is settled halfway through without an order having been made, or if an order is made based on agreement.

Only if the property was genuinely never in dispute would there be no risk of the statutory charge applying in the end. For example, if you had come to a final agreement before the application for legal aid was made, or if, in correspondence, it had been conceded that the other party always had the property rather than that it was now being transferred, this would be evidence that there was no element of dispute. Ideally you could send an agreed statement with the application for legal aid, so that the Legal Aid Board would know from the start that no property would be gained or preserved in the proceedings.

Postponement

Where the property is being transferred to a legally aided spouse rather than sold, and is to be used as a home for the assisted person (or his or her dependants), that spouse does not have to pay the statutory charge there and then. Instead, the charge is put on the house but is not enforced until the house is sold (provided the conditions below are satisfied).

The fund's postponement of enforcing the charge is relevant also when property has been preserved. For example, if the house belongs to the wife, and the husband's application for a share in it does not succeed, the wife has preserved her ownership of the house and the statutory charge will be enforced – but only when she comes to sell the house.

When the house is being sold so that another house or flat can be bought with the proceeds of sale or where, under any court order or by agreement, other money is to be used to purchase a home, the Legal Aid Board can agree to put the charge on the new home, provided that:

- it is expressed specifically in the court order or agreement that the

property or money is to be used as a home or to purchase a home for the legally aided person or his or her dependants
- the Legal Aid Board is satisfied that the net value of the new home will cover the amount of the charge and the legally aided person agrees in writing that a legal charge can be registered against the new property and that interest will be paid on the outstanding amount.

There is a further proposal to end this concession too, thereby making the statutory charge payable immediately after the end of a case without any postponement. Check with your solicitor or CAB for details.

Interest on the charge

Whenever payment of the statutory charge to the Legal Aid Board is postponed, simple interest at the rate of (at present) 8 per cent per year is payable from the date of registration of the legal charge until the date the sum secured by the charge is paid off. This means that if you do not pay your statutory charge when it arises, you will have to pay interest until it is eventually settled. In times of rising house prices, the increase in value of your home should offset the interest accruing, but you should be aware, particularly now because house prices are rising only modestly, of your liability to repay the statutory charge with the accrued interest. If you do not agree to pay the interest, the charge cannot be postponed and must be enforced immediately.

No charge

In some current cases, the statutory charge will not apply. Here is an example.

A husband and wife and two children live in a council house. The husband walks out on the wife and pays her no maintenance. The wife, who does not work, claims income support. The husband admits adultery, and asks for a divorce. The wife goes to a solicitor for advice under the green form scheme (no contribution is required from her because she is on income support) for help with her divorce petition and also advice on transferring the tenancy wholly to her.

The husband becomes violent towards the wife and the children, and she has to apply for an injunction. He seeks a residence order and causes difficulty over agreeing about contact (see Chapter 8).

For all of these matters, the wife gets legal aid (no contribution required).

Irrespective of how many hundreds of pounds are run up in legal fees on her behalf, she may never have to pay a penny to the legal aid fund because no property on which any value can be placed has been recovered or preserved. The local authority tenancy has no value in this context.

The husband applies for legal aid to defend the transfer of property application and the injunction and to apply for a residence order. He gets a legal aid certificate subject to a contribution.

Win or lose, however, he will not be required to pay anything more towards his own legal costs.

The net result is that the legal aid fund ends up paying virtually the whole of both parties' costs.

However, a reform option still at large is that the statutory charge should be extended to cover all proceedings, even those where no money or property is recovered or preserved, for example. So applications over children or domestic violence could be covered by the statutory charge, but of course this could apply only if the legally aided applicant had owner-occupied property. Applicants living in rented property will still be protected from the worst effects of the statutory charge.

Running up legal aid costs

High legal costs can be run up over what may in essence be quite trivial disputes. Solicitors' duty to the legal aid fund requires them to report to the Legal Aid Board if they consider that the client is acting unreasonably – for example, by refusing to accept a sensible offer of settlement.

Even if you are on legal aid, it is important to ask your solicitor to keep you posted on the costs of the case, particularly where the house or a lump sum is being negotiated for, and to explain to you what the statutory charge entails.

How the statutory charge gets paid

In legally aided cases, any lump sum payment ordered by the court has to be paid to the solicitor: only he or she can give a receipt for it. He or she has to pay it all into the legal aid fund – the recipient has to wait until the legal aid fund has settled up the costs before being paid the balance. But if a solicitor's undertaking is given that the cost of the case will not be more than a specific amount, he or she can pay just that amount into the fund and hand over the rest direct to the recipient. This is subject to authorisation from the Legal Aid Board and applies only if the money is not to be used for the purchase of a new home.

If the money is being released for a home purchase and payment of the statutory charge is being deferred, once the Legal Aid Board has agreed to defer payment of the charge, your solicitor can use the funds for the new property purchase.

Costs in the proceedings

Irrespective of whether or not you obtain a Legal Aid certificate, and particularly if you have to pay the solicitor yourself, it is important to explore whether you may be able to get some of your legal costs paid by your spouse or whether you are laying yourself open to an order for costs being made against you. The issue of costs is complex and, remember, whether the costs are paid by you or your spouse, ultimately they will considerably reduce the amount of money available in the 'pot' for later division.

How solicitors charge

Solicitors basically charge by the hour, so that every interview, telephone call, letter and indeed every time the solicitor opens your file, means additional expense to you, the client. Most solicitors charge out their time in units of five or six minutes. Short letters or telephone calls count as one unit each. Work that takes longer will be rounded up to the nearest unit.

Ask what the solicitor's hourly charging (or 'charge-out') rate is, preferably before making an appointment. If you are seeing a solicitor under the low-priced interview scheme (see Chapter 3), you can ask him or her what the usual charging rate would be. Remember that the charges apply to the time spent not only with you but also on writing letters, talking to witnesses or to the other spouse's solicitor, and attending court. Check whether the rate includes a percentage mark-up for 'care and attention' (an increase of anything over 25 per cent in the solicitor's legal bill if the case has been complex or has had to be dealt with especially quickly) or whether that is additional. Ask the solicitor to let you know whenever the charging rate is reviewed and changed, although he or she should do this automatically. Value Added Tax (17½ per cent) is payable on fees and on some out–of–pocket expenses, like travel costs.

There will be additional costs (often called disbursements) such as court fees, fees of any barristers engaged and, if there are major areas of dispute over the value of items of property, valuers' fees as well. In complex cases involving a business, your solicitor may also advise you that an accountant should be instructed to prepare a report on the business.

If you are paying privately you may be asked to pay a sum of at least £500 on account of your future costs. Some solicitors deliver interim bills on account at various stages, which you will have to pay. Although this will increase your outgoings, interim billing is a good practice as it gives you a clear idea of where you stand, and paying as the case proceeds avoids the problem of having to find a large amount to cover all the costs at the end. You can sometimes arrange with your solicitor to pay monthly instalments on your fees to keep costs manageable.

A solicitor's hourly charging rate can be anything from £80 upwards (plus VAT) in a provincial firm; in London it may range from £90 to £180 (plus VAT), and, in really upmarket firms, hourly charging rates of £250 (plus VAT) are not uncommon. So, using your solicitor as an emotional prop rather than as a legal adviser can turn out to be an extremely expensive luxury.

You are entitled to query your solicitor's bill and disbursements, and to ask for a fully itemised account. If you are still dissatisfied, you are entitled to have the bill 'taxed' (see below). Normally, you should do this within one month of the date on the bill.

A solicitor is not entitled to sue for his or her bill on a contentious matter unless a month's notice has been given to the client with a reminder of the client's right to have the bill taxed.

Taxation of costs

Taxation is the process whereby the district judge at the county court considers the solicitor's bill and decides whether the charges are fair and reasonable given the circumstances of the particular case.

For taxation, the bill has to be drawn up in a specially detailed form, in chronological order of the steps taken. If a court appointment is made for taxation, the solicitor can also charge for attendance at court. There is a court fee for taxation of costs, currently £7.50 per £100 of the final taxed costs (since January 1997 half of this fee has to be paid up-front on lodging the bill to be taxed at court). Usually, the party asking for the fees to be taxed has an order that the other party will pay the costs. Sometimes, however, the former will end up paying the bill him- or herself, in which case the up-front fee for lodging the bill of costs drops to £50 (unless the district judge orders otherwise).

The Office for the Supervision of Solicitors★ produces a free leaflet about querying your bill. It is called *Are your solicitor's charges fair and reasonable?*

Reducing the chances of paying your spouse's costs

You can reduce your potential liability for paying your spouse's costs by making a reasonable offer by letter to settle the financial claims. (This offer, often called a 'Calderbank letter' is discussed in Chapter 10.) If the offer that you make is fair, and your spouse chooses not to accept it and proceeds to a full financial hearing, he or she places himself or herself in a much riskier situation. If the court ultimately makes an order which is similar or less generous than the offer that you made, your spouse may be ordered to pay not only his or her own costs but also a contribution to yours as a penalty for stubbornly increasing costs without merit.

Costs awarded

If you want your spouse to pay at least a part of your legal costs, you must make a request 'for costs' at each stage of the proceedings, whenever orders are sought.

In a divorce, there is usually not just one set of proceedings: apart from the obtaining of the divorce decree, there may be matters of litigation on spousal maintenance, property adjustment or financial applications under the Children Act, all of which run up costs. On applications on any of these proceedings, or any 'interlocutory' (i.e. interim) hearings, costs will usually be 'reserved' by the district judge to be dealt with on the final hearing or outcome of your case. At an interim hearing, a party will be ordered to pay the costs only if that party is in some way at fault at that time. At the conclusion of any final hearing, you can or should ask the district judge or judge to make an order for costs; he or she decides there and then whether to make such an order.

If you are asking the court to make an order by consent (that is, in terms agreed by you and your spouse), one of the agreed terms can be in respect of costs.

The court will bear in mind, at a financial hearing, the effect of any order for costs and will be conscious, for example, that such an order will still leave the recipient with a part of the overall bill to meet. Sometimes, the amount of a spouse's share in any property is increased to take account of his or her liability for his or her own costs instead of an order for costs being made against the other spouse.

Where an order for costs is made in favour of a party who is legally aided against the other spouse who is paying privately, certain rules apply if the legal aid certificate was issued after 25 February 1994. According to the rules, the legally aided party's solicitors can claim legal fees worked out on private rates against the party ordered to pay the costs and can get back these higher fees from him or her. The legally aided spouse will not be affected directly by the fact that his or her solicitor will be able to charge extra fees, but indirectly by a reduction of the family's money 'pot'. (The new rules were brought in to try to stem the numbers of solicitors refusing to take on legal aid cases because of the low hourly legal aid rates.)

If someone on legal aid is ordered to pay the other party's costs (this happens, but not that frequently), the legal aid certificate does not cover this: the person is likely to have to pay out of his or her own pocket. The court must determine the amount that is reasonable for the legally aided person to pay and will usually say that an order for costs cannot be enforced without the court's permission. It may limit the amount of such costs to the equivalent of the person's legal aid contributions and make the costs payable by instalments over 12 months.

The costs may be awarded by the court on a standard basis or (the higher level) an indemnity basis.

Unless otherwise specified, an order for costs usually means 'standard' costs. This means that you will recover from the person ordered to pay the costs usually between 60 and 80 per cent of your own bill. The term 'indemnity costs' is used to mean that your bill for legal costs (whether you are legally aided or not) will be met in full. When an order for costs is made and a figure cannot be agreed, the bill will be taxed. The bill should be sent for taxation within three months of the date of the order for costs.

Costs in different types of proceedings

The issue of costs is fairly complex and confusing, not least now because of the various sets of rules that apply, and you can expect a different approach to the question of costs depending on the type of proceedings. Set out below are some practical examples.

For the divorce

The petitioner can ask for costs (although this is not usual where the petition is on the basis of two years' separation with consent). If an order for costs is made, the petitioner's solicitor has his or her charges assessed by reference to scales laid down by special rules.

For example, a wife goes to see a solicitor to obtain a simple divorce based on her husband's adultery. She has to settle up with her own solicitor. She obtains an order for costs, assessed on the appropriate scale, at £250, plus court fees. But she has insisted on 'five star' service, requiring the solicitor to come personally to her house, spending many hours discussing the matter, and speaking to him many times on the telephone to find out how the case has been progressing, and her solicitor's bill comes to £2,250, plus court fees. She has to pay the £2,000 difference herself.

For an injunction

Injunction proceedings can run up very substantial costs. The successful applicant should obtain an order for costs against the other spouse. But, in many cases, this may not be worth the paper it is written on, either because the latter disappears or because he or she has no funds.

For residence, contact and other orders

Considerable costs can be run up in disputes over orders made under the Children Act, such as for residence or contact with the children. The fact that one parent obtains an order stating that the children would reside with him or her instead of the other does not necessarily mean that that parent has 'won' in the same sense as would be the case in, for example, a claim for damages for personal injuries, so both parties may be left to bear their own costs. The court is likely to order one party to pay the other's costs only if the former's behaviour during the proceedings has been in some way quite unreasonable, causing unnecessary delays and expense.

Financial matters

Theoretically, the costs of a financial case ought to have been pruned since a court practice direction of January 1995 ordered solicitors to control costs more strictly. In certain areas, a new ancillary pilot scheme in force since October 1996 also has the potential to make costs savings.

The fact that the wife (or, rarely, the husband) obtains an order for spousal maintenance or an order relating to the matrimonial home does not necessarily mean that she (or he) will be awarded costs, but the impact of costs is likely to be taken into account in making the overall order.

Sometimes a spouse's solicitors will at an early stage make a Calderbank offer (see Chapter 10) to include payment of the other's costs, only up to the date of the financial offer, in order to try to force a settlement. If the latter refuses to negotiate or in any other way unreasonably presses ahead for a court hearing after receiving a sensible offer, he or she puts him- or herself at risk of having to pay not only his or her own costs but also the spouse's costs since the offer was made.

When costs are paid

The theoretical (and usually the practical) position is that the successful party has to pay his or her own solicitor's bill first, and then recover any contribution ordered by the court from the other party. Usually, the solicitor will continue to act by preparing the bill and having it taxed and enforced against the payer.

Sometimes the solicitor may not press his or her client for payment of that part of the costs which are recoverable from the paying party, but that is entirely a matter of the solicitor's benevolence and is based on his or her assessment of the prospect of the other side paying up.

Costs and the Child Support Agency

If you are seeking or will be paying child support, this will usually be dealt with by the CSA rather than through solicitors and the courts. Fees were charged by the Agency up to April 1995. It then waived its fees for a two-year period, and this period was subsequently extended to April 1999. If and when the CSA does reintroduce fees, the rates might be similar to the old rates of £34 for assessing child support and £44 for enforcing payment – both fees payable by each parent. These fees are much lower than legal costs for dealing with maintenance are likely to be, but then unfortunately the CSA does have a reputation for slowness and inaccuracy. (See Chapter 5 for details.)

Chapter 2

Financial planning for divorce

Planning for divorce can be done at any time. It may be something you have been engaged in for some time, waiting just for the right moment to act. On the other hand you may be the spouse who has suddenly (and painfully) been deserted and you cannot see how planning can possibly improve things.

Certainly, in times of emotional crisis it is often difficult to make well-thought-out decisions for the future. In the heat of the moment, when the separation is very recent and the emotional atmosphere charged, it is sometimes best to avoid making long-term decisions, concentrating your energies instead on getting through the next week or even the next day. But as time goes on, the importance of planning for divorce, even if you never wanted the separation to happen, cannot be over-emphasised.

By planning you can frequently help minimise what can be the crippling financial effects of divorce. You can work out in advance how best to divide the income which formerly supported one home but which must now support two. Not only can you clarify your existing financial position but you can also explore how you could improve it: cutting down on outgoings, seeing if there are any ways of increasing your income, minimising the tax consequences of longer-term decisions and perhaps seeing whether there would be any financial help from the state (see later in this chapter and Chapters 5 and 10).

Financial planning and child maintenance

Since the Child Support Act 1991 came into force in April 1993, different rules apply to claims for child support. If you have children, these rules can affect your control over financial planning for your situation following a separation or divorce.

A parent who needs financial help from an ex-partner to look after children may be required to use the Child Support Agency (CSA)★ to claim the child support from him or her. If the parent who looks after the children already receives or will claim income-based jobseeker's allowance, income support, family credit or disability working allowance, then she (or, more rarely, he) will be referred to the CSA by the Department of Social Security (DSS) and asked to make a claim for child maintenance. If none of these benefits is claimed, the parent looking after the children can still use the CSA (but will not be forced to do so – voluntary agreements can be made as an alternative).

The amount of child support will be worked out according to a special, quite complicated, formula which, together with the procedure for claiming an assessment, is explained more fully in Chapter 5. If you are likely to be making a claim for or paying child maintenance, you should read Chapter 5 now before continuing to make financial plans.

Debts

For an increasing number of families, the financial issues involved in divorce are less about dividing up assets than about dealing with the heavy burden of debts and who will or should take them on. Although it may be of little comfort to those in debt, it is a fact that getting into debt has become a common problem. Over 2.5 million families in Britain are estimated to be heavily in debt, two-thirds of whom are behind with their mortgage repayments. The stresses caused by financial debts can indeed often be the cause of the family break-up.

Broadly speaking, a spouse will not be responsible for debts incurred by the other spouse alone. But there are exceptions: a spouse will usually be responsible for the other's unpaid council tax bills and sometimes other outgoings on the home. Spouses also share responsibility for joint debts, say from a joint account, or for joint mortgage repayments or rent.

If your spouse has deserted you, leaving behind high unpaid household bills, the date of separation is important. If your spouse has failed to pay his or her council tax, you must inform the local authority of the date of separation and thus at least cut off your responsibility for paying your spouse's share of the council tax debt accruing after that.

Your council tax bill will also be cut if there is now only one adult living in the home. By advising the gas, electricity and telephone companies, you can also get the meters read as near to the separation date as possible and ask for a transfer of the accounts into your own name. This will, obviously, leave you with having to pay future bills and so may not be appropriate, but it can be one way of avoiding responsibility for some previously built-up debts.

If on the other hand one spouse is paying maintenance, but the other does not pay the bills, what responsibility does the former have for the unpaid bills? The answer lies in what the maintenance is intended to cover. If the paying spouse makes it clear that the maintenance should cover, for example, the payments of electricity and gas bills (and if the amount of maintenance is adequate for this purpose), then he or she should be relieved of the obligation to pay those bills. Asking the utility companies (for example) to change the accounts into the name of the spouse now living alone in the property clarifies who will be responsible in future.

Working out debt repayments

The first step is to assess the priority of debts with the help of expert counselling – see overleaf. You will probably be advised not simply to pay off the creditor who shouts the loudest. A credit card company, say, may telephone and write a string of letters in an endeavour to get money from you, but that bill may have to be left, if necessary, to enable you to pay for housing. The credit card company may take you to court: at worst the court could send in the bailiffs to take away some possessions, but that would be preferable to losing the roof from over your head.

Once you have worked out the total amount of your debt and (preferably with assistance) a list of priorities for repayment, see also whether you can increase your own income – perhaps by getting a part-time job or by applying for welfare benefits to which you may be entitled (see page 53). Look at ways of cutting your own expenditure: by going to markets instead of superstores, say, or by walking or cycling instead of going by car. If you belong to a pension scheme you could ask for your payments to be frozen until you can once more afford them, but check whether you will be financially penalised by making such a decision.

Although it may be tempting to try to avoid your creditors, you may well find that by contacting them and showing that you are willing to try to repay them you can work out a realistic level of repayment. Creditors will very often accept a reduced payment made regularly rather than nothing at all, and will feel happier knowing that you have not fled the country. Also, it will be less expensive for them to agree a repayment with you rather than incur extra legal costs in having to take you to court.

As an alternative, you may wish to roll up your debts into one loan and then pay a monthly amount. A problem with this is that the loans advertised for such purposes can charge extortionate rates of interest. Even if your own bank is willing to make you a loan, the interest rates charged may differ little from those charged by credit card companies. Debt-advice agencies also advise strongly against taking out a loan to help pay off your mortgage repayments (often termed 'distress borrowing'): this only serves to dig you deeper into debt.

If you find it impossible to pay off your debts or to repay a creditor you owe over £750, you could ask the court to make a bankruptcy order. If you take this action yourself it will cost you a deposit of £200 plus court fees. You will thus largely be relieved of the burden of your creditors.

However, once you are made bankrupt, there are limitations: you cannot hold a bank account or obtain credit of over £50, nor be a company director (or a solicitor, for example). Depending on the circumstances, most bankrupts are discharged after two or three years, when they have a clean sheet. But even if you think this is the only way out of your debts, obtain legal advice before going ahead.

Special help and advice about debts

Your best bet for advice and help about debts is likely to be your local Citizens Advice Bureau (CAB), money advice centre or law centre; many of these have special sessions for debt problems. For further advice try contacting the National Debtline,★ the Office of Fair Trading★ and the Council of Mortgage Lenders.★

Many local authorities and some banks have free information leaflets. You can also get help from your solicitor, and green form advice is available if you are eligible (see Chapter 1).

If you are not in debt

Even if you are not in debt, you may need to take steps to protect your position.

The home

If your home is registered in your spouse's name alone, you need to register a charge on the property to make sure that outsiders are aware of your interest in the home. This will also ensure that your spouse will not be able to sell the home or remortgage it without your consent (see also Chapter 9).

Joint accounts and credit cards

With a joint bank or building society account on which either of you can draw, there is the risk that the account could be cleared out by one partner without the other knowing about it. To prevent this, the bank or building society manager should be told to change the arrangement so that cheques can be drawn only with both signatures. Alternatively, you could ask for the account to be frozen (although then neither of you would be able to draw out funds).

Similarly, where each of you has a credit card or cash withdrawal card for drawing against one account, it is usually wiser, from the main cardholder's point of view, to put a stop on the cards. The card company must be notified and the cards (including, if possible, the other spouse's card) sent back. A new card will then be issued to the main cardholder.

Preventing disposal of assets

If you strongly suspect your spouse of intending to dispose of assets to try to escape his or her financial obligations, you can ask the court to make an application under Section 37 of the Matrimonial Causes Act to prevent him or her from doing so. You will need to instruct a solicitor (see also Chapter 3).

Working out your financial position

The following pages set out guidelines for working out a fairly detailed picture of your and your family's current financial position. It is only once you have filled in the detail of what actually happens in the present that you may be able to start making plans for the future. If you can, try to project ahead for the future what your likely income and outgoings might be.

You may not be able to work out all the figures by yourself: your spouse's position may be a blank to you, for example. But you should still fill in as much of the picture as possible. By undertaking this preparation yourself you may well be able to save on a solicitor's time (if you are going to use one) and thus on legal costs.

If you have not been responsible in the past for paying the bills, try to find out how much recent bills have been. Your spouse may be willing to cooperate; otherwise you could contact the companies direct – for example, the utility companies (about the gas and electricity bills), British Telecom, Mercury and other telephone companies (about the telephone bill) and the local authority (about your council tax) – and ask them to send you copies of your old bills.

If you still feel at a loss, use these guidelines to prepare a summary of information for your solicitor, who could then help you to sort through them and assist you in planning for the future.

The home
If you own your home:

- what is it worth now? An approximate estimate can be obtained by telephoning two or three local estate agents to ask them for a rough guide of what your property would be worth if you put it on the market now. The estate agents will not usually charge for making informal estimates of your house's worth like this
- when was it bought and for how much?
- how did you arrange your finances to pay for the house or flat?
- who put down the deposit, and where did the money come from?
- what substantial improvements have been made to the property since you bought it (e.g. central heating)? when? what was the cost and how was it paid for?
- is the house or flat in joint names? This is important – if you find that the property is in your spouse's name only, it could be sold without your agreement or knowledge, but you can take steps to prevent this happening by registering your 'matrimonial home rights' – see Chapter 9
- is the title registered?

If you own a leasehold property:

- what is the ground rent?
- what is the service/maintenance charge?
- how long is the lease?

If there is a mortgage:

- name, address and account/reference number of the building society, bank or other lender
- how much is outstanding?
- what are the monthly payments?
- when will it be paid off? Ask the building society or other lender for any of these facts if you do not know them
- if it is an endowment mortgage, when is the policy due to mature and for how much? What is the current surrender/paid-up value of the policy? Ask the insurance company.

If either you or your spouse owns other properties (e.g. a country cottage, villa abroad, time-share, all or part of a parent's home), include its approximate value.

If you rent your home:

- is it rented from a private landlord, the council, a housing association?
- how much rent do you pay (weekly, monthly, quarterly)?
- is there a service/maintenance or management charge? If so, how much?
- what type of tenancy is it?
- in whose name is the tenancy? Check the contract, tenancy agreement or rent book, if you have one.

Car or other vehicle

- do you own a car? If so, what is the make, model, year, value?
- does your spouse own a car? If so, what is the make, model, year, value?
- will you and/or your spouse need a car in the future?
- do you or your spouse have the use of a company car? If so, what model is it and how often is it replaced? What is paid for: car tax? tax on the benefit of having the car? insurance? servicing? repairs? petrol?

- do you and/or your spouse own a motor-bike? caravan? boat?

Employment

If you are self-employed:

- what income have you had for the past three years? Any regular earnings from occasional freelance or part-time work at home should be included.

If you are an employee:

- name of employer, nature of job, whether full- or part-time. If you are currently not employed, include details and dates of last employment and qualifications
- normal weekly or monthly earnings – form P60 shows the total amount of pay for income tax purposes including any bonus or commission and what tax and National Insurance payments were made for the previous tax year
- any other relevant information, such as imminent promotion or redundancy, dates of pay reviews
- any fringe benefits, commission or bonuses regularly received e.g. private medical insurance, subsidised loan, expense account, company car (a company car will be treated by the Inland Revenue as 'deeming' extra income, the amount of which will be determined by the year of the model, how many business miles you do and what type of car it is)
- expenses of any clothing and equipment essential for your job
- cost of childminding or nursery school for your child(ren) while you are at work
- details of additional casual or freelance work.

You will also need to look at details of your spouse's income if known.

Pension

- details of any occupational pension or superannuation scheme or personal plan to which you belong
- does the pension scheme provide any benefits for a widow or widower? She/he will probably lose any benefits as a result of divorce (but see Chapter 11 on Pensions for what orders the court can now make over pensions).

Try to obtain a copy of the rules relating to the occupational pension scheme and an up-to-date statement showing the present value of your pension and the estimated value on retirement. (Another common valuation method is the 'cash equivalent transfer value', i.e. how much your existing pension scheme would pay into a new pension scheme that you were to transfer to – this is likely to be much less than the figure for the present value of your pension). An up-to-date value is more difficult in the case of 'unfunded' occupational pensions, which are worked out on the level of your final salary and how many years you have worked for that employer. You can apply for details direct to the pension company or to your personnel office, which should have the necessary information.

Note that there may also be a hidden matrimonial asset if you or your spouse have been mis-sold a personal pension in place of an occupational pension (or other more protected form of pension). Although new rules are now supposed to protect against mis-selling, a number of people in the late 1980s and early 1990s gave up valuable occupational pensions in the mistaken belief that a personal pension would give them better benefits. Compensation for having had a mis-sold pension may be payable, and since 1 January 1997 reinstatement to the old pension may also be possible. See Chapter 11 for details.

Other assets and income
- any joint current accounts or savings accounts you have
- your own savings in building society, bank, National Savings accounts, with details of the account(s) and current balance(s)
- stocks and shares, and unit trusts, with a current valuation of your portfolio
- Personal Equity Plans (PEPs), Tax-Exempt Special Savings Accounts (TESSAs) or any other type of investment (these may be affected by changes in the Budget from the new government)
- endowment policies and/or life insurance policies: how much? when do they mature? You could ask the insurance company or broker for current surrender values and check whether any policy has been written in your spouse's favour
- the income from your investments over the past two or three years, e.g. dividends, building society account interest
- future income or redemption value of investment that will mature in some years' time

- valuables, such as jewellery, antiques, with estimates of their value and brief details of how and by which of you they were acquired (bought, inherited, gift, etc.).

General contents of the house are rarely realisable, and proposals on how to divide these between you should be considered separately. This is better done after you have reached a general agreement on the broader issues otherwise you may get bogged down in minutiae.

Outgoings

Summarise as precisely as possible your necessary outgoings. These would probably include:

- tax and National Insurance contributions
- travel to work
- childcare costs: childminding, or nursery fees or pay to an au pair or nanny
- car expenses, including hire purchase (HP) payments, insurance, road tax, petrol and repairs
- any other HP commitments
- mortgage payments or rent and service charges
- council tax and water charges
- gas, electricity, telephone bills
- house insurance and all other insurances
- payments into pension schemes
- housekeeping – food costs, toiletries, etc.
- home repair(s) and maintenance
- television rental/licence
- holidays and entertainment
- all and any payments involving the children
- vets' bills.

Try also to project what your outgoings might be in your new home (and, if you can, those of your spouse).

Expectancies and trusts

Are you and/or your spouse likely to come into an inheritance in the foreseeable future? Does either of you have interests under a trust (perhaps as a result of tax planning by you or your parents)?

Child maintenance

Special rules apply about payment of child support since the Child Support Act 1991 changed the law in April 1993. Instead of you having to work out how much you think you and the children need in terms of maintenance, or how much you think you can afford to pay, a special formula, which is not only complex but usually fixed, is now used to calculate maintenance for the children payable via the Child Support Agency. Although the formula is based on both parents' incomes, only certain limited outgoings (such as tax, National Insurance and housing costs) are taken into account, and other outgoings (such as debts and childcare) are usually ignored. However, a new 'departure system' was introduced in 1996 which may enable you to ask for extra outgoings to be taken into account when working out the formula.

The rules are explained in more detail in Chapter 5.

Other maintenance

- any maintenance payments made to spouse (or an ex-partner from a previous marriage) and/or to your child(ren)
- children's maintenance payments received from a former husband or wife of yourself or your spouse
- any regular provision to or from someone else, e.g. deeds of covenant from grandparents
- maintenance payments you would expect to receive or pay in the future.

New partner's finances

If you and/or your spouse are cohabiting on a long-term basis with someone else, and/or have plans to marry, you should include what you know of that person's financial circumstances.

Payments from DSS

What money do you receive or could you claim from the DSS? For example:

- jobseeker's allowance
- income support
- family credit
- child benefit

- state pension
- incapacity benefit or other disability benefits.

Debts

Make a list of all the money you owe: for example, tax arrears, what is outstanding under any hire purchase agreement(s), bank overdraft, credit card, other loans. For a loan or credit agreement or other liability which requires payment regularly, note the arrears and the total amount outstanding.

Note who is responsible for each debt – you or your partner or both of you. You are not responsible for each other's individually incurred debts.

Preparing a budget

When preparing the financial summary, the most difficult item to assess can be your outgoings. You do not need to calculate everything precisely to the last penny. But gaining a clearer picture of your current outgoings will help you prepare a budget for your future outgoings.

If you have no idea of how much you do spend on what, get a notebook and write down the cost of your shopping as you pay for it. If your children are old enough to understand, encourage them to note down what they spend (it may also make them feel less excluded from the plans you are making for the future).

For major recurring bills, for example, gas and telephone bills, make sure that you try to add these together over a period of, say, 12 months, before dividing to create a monthly sub-total, to allow for seasonal fluctuations.

You should also make a note of necessary expenditure that may be looming, such as major car repairs or kitting out a child in a new school uniform, and of longer-term needs, such as replacing a car, re-roofing the house, and so on.

Not all items will be doubled when you split up: some will be halved, some reduced, and some will stay the same and may be paid for by either of you. For instance, electricity will be paid twice, toiletries divided, school meals and any private lessons for the children will be unchanged. A probable future spending pattern for each of you should emerge from this preparation of a budget.

Making plans for the future

By now you could be thoroughly depressed. You will have spent many hours producing meticulous sets of figures and, almost inevitably, they will paint a grim picture. You may wonder how you ever managed to afford living under one roof – let alone how you will juggle two households.

See whether there are any ways you can improve on your financial position – by cutting down on expenditure as well as seeing whether your income can be increased in any way. You could perhaps think of renting out a room to a lodger – under the 'rent a room scheme' you can receive up to £4,250 per annum tax free (1997/98 figures).

Try to consider all the possible scenarios for the future. You strengthen your position by having worked out in detail the likely consequences of plans that you and your spouse may each be putting forward, even if (or particularly if) you are convinced that your spouse's suggestions are ridiculously unrealistic.

In practice, you may have little choice, and what options there are will be fairly stark. Inevitably, you will have to make compromises. It is only by having thought through your priorities that you can mould the eventual compromise into a shape that best suits you and your family. Sometimes professional help from a mediator may be exactly what is needed.

Making plans for the future revolves primarily around accommodation and income.

Where to live

Your first priority, if you have children, will of course be to ensure that they have a roof over their heads. Work out what it would cost you to stay on in your home, and where you could move to if you were to move, and how either option would leave you and your spouse financially.

Factors such as the location of children's schools and being near to helpful friends or willing parents can be important, particularly now that you are going to be on your own.

If you own your home but are likely to have to move, ask two or three local estate agents to tell you what they think it might fetch. There should be no charge for such a valuation if you explain that you may be selling but have not yet decided to. These figures may not be exact (some estate agents tended to undervalue when the housing market was depressed) but they will be a guide. Deduct the likely agent's and conveyancing costs and moving costs (say, around 5 per cent of the house value), plus what you will owe on the mortgage, and you are left with the 'net equity'. From that, you would have to pay the costs of setting up a new home or possibly two – one for each of you. Work out what sort of mortgage you and your spouse could each shoulder and then investigate the property market.

If you are in rented accommodation, and indeed even if you are not, investigate the rented sector – private, council and housing association.

This can be a disheartening business at the best of times, but it is only by exploring what might be possible that you can work out what the options are, and the respective advantages and disadvantages of each option.

What to live on

In respect of capital, look at your schedule of assets, having worked out the net equity in the house (if you own it) and the net value of all other realisable assets after meeting outstanding liabilities (including legal fees for the divorce, if you are consulting a solicitor). What is realisable will depend upon your circumstances – cashing in a life insurance policy or selling the car might be foolish in some circumstances but unavoidable in others. Everyday household belongings are rarely realisable and should preferably be linked to need: the parent with the children, for example, is likely to need the washing machine and the majority of the furnishings. The other parent, however, may need to buy, either immediately or in due course, his or her own household equipment and furniture.

Starting off calculating maintenance

If you have dependent children, first work out how much child support might be payable under the formula laid down by the Child Support Acts. This usually has to be the first step because the amount can be precise, whereas other payments tend to be up in the air at this stage. Turn to Chapter 5 to work out how much child support is likely to be payable.

A mother who will be looking after children may be able to claim maintenance for herself to top up her child support. As the Child

Support Act 1991 increased the amounts of child support payable, conversely the amount she might expect to receive in her own right has (broadly) tended to decrease.

A wife who does not work outside the home or who is on a low income may also be entitled to spousal maintenance from her husband if he earns enough. Exactly how much he should pay is not easy to quantify as the court will take a number of factors into account. If sufficient income is available, a wife could expect to receive enough to meet her reasonable needs (based on the court's pragmatic 'needs and resources' approach – see Chapters 6 and 10) but the court may also expect a wife who is not currently earning to make endeavours to support herself financially in the future.

Figures and forecast

Once you have worked out what money will be available, compare the figures with a forecast for the needs of both new households. This may show that one of you has, or both of you have, got nowhere near enough to meeting your projected expenses. Remember that the needs of the children will take priority.

Looking at your incomes, needs and available capital (if any), a decision must be reached on how things can be arranged, but with realistic figures. In many cases, it will just have to be accepted that both of you are going to be very hard up, at least for a while.

Negotiating a financial settlement

You do not need to leave it to the courts to decide how much each of you can have. By negotiating directly with your spouse (or through a mediator or solicitors) you can save legal costs. It is a good idea, however, to get about an hour's advice from a solicitor to find out properly what your own rights and responsibilities may be before launching into negotiation uninformed.

For reasons of professional etiquette, it is not usually possible to have the same solicitor acting for both of you (unless the solicitor is acting as a mediator for the two of you – in which case he or she will not be able to give advice, but instead information). Some solicitors may be willing to see you and your spouse together, strictly on the basis that he or she will act only for one of you.

Remember that the amount of child support will usually be fixed and really only then will you be able to negotiate about financial matters, excluding maintenance for the children.

In your negotiations, your objective must be to achieve a workable financial settlement with your spouse. If you have carefully prepared an overall summary of your financial circumstances and calculated how a division of your income and assets might work out in practice, you will have a good idea as to whether the proposals that you intend to make are realistic or not.

Proposals

Once you are satisfied that you have a clear view of the overall financial picture and that both sides have fully disclosed their financial positions to each other, you can put forward proposals for settlement on a 'without prejudice' basis. This means that if the proposals do not result in settlement and litigation does follow, they cannot be referred to in argument before a court. Your or your solicitor's 'open' negotiations (as against 'without prejudice') would place you in a vulnerable position in that your spouse could later use in court any admissions you have made. Accordingly, if your solicitor is conducting negotiations for you, he or she will automatically head proposals with the words 'without prejudice'; if you are conducting negotiations yourself, you should do likewise.

Usually it is the spouse who will be paying maintenance and/or a lump sum who puts forward the first proposals; frequently (but not always) these result in counter-proposals from the other spouse. Generally, the eventual agreement will fall somewhere between these two sets of proposals.

You may, therefore, be tempted to pitch your first proposals very low (or very high as the case may be). This is, on the whole, not a good idea. Although whatever proposals you make may be interpreted as just an opening bid, unrealistic proposals will sour the atmosphere and prolong the agony, with inevitable consequences in terms of both acrimony and legal costs. They are also likely to prompt your spouse into being equally unrealistic when it comes to counter-proposals, and you will be faced with what appears to be an unbridgeable gulf.

Compromising

Carefully timed, well-thought-out and realistic proposals should mean that there is not too wide a gap between you. The question then is one of how to close that gap altogether. Look at the calculations you have made and put yourself in your partner's shoes. You have the advantage of knowing your spouse well and you are likely to know what will be attractive and what will be abhorrent.

Ultimately, you may have to split the difference between you and/or reach a bargain over household goods or the car, for example, to offset an imbalance in terms of hard cash. Reaching a compromise, however, should not mean bullying your spouse into submission or allowing yourself to be bullied. If you feel this is happening, talk it over with your solicitor to get an objective view as to whether you or your spouse are being unreasonable. Similarly, if you feel that your spouse is not giving full disclosure or is deliberately disposing of assets, make your worries clear to your solicitor without delay – the court has powers to deal with tactics such as these.

Financial help from the state

When the marriage breaks up and you have separated, you may find that you need – and now are eligible for – financial help from the state.

State benefits (that is, payment of one kind or another) have over the past few years been radically reorganised. Old familiar names such as supplementary benefit and family income support have been replaced by new types of benefits.

The seven main types of new benefit which you could be eligible to apply for are:

- jobseeker's allowance
- income support
- family credit
- one-parent benefit
- housing benefit
- council tax benefit
- loans from the social fund.

Income-based or non-contributory jobseeker's allowance (JSA), income support (IS) and family credit (FC) can lead to the recipient being entitled to other benefits, for example, legal advice and assistance under the green form scheme (see Chapter 1). However, since hikes in court fees were introduced in a new scheme in January 1997, only people in receipt of IS, FC, JSA or those getting advice under the green form scheme will be eligible for a reduction in court fees.

For JSA, you must go to the Jobcentre in person and ask to make a claim. You can claim by post only if your door-to-door journey to the Jobcentre is longer than an hour and you will be away from home for more than four hours. You will need to complete a JSA claim form and a form called 'Your Job Search'. Availability of IS has been much reduced since the introduction in 1996 of JSA (although lone parents can still get it), but if you still can claim IS or want to claim FC, you have to apply to the DSS on the appropriate forms, which are available from post offices, Benefits Agencies and CABx.

As we go to press, governmental plans to reduce welfare benefits to lone parents are under discussion, coupled with potentially more positive plans to help lone parents get back to work if they are able to. You may need to make more enquiries about this – the National Council for One Parent Families★ is a good source of up-to-date information on all issues for lone parents.

Welfare benefits, child support and court orders

Occasionally a child support assessment or even a court order for maintenance could increase a wife's income such that she is no longer eligible for her usual benefits. As a knock-on effect she might suffer real hardship: she may lose her 'passported benefits' like her right to have free school meals for her children, her right to apply for loans from the social fund and, most importantly, her right to have her mortgage repayments or rent paid. When child support is assessed by the CSA, there is no flexibility in cases where wives are 'floated off' IS and thereby lose their passported benefits. However, no such rigidity prevails when spousal maintenance and other financial matters are worked out. Here care must be taken when calculating maintenance: consider whether proceeding with a claim through the courts will really be worthwhile.

There are other effects to be aware of when working out entitlement to welfare benefits:

- *Maintenance and welfare benefits*
Payments of maintenance will reduce the amount of IS pound for

pound. However, with FC, housing benefit and council tax benefit, the first £15 of maintenance will be disregarded, so paying maintenance results in a real financial benefit to the family.

- *Lump sums*

If a lump sum is ordered through the courts, the amount may take a wife above the capital limit, and IS (or FC) would then cease. The interest which the DSS assumes to be coming from the lump sum may also make her ineligible.

- *Arrears*

If a woman has to claim IS because her husband is not paying the maintenance he was ordered to pay, and he later does pay off the arrears, she will be asked to repay any benefits she has received in the meantime.

- *The CSA*

Since April 1993 claimants of IS, FC or disability working allowance (DWA), and, in some circumstances, JSA must approach the CSA for calculation and collection of maintenance payments. Others can also do so and since the Agency has waived its fees until April 1999, no fees are payable until then. For more about child support via the CSA see Chapter 5.

The various benefits and how they will affect you as a one-parent family under the new system are summarised below.

Jobseeker's allowance

JSA, introduced in October 1996, replaces unemployment benefit and to some extent IS too. IS has now been abolished for all those required to sign on for work, but is still available for lone parents looking after children under 16 (or those who are caring for a household member who is ill or is disabled), so JSA is likely to apply to you only if your marriage breakdown has unfortunately coincided with the loss of your job and you are not looking after the children on a day-to-day basis or your children are older than 16 (and not disabled).

There are two kinds of JSA – contribution-based and income-based. The former is similar to the old unemployment benefit. It lasts for 26 weeks and is available as of right to those who have the necessary National Insurance credits. Once the 26 weeks run out, income-based JSA replaces it; it is subject to means testing. The income-based

JSA has passported benefits like housing benefit, free school meals and legal aid.

To qualify for JSA, a claimant must satisfy certain 'labour market conditions':

- he or she must be capable of work
- he or she must be available for employment
- he or she must be actively seeking work and
- have a current jobseeker's agreement.

Capital of over £8,000 will disentitle a claimant to income-based JSA. Applicants are also means tested. The benefit rates paid are by and large the same as for IS and there are similar restrictions on mortgage interest payments.

Income support

This benefit, which originally replaced supplementary benefit, is now much curtailed since the introduction of JSA, but it is still available for lone parents looking after children under 16 (see above). It can be claimed by lone parents who are not working or are not in full-time work (for DSS purposes, full-time work is 16 hours or more a week).

For those still eligible, even an owner-occupier with savings of up to £8,000 who has not paid National Insurance contributions can claim IS. The amount you can get depends on your age and whether there are children in the family, as well as on how much you have coming in from other sources such as benefits, maintenance and part-time work. Savings of between £3,000 and £8,000 will also affect the amount, as you will be deemed to have an income of £1 for every £250 (or part of £250) over and above £3,000. After you have returned the tear-off slip on form IS1, you will receive a claim form on which you must give full details of your situation. If you prefer not to fill in the form, you may be able to ask for an interview with someone from the Benefits Agency.

At present (1997/98 rates) the maximum IS for a single person over 25 is £49.15 a week plus £16.90 for each child under 11 (more if the child is older), plus 'premiums' for people with extra needs such as being a lone parent.

Changes to lone-parent benefits

In April 1996 the government started restricting benefits to lone parents. The restrictions are quite complex but in essence involve the freezing of certain benefits to lone parents and the phasing out of benefits too. In 1997, for example, the child benefit payable to lone parents for the first child remained at £17.10 (frozen since 1996, although the rate payable to couples increased). From June 1998 this augmented child benefit will not be available to new claimants. If you wish to find out more, the National Council for One Parent Families* has a booklet called *Benefits and tax* available free to lone parents.

Income support and mortgage repayments

If you pay a mortgage, IS will pay only the interest, not the capital repayments. There are other limitations about how much the DSS will pay. Since October 1995 homeowners claiming IS for the first time will be paid no interest at all for the first two months, and half the interest for the next four months (this replaces the old 16-week rule). The maximum mortgage loan taken into account for IS has also been capped – at £100,000 – so if the mortgage is more than that, the DSS will not meet the extra payments.

If you are unlucky enough to have bought a house with the aid of a mortgage or switched your mortgage to a new mortgage company (like a bank or building society) *after the beginning of October 1995*, IS will not cover any mortgage interest at all. However, you may be covered by an insurance policy, which the government has identified as the safety net for homeowners. Check the terms of the policy carefully – most policies cover the risks of only redundancy, not separation. Even then, most policies do not kick in until three months after redundancy, and some are limited to payments for, say, a two-year period.

Family credit

You can claim FC if you or your partner are working for 16 hours or more a week and are responsible for at least one child who is a member of your household (you do not have to be the parent). The amount you get depends on your income, the income of your partner (if you live with one), and how many children you have.

To calculate how much you might be entitled to, add together your take-home pay, your partner's take-home pay, any welfare benefits you are receiving (excluding child benefit and one-parent benefit) and any other money coming in from, say, maintenance payments or rent from a boarder. For these two latter categories, some of the monies received will be disregarded (ignored) when calculating your eligibility:

- maintenance – disregard the first £15
- income from boarders – disregard the first £20 plus 50 per cent of the balance.

If you are self-employed, use the amount of your profit after deducting allowable expenses as the figure for take-home pay.

To get the maximum amount of FC your net income must be less than £77.15 (1997/98 rates) a week (although if it is more than that you may still be able to qualify). For example, a parent with one child under 11 years old, earning up to the threshold of £77.15 a week, would be able to get £47.65 adult credit (plus an extra £10.55 for working more than 30 hours per week) and £12.05 child credit.

Housing benefit and council tax benefit

You can get help to pay your rent and council tax if you are on a low income and have savings of less than £16,000. If you have savings of less than £3,000, your capital will be disregarded; over and above this, up to £16,000, you will be deemed to have an income (called a 'tariff income') of £1 for every £250.

The rates used for calculating payment of housing benefit payment and council tax benefit are generally similar to the premiums that make up IS. For example, childcare costs of up to £60 and the first £15 of maintenance payments will be disregarded. The maximum you can get is 100 per cent of your 'eligible rent' (this may not be the same as the amount you pay your landlord – check with your CAB or Benefits Agency for details) and also 100 per cent of your council tax bill. Other discounts on council tax, for example the 25 per cent sole-occupancy discount for occupiers who live alone, may also be available.

If you have more money coming in than the allowances and premiums you qualify for (the money you need to live on, according to official calculations), you get less benefit.

Housing benefit cannot help with mortgage interest payments and other expenses, such as fuel bills. You may be able to get more advice from Shelter National Campaign for the Homeless.★

Loans from the social fund

There are several types of payment which you may be able to get from the social fund. If you need help to buy things for a new baby and are getting IS or FC, you may be able to get a maternity payment.

To spread the payment for an exceptional expense you may be able to get a 'budgeting loan'. This is interest-free but repayable, normally from your weekly IS or other benefits.

If you are not receiving any IS, you could still get a 'crisis loan' to help pay for living expenses, or for something you need urgently following an emergency or disaster, if you have no other way of meeting your needs. You have to apply in person to the social fund officer at your local Benefits Agency; however, entitlement to payments depends on available resources and if the fund has reached its limit for the period your application may be refused.

If a single parent is unable to repay a loan, social fund officers are entitled under certain circumstances to try to recoup the money from any person liable to maintain the children.

Making agreements over money

You may be relieved to know that only a small percentage – about 10 per cent – of divorce cases end up in a full-blown battle over money. The rest are settled by agreement at some stage along the line: at the very beginning of the separation (or before), or even on the steps outside the court doors just before the final financial hearing is to be held. The fact that mediation is now more widely available and can be used by families who want to save on legal costs also offers another option to come to a resolution of family disputes speedily, efficiently and effectively.

Whenever an agreement is made, the family as a whole is likely to save significantly on legal costs. There are rare cases where a spouse pretends to make an agreement while in reality being determined to drag out the process of resolution, but as a general rule making agreements will save you money, and the earlier you can do so the more money will be saved on legal fees.

Although you have the option of keeping your agreements oral and relying on your spouse's sense of honour, the problem is that such agreements have a habit of unravelling over time as one or other spouse claims no longer to be able to 'remember' the terms. So, to protect yourself properly, an agreement should be drawn up in the form of a separation agreement or deed, or, far better still, a consent order made by the court. If you have reached a settlement through mediation, this will usually be drawn up in the form of a 'Summary' or 'Memorandum of Understanding' which again should be translated, usually by solicitors, into a court order which you seek from the court to make it financially watertight.

Financial agreements and child support

Since the Child Support Act 1991 came into force in April 1993, agreements about how much child support should be paid cannot always be properly made in practice. Claimants of income-based JSA, IS, FC or DWA will automatically be referred to the CSA for the Agency to assess child support and collect the amount calculated to be due from the parent who has left the family home. Any agreements made can be overridden by the CSA. Non-claimants, on the other hand, have a choice: either to use the CSA or to make a voluntary agreement about how much should be paid, which can be translated into a court order made by consent. (They will, however, no longer be able to ask the courts to make an order for maintenance for the children if there is a dispute about how much should be paid, because the courts have lost their powers to make orders in disputes over maintenance for natural and/or marital children – they still can deal with maintenance disputes over stepchildren).

Any agreement about child support will last for only as long as it is a real agreement – if one parent chooses to back out of it, it will be open for him or her to use the Agency for a child support assessment. Even if parents choose to make agreements rather than use the Agency, it is sensible to use the formula for working out how much child support should be paid as a bench-mark, otherwise the paying parent could go to the Agency in the future.

There is one significant practical advantage to making agreements over using the Agency. The CSA has a huge backlog of claims built up over its early years in operation, sometimes resulting in waits of many months for those submitting claims. It is taking steps to tackle the backlog but it is still criticised for being too slow. So where parents can, making an agreement themselves could speed up the settlement process.

Separation agreements

Separation agreements are sometimes simply referred to as agreements, sometimes as deeds. The distinction between the two documents is that the latter is drawn up 'under seal', which is sometimes necessary if the document provides for a transfer of capital assets (like the home). A deed will have small circular red stickers placed by the side of your signatures, which must be witnessed.

Before making a separation agreement, be sure that you are both fully aware of each other's financial situations, what each earns, owns and owes. It is sensible to consult a solicitor to check the terms you and your spouse have in mind, and perhaps to draft the appropriate documents.

The form of a separation agreement or even a deed is fairly flexible and it can be designed to suit your own particular requirements. The issues that are usually covered include:

- an agreement for spouses to live separate and apart
- agreements about whom the children will live with and how often the other parent will see them and/or have them to stay
- any agreement concerning the house, for example who will live there, whether and when it might be sold, how the sale proceeds will be divided
- agreements to pay sums of spousal maintenance; over what period and how much
- any agreements for the payment of capital sum(s) and/or the dividing up of other assets.

Courts do not like seeing any curbs on their own power, so any provision which supposedly ousts the jurisdiction of the courts (for example, saying that neither party is allowed to go to court over any financial issues) will be void. This in effect means that an agreement or deed could later be challenged in the courts. However, the courts are most likely to uphold the agreement or deed unless, for example, it was made with one spouse being unaware of the full extent of the other's wealth or unless one spouse was forced to sign by the bullying behaviour of the other (sometimes known as 'duress').

Care should always be taken about what separation agreements or deeds contain. Even though they may appear quite informal, they pave the way for future long-term financial arrangements and can have serious repercussions in the form of tax consequences (for example, increasing the likelihood of Capital Gains Tax being payable if the home is kept on in joint names in the longer term after one co-owner has left).

Separation agreements or deeds can be enforced by an application to the county court (such applications are rare) if either party later proves reluctant to keep to them. Although such agreements and deeds are not absolutely watertight, the court is more likely to uphold the original terms if both spouses had received independent legal advice, there had been full financial disclosure and there had been no duress.

Financial agreements and divorce

Once the divorce has been started, an existing separation agreement or deed should be converted by applying to the court for a consent order to be made. The parties may also reach an agreement over money at some later stage when or after the divorce papers are filed; again, they can then apply for a consent order.

An application for a consent order involves the drawing up of a draft court order which the parties would like the court to make: this is usually called by lawyers 'minutes of agreement and consent order'. This too can be tailor-made to fit your own requirements (and so can often suit an individual family far better than can a court order made by the court after a battle).

One of the main reasons why lawyers emphasise that a court order should be drawn up instead of leaving an oral or written agreement as it stands is the issue of a clean break. The husband and wife may have amicably agreed to a clean break: that they will divide their assets to give the wife a greater share to compensate her for giving up her claims against the husband for maintenance. But so long as no court has formally ordered a dismissal of the wife's maintenance claims, they can still be activated at a later stage. If she were to fall on hard times or were to see her husband's financial standing improve, she would still be able to make a further claim for maintenance from him (unless she had remarried). Indeed, as long as she had included capital claims, say, in the petition, these would continue, even after remarriage, unless dismissed by the court.

To ensure that the form of a proposed consent order is as watertight, tax-efficient and comprehensive as possible, a solicitor should be instructed to draw up the documents. Note that making a clean-break order by consent will not preclude a future application for child support via the CSA. A 1993 case confirmed the long-standing principle that clean breaks can end only a wife's (or, more rarely, a husband's) right to maintenance and never a parent's responsibility to maintain the children. Some parents who had previously agreed clean-break orders are now finding that the amount of child maintenance, if the Agency becomes involved, dramatically increases beyond their initial expectations. Since 1996 parents can apply for a departure direction in the departure system if the result appears unfair – see Chapter 5.

The consent order

An order made by consent can be much more comprehensive than an order made after a contested hearing. This is because you and your spouse can include undertakings (formal promises) in respect of matters over which the court could make no order: for example, an undertaking by a husband to retain sufficient funds in his own bank account to meet his obligations, to arrange the transfer to his wife of a car owned by a company of which he has control, and so on. Undertakings are enforceable, so make sure that you do not undertake to do anything which might turn out to be impossible.

You can also include 'recitals' setting out the background to the order: for example, that you intend it to be in full and final settlement of any claims. If you have agreed the form of a clean break, it is also wise to include a recital that neither you nor your spouse will be entitled on the death of the other to make a claim against the estate of the deceased spouse under the Inheritance (Provision for Family and Dependants) Act 1975 as amended by the Law Reform (Succession) Act 1995. You can also note 'for the record', for example, that the family home has been sold and the proceeds divided (and, by implication, taken into account in the overall settlement).

Do not forget to include reference to costs, whether for payment by one party of the other's costs or 'no order for costs', and deal, too, with orders for costs 'reserved' on any interim applications where there has been some litigation between the husband and wife before reaching the stage of applying for a consent order.

The words 'liberty to apply' are sometimes written into the wording of consent orders. This confirms that either spouse can go back to the court for implementation of the order. It does not allow either party to seek in any way to vary the terms of an order for a lump sum or of a property adjustment order.

An application can be made by a couple at any time within the divorce proceedings for an order to be made by consent for maintenance pending suit (temporary maintenance payments made to a spouse until the decree absolute) and for interim periodical payments for children. For a final order (lump sum, property adjustment, periodical payments) the application cannot be made before you apply for 'directions for trial' under the special procedure. The order will not be made until the decree nisi has been pronounced and will not become effective until decree absolute.

To apply for an order, you will need to lodge with the court:

- agreed 'minutes of agreement and consent orders', signed by both parties and their solicitors if instructed, in duplicate; only one copy need be signed
- a short synopsis of the family's financial circumstances (known as form M1)
- if financial applications have not already been made, a formal application (form M11 or M13 as appropriate) by both parties
- court fees – £20 for the consent order and £50 for form M11 or M13 (reduced to £30 if the application is made by consent right from the start).

Form M1. Financial information form on the lodging of a consent order

This form is obtainable from the divorce court office. The information it seeks includes details of:

- the length of the marriage, the age of each party and of any minor or dependent child of the family
- an estimate in summary form of the approximate amount or

value of the capital resources and net income of each party and of any minor child of the family

- what arrangements are intended for the accommodation of each of the parties and any minor children, and what child support payments are being made
- whether either party has remarried or has any present intention to marry or to cohabit with another person
- where the terms of the order provide for the transfer of property, a statement confirming that any mortgagee of that property has been served with notice of application and that no objection to such transfer has been made by the mortgagee within 14 days from such service
- any other especially significant matters.

There is a very serious obligation on each party to give full financial disclosure. Just how serious that is was shown by a decision by the House of Lords, the highest appeal court in the country. In the particular case, decree absolute was pronounced in April, terms of agreement were reached in August and about one week later the ex-wife became engaged to be married without telling the court or her ex-husband. On 2 September an order was made by consent; on 22 September, in accordance with the order, the husband transferred his half-share in the home to the wife who, two days later, remarried. In these circumstances, the court order was held to be invalid for lack of proper disclosure and the ex-husband was entitled to have it set aside.

These circumstances were somewhat exceptional. You would not be able to have an order set aside on the grounds of failure to disclose some minor matter which would not have made any difference to the order the court would have made.

Financial applications

If the court order is to provide for the dismissal of either party's claims (so as to achieve a clean-break situation), it is essential for the court to have the claims before it in order to dismiss them (or to deal with them generally). Both petitioner and respondent should file form M11 or M13 as appropriate drafted so as to include all the financial applications that each party is entitled to make. A fee of £50 is usually payable to the court unless the application is by consent from the start, when the fee is reduced to £30.

Making of the consent order

Once the consent order minutes, financial statement and applications have been lodged at the court, the district judge will review them. Provided the district judge has sufficient information to be satisfied that the proposed terms are reasonable and both parties are in agreement, he or she is likely to accept the agreement and issue a formal consent order as requested.

If the agreement is put forward by solicitors on each side, the district judge may approve it without either spouse having to attend in person, but if you are acting for yourself, the district judge will probably make an appointment to discuss the proposed order with you and your spouse, and may require further evidence, especially if no affidavit has been filed. Approval by a district judge is not a rubber-stamping procedure: in certain cases, where the district judge feels that the order is unfair to either party, he or she may refuse to make it (although, again, this is unlikely if you have negotiated terms through a solicitor).

Effect of a consent order

Consent orders, once made, are as effective as orders made by the court after a full hearing. You can apply to have a consent order set aside only on grounds of:

- fresh evidence that could not have been known at the time
- fundamental mistakes, such as wholly erroneous information on which all parties, including the court, relied
- fraud (which may include evidence that the other party had no intention of ever abiding by the terms of the order)
- lack of full and frank disclosure if such disclosure would have resulted in an order substantially different from that which was made
- in certain rare circumstances, where the fundamental basis on which the order was made has been destroyed.

Chapter 3

Legal advice

At an early stage in your divorce/separation process, you should consider obtaining legal advice about your best future course of action. While a do-it-yourself divorce is relatively easy if you agree that there is to be a divorce and on what basis, you will almost certainly need a solicitor's help if there is little or no common ground between you. Wherever financial arrangements and division of property are at issue, or where there is uncertainty about the children, an initial advisory meeting with a solicitor specialising in divorce problems has much to recommend it, if only to avoid giving up rights in ignorance of the law.

If you can sort out your financial affairs as equal partners, between yourselves or with the help of a mediator (see Chapter 4), so much the better – although even then it is wise for you both to ask a solicitor whether the arrangements seem fair, and to ensure that they are framed in a watertight manner so as not to leave you open for future unexpected financial claims and that they do not result in any unnecessary payments of tax.

If you are intending to use mediation as the primary means of sorting out your arrangements comprehensively, ask your solicitor about his or her attitude towards mediation. Some solicitors have now been trained as mediators themselves and are likely to have a more constructive approach towards agreements worked out through mediation, as long as they do not work against your (and the family's) best interests. There are, however, a few, perhaps more old-fashioned, solicitors who may be instinctively anti-mediation and may thus not be helpful in advising you objectively if you do reach arrangements through mediation.

If it is not possible for the two of you to achieve a fair agreement on your own or via a mediator, a solicitor can negotiate on your behalf. As pointed out in Chapter 2, it is not usually possible for you and your spouse to instruct the same solicitor as there is a potential conflict of interest between you (although services such as the Cambridge Family and Divorce Centre★ can arrange a joint appointment with one solicitor; see Chapter 4).

A solicitor can be of great help, but try to use his or her services efficiently and economically. Ask yourself whether you want to obtain legal advice or want someone to 'fight' for you. Wanting a solicitor to act for you in a contentious way will involve you in expense which may be out of proportion to anything gained. It is also extremely non-cost-effective to use a solicitor as an emotional support, whatever the temptations.

Time and money are invariably interlinked. The more you use a solicitor's services, the greater the hole that will be cut into your financial budget. What a solicitor can effectively do for you is explained in detail in this chapter. It is of the utmost importance that you consider the question of costs before launching into a major battle. Of course, how much you want to (or are forced to) involve your solicitor may be constrained by how much you can afford to pay. Explanations and warnings about the problem of costs have already been given. If you have not already done so, read Chapter 1 now.

Future changes in the law

The Family Law Act 1996, if and when it is fully implemented in 1999, will make many changes in peoples' experience of divorce. At present, when someone is considering divorce, a first step may be to go straight to a solicitor. The Family Law Act would probably change all that. Divorce information meetings – where people can gain more information about the process of divorce and the services available – will be offered and attending such a meeting will be a required step three months before a divorce application can be made under the new law. Mediation services are likely to play a greater role, and as we go to press the second phase of a Legal Aid Board pilot scheme offering free mediation to people who live in the pilot areas and who are getting advice under the green form scheme is about to start. Marriage counselling under the new framework may also be provided for free where both partners are eligible for legal aid. What this means for solicitors is that their role in divorce might well diminish. But as long as the divorce process remains a legal one and is not converted into a purely administrative one, and family law remains flexible enough to suit individual family circumstances, spending an hour or so (at the very least) with an experienced and competent solicitor to get advice on your legal position is likely to be a worthwhile investment.

What a solicitor can do for you

A solicitor should discuss your position dispassionately and advise you from the benefit of his or her experience what is likely to happen about the separation, the divorce (if and when that happens), the children and money matters. Good advice early on may prevent matters becoming complicated, or one party getting less than his or her entitlement, and can generally help to take the heat out of the situation.

Handling your divorce

An undefended divorce is possible to do yourself without a solicitor, although it is probably fair to say that it is at least as hard as doing your own conveyancing on your house (and the financial pitfalls can be worse if something goes wrong). Do-it-yourself divorce packs are widely available but the packs may contain out-of-date forms, so you should double check these with the court. Be wary of taking important steps without legal advice: the packs can give you general but not individual advice, which can be provided only by solicitors or Citizens Advice Bureaux (CABx). Be particularly wary of the common assumption that getting a divorce means an end to your financial obligations to your ex-spouse – divorce and money matters are considered quite separately by the courts and getting a divorce does not mean an automatic end to your money concerns. In any event, if a divorce petition arrives through your letterbox and you are unsure what to do about it, or if your spouse flatly refuses to cooperate in any way, a solicitor's advice would be useful.

Sorting out problems over children

Protracted litigation over the children can be extremely expensive. Also, it is harmful to the children and you, and rarely produces a satisfactory result. If you cannot come to an agreement by yourselves or through mediation, see if you can arrange a meeting for both of you and your solicitors. Disputes over children cannot be 'won' or 'lost', and ultimately you are likely to prefer a solution that you reach yourselves, rather than having to accept one imposed upon you by a judge who, however wise and well meaning, does not – and cannot – know you or your children.

Getting a court order for maintenance and division of property
A solicitor will know the appropriate court (see page 289) for the particular order you require and the procedure for applying.

Getting information about finances
You may find that you are faced with a long uphill battle to get financial information out of your spouse. However much you want to be reasonable over things, and whatever you do, he or she may refuse to disclose assets.

Withholding information at the early stages does nothing but run up costs and will reduce the amount that there is to go round. If you go to see a solicitor, your spouse may then do so too, and may be persuaded to come clean about details of his or her financial situation. You will both need to disclose your finances fully to each other before a proper agreement can be reached.

Getting an agreement about finances
Good solicitors will impress upon both of you the advantages of cooperation and help you to negotiate an agreement about finances.

If your resources leave very limited room for manoeuvre, fighting it out in court may not be worthwhile. It is pointless getting your solicitor to try to push for more, or less, if the cost of getting it is going to be more than the amount you are asking for. If money disputes go on for months or years, the costs will run into thousands of pounds even where small amounts are in dispute. Even if you are in receipt of legal aid and do not initially have to pay your solicitor's charges as they arise, you have to do so ultimately under what is known as the Legal Aid Board's 'statutory charge' (see Chapter 1).

If you have reached an agreement with your spouse and the issues seem fairly clear cut, it may still be worthwhile considering having one interview with a solicitor to check over the terms of that proposed agreement, particularly if you have reached agreement only about the broad outlines of how you are going to split your finances. Sadly, agreements, especially unwritten, have a habit of unravelling over time unless all their consequences are thought through and the agreements recorded officially. Formalising an agreement need not jeopardise amicable relations with your spouse: indeed, doing so could pave the way for a more painless divorce.

A solicitor may also be able to:

- put an agreement into wording that is clear and will be acceptable to the court
- arrange maintenance and the division of property in a more tax-efficient way
- draw up a 'clean-break' settlement where appropriate (particularly where there are no young children)
- point out things that you may not have thought of: for example, that a wife may be losing substantial widow's pension rights under her husband's pension scheme
- explain how the new pension law works and what changes are in the offing that may affect you
- take into account the effects of any proposed order on welfare benefits entitlements
- advise you whether it would be better for you and your family to go ahead with a divorce now before the new law comes in or wait until after its implementation.

Finding a solicitor

When you have decided to consult a solicitor, choose one who is experienced in and up-to-date about matrimonial work. This will not necessarily be the solicitor with whom you have previously dealt (perhaps about buying the house or making your will) unless he or she is also experienced in family law. But a solicitor you have used before may have a colleague who specialises in divorce matters, to whom you can be referred. If the firm has acted for both of you (husband and wife) in the past, there is likely to be a policy of acting for neither in a matrimonial dispute. A solicitor should not act for you if he or she has previously acted for your spouse.

Ask acquaintances who have been divorced whom they used, although you should be wary of recommendations in cases which are very different from your own. It is also worthwhile making enquiries at your local CAB or advice centre or even your local county court (each court keeps a list of solicitors who appear before the court). The Law Society's *Regional Directories* of solicitors practising in the area and showing the categories of the work they undertake are available in CABx, public libraries and court offices throughout the UK. The *Directories* and CABx should also be able to point you in the direction of lawyers willing to do legal aid work. If you qualify for legal aid there are significant advantages, not least exemption from court fees.

The task of finding a solicitor through *Yellow Pages* if you do not have any recommendations is also now easier since *Yellow Pages* has created in most of its directories special sections for solicitors who are members of the Solicitors Family Law Association (SFLA – see below)* identified by the SFLA logo, as well as another section for solicitors who offer legal aid. Look under the heading 'Solicitors' (usually there is very little listed under 'Divorce').

When you telephone or write to a firm of solicitors asking for an appointment, say that you wish to be advised in connection with your matrimonial difficulties and ask if they have a solicitor specialising in divorce and related financial matters, preferably one who is a member of the SFLA.

The SFLA is in practice a very good source for tracking down a specialist family lawyer. It is an association of around 4,000 matrimonial lawyers in England and Wales who must subscribe to a code of practice designed to encourage and assist parties to reach acceptable arrangements for the future in a positive and conciliatory – rather than in an aggressive and litigious – way. This does not mean that an SFLA solicitor will be 'soft'. His or her advice to you will be positive and so, too, should be his or her manner of dealing with the various issues that arise. You can request a copy of the SFLA Code of Practice which tells you more about the goals of your SFLA solicitor's practice.

You can also ask the administrative secretary of the SFLA for a list of the solicitor members in your region. If there are no SFLA solicitors practising in your area, you can telephone the Records Section of the Law Society of England and Wales,* which can give you the names of three solicitors local to you.

Using the Internet

With an estimated one in three households with children now

having a home computer and with the Internet, or World Wide Web, being an increasingly used source of information, some readers may wish to use the Internet as a method of choosing their solicitor. The usefulness of the Internet for people who want to find a solicitor and/or a mediator and perhaps also find out more about what's in store in their divorce is still somewhat limited but improving all the time. Family lawyers have been slow to use the Internet as a means of contacting potential clients via creating their own web sites, but there are some exceptions (you will see that some of the addresses listed at the end of this book have their own web sites). Your chances of success of finding a local solicitor on the Internet are closely linked to where you are – London and other major cities are generally better served. You can take advantage of the search facilities offered by the Web by searching for particular key words – 'divorce', 'family lawyer', 'family mediation' – ensuring that your search is limited to the UK. You could also type in your locality (e.g. Manchester) and see what comes up. Many legal web sites are somewhat 'boring' but at least they should give you an idea of what is on offer at a firm. Others will include full explanations of their services and fees, pictures of solicitors (so you can see what they look like) and sometimes 'update' pages which you can visit to get free information.

Accreditation scheme for family lawyers?

Another possible means of finding a specialist family lawyer should be, in future, via an accreditation scheme, still in its planning stages as we go to press, but which should cover specialist and experienced family solicitors nationwide. Contact the Law Society for more details.

Low-priced interview

The old-style, fixed-fee interview, under which you could get up to half an hour's legal advice for £5, was abolished in 1993, although you may still find some solicitors' firms offering it. Officially, there is a new scheme in its place called the 'low-priced' interview. Irrespective of your financial means, under this scheme you are allowed half an hour's advice from a solicitor at a reduced cost. The maximum chargeable for this is £25, and in some parts of the country this half-hour session may even be free. Various local schemes have been set up by

CABx, so try your nearest bureau first. Otherwise, you can track down firms of solicitors who offer low-priced interviews (not all do) in the Law Society's *Regional Directories*.

You must make it clear when making an appointment that you wish to see a solicitor on the low-priced (or fixed-fee) basis. You are more likely to see a junior than an experienced solicitor under the scheme.

The Bar Council's Pro-Bono Unit

With the numbers of people who are potentially financially eligible for legal aid now shrinking, one possibility of getting legal advice for free, which might be worth looking into, is the Bar Council's Pro-Bono Unit. The Bar Council★ is the barristers' equivalent of the solicitors' Law Society and runs a scheme whereby barristers (or counsel) offer free legal advice to deserving cases. Normally barristers cannot advise members of the public direct – their clients are the solicitors – but this scheme operates so that barristers can give direct advice. The scheme, which covers many other areas of law too, is limited to those without financial resources who would otherwise be unable to have their case heard. In most cases a solicitor will still need to be involved, but it might be worthwhile enquiring. The address and contact details are at the back of the book.

Seeking advice from solicitors

Remember that time is money, so try to use your solicitor's time as efficiently as possible. A succinct letter to him or her setting out what you want to do (your 'instructions') may well be more cost-effective than a long rambling telephone conversation. If you can go prepared for your first interview, so much the better. Some solicitors send a questionnaire to their clients before the first interview, to be completed and returned in advance of the interview. Otherwise, try to take along with you, on your first appointment:

- your marriage certificate (if you can find it)
- any correspondence or assessments from the Child Support Agency
- copies of any court orders made in respect of this marriage or any previous marriage – or in respect of your children
- typed or neatly written note setting out:

- your name in full, and those of your spouse and children
- dates of birth of yourself, your spouse and children
- details of any children in the household who are not children of the marriage
- your address and (if different) that of your spouse
- your home and work telephone numbers (and perhaps your email address if you have one)
- your occupation and that of your spouse
- names and addresses of the children's schools
- dates of any previous marriage of yourself and/or your spouse and dates of decrees absolute
- if you have already separated, the date and circumstances of the separation
- a summary of your financial position (include details of your and your spouse's income including welfare benefits; details of the home and its approximate value, and the name and address and mortgage account number of the mortgagee; any other capital assets and any debts and liabilities)
- any correspondence that you might have received from your spouse's solicitor.

To use your solicitor to the best advantage do not hesitate at any time to ask him or her to explain and discuss any points about which you are not clear. It may help to go prepared with notes of what you want to ask and then to take notes of the advice given. Indeed, this is a sensible precaution as otherwise it is all too easy to forget everything your solicitor has told you.

Remember that you can accept or reject advice as you wish. But before you reject advice, make sure that you understand the point.

Using your solicitor's time wisely and cost-effectively means not leaving it to your solicitor to do everything: because of the time basis of costing the bill, the more time he or she spends on the case, the higher the bill will be. Quite a lot can be done by you yourself that will save solicitor's costs, but tell your solicitor first what you plan to do.

Open your own file at home and be organised about keeping correspondence and any relevant documents safe, and keep copies of letters that you send to your solicitor.

You are entitled to be told at any stage how the case is progressing and how much it is costing. Your solicitor should send you a client care letter (see below) at the outset. Remember that you can ask your solicitor for interim statements of how costs are building up if they are not supplied automatically (many firms will do this now).

Although it can be tempting to forget about the question of costs, this is an area which you ignore at your peril. Running up hefty bills of costs, whether you are paying privately or have legal aid, will severely damage the ability of both partners to begin their lives afresh. Costs are dealt with at length in Chapter 1: read this now if you have not already done so.

'Client Care Code'

All solicitors are now supposed to comply with a 'Client Care Code', which sets out how clients should be kept informed and advised on who will be handling their case.

One of the Code's particular objectives is 'to ensure that the client who is unfamiliar with the law and lawyers receives the information he or she needs to make what is happening more comprehensible and thus to reduce areas of potential conflict and complaint'.

What this could mean in practice is that at the outset of your case – once you have seen and informed a solicitor that you want him or her to take on your case – you should receive a fairly detailed letter (sometimes called a 'client care' letter) which complies with the code. This might tell you, for example, the name of the person dealing with your case, the name of the head of the department and information about costs. It should also identify the person to complain to in the firm if you think you have got poor service. If your solicitor does *not* send out such a letter, it may be an indication that he or she is not really on the ball – so you may get better service elsewhere.

Complaints about solicitors and barristers

Solicitors

Occasionally the relationship between a client and a solicitor can break down. If you have a real, not an imagined, grievance against your solicitor (for example, if he or she persistently fails to return your telephone calls or to respond to your letters), it may be worthwhile having a word with the person identified in the client care letter as the one to complain to, or the head of the matrimonial department, or otherwise the senior partner of the firm (the name on the top of the notepaper). Switching to another solicitor can be an expensive process, as the new solicitor will have to read through all the paperwork that has already been produced: this can itself cause extra delay. So, if a sincere personal intervention can restore a good working relationship with your solicitor, this can often be the best action to take.

If, however, the situation fails to improve, you may wish to complain formally about your solicitor. Address your complaint in writing to the Office for the Supervision of Solicitors (OSS).★ The OSS produces a leaflet called *What to do if you are dissatisfied with your solicitor*, which may be useful, and also operates a helpline.

Once your complaint has been investigated, the next stage, if you are still unhappy, is to write to the Legal Services Ombudsman.★ Appointed under the Courts and Legal Services Act 1990, he or she oversees the handling of complaints against solicitors, barristers and licensed conveyancers.

Barristers

Another possibility is that later on you may have a complaint against your barrister or counsel, if instructed by your solicitor to act on your behalf – say, at a court hearing. Complaints about barristers can be hard to succeed with, but it is a good idea to check with your solicitor first to see if your grounds for grievance are well founded. Many courts carry a leaflet called *How to Complain about a Barrister* issued by the Bar Council complaints system. You can get hold of this leaflet from the Bar Council, Publications Department.

Other sources of advice and help

Anyone in difficulties over finance, tax, housing, the children, or rights generally, can go for advice to a CAB. All CABx have numerous leaflets and information about local sources of help and services. They differ across the country but many can provide you with everything from an impartial listener to representation at social security appeal tribunals or advice about money and county court representation. CABx are especially good at providing debt counselling services. You can find the address of your local branch in the telephone directory.

Other agencies which offer specialist help are listed at the back of the book.

Chapter 4

Mediation

> *No arrangement will work unless those who make it see the sense of it*
>
> Divorce Mediation and Counselling Service Guidance Notes

Many divorcing couples fear that if each spouse goes and sees his or her own separate solicitor the gulf between them will widen. This need not necessarily be the case, but in any event couples facing separation and divorce probably have a wider choice of services to help them get through the situation than ever before. This chapter deals with *mediation*: how separating couples can get skilled help to sort out their disputes over the divorce and all the issues involved with getting a divorce – money, the home, businesses, debts, pensions, and not least the children – without building up unbearably heavy legal costs. It covers what mediation is (and is not), the types of mediation available, what is likely to happen in the mediation process, who it is likely to work for and how to go about finding a mediator.

Going to an independent mediator is entirely a matter of choice: the services on offer are both voluntary (no one is forced to go and the sessions can be terminated by either of you if you so choose) and confidential. Mediation can take place at any time, even before divorce proceedings have been started. Sometimes it can be of help where the divorce ended years ago but where there are still intractable problems for example over the children.

Mediation is 'legally privileged', which means that nothing said in the context of the sessions can be used in evidence at court, if, eventually, legal action through the courts has to be taken. Documents disclosing financial information in a mediation are, however, usually treated as 'open', which means that they could be disclosed as evidence in court if a court case over money issues happens later. Also, any wish not to disclose an address to the partner will be respected. However, there is an important exception to both the confidentiality and privilege attached to mediation: where someone, particularly a child, appears to be suffering or is likely to suffer 'significant harm' (e.g. sexual abuse), the mediator may have to stop the mediation process, for example, and take steps to protect the child. What steps will be taken in practice may very often form part of the discussion between the mediator and the couple.

What is mediation?

Family mediation has been developing in the US from the 1960s and emerged in the UK in 1977: it was first used in Bristol in relation to disputes involving children in Bristol County Court. Since then it has grown to become a voluntary process encompassing all issues which arise in the wake of separation or divorce.

Defining exactly what mediation is is not easy. Dictionary definitions of the word do not capture the complex nature of mediation as practised in family matters. The Code of Practice for Family Mediators, produced by National Family Mediation (NFM)* and the Family Mediators Association (FMA),* defines mediation as 'a process in which an impartial third person assists those involved in family breakdown, and in particular separating or divorcing couples, to communicate better with one another and to reach their own agreed and informed decisions about some or all of the issues relating to or arising from the separation, divorce, children, finance or property'. Another, more technical but precise, definition comes from the Family Mediation Code of Practice produced by the Solicitors Family Law Association (SFLA).* It describes mediation as a process in which

1.1   a couple or any family members

1.2   whether or not they are legally represented

1.3   and at any time, whether or not there have been legal proceedings

1.4   agree to the appointment of a neutral third party (the mediator)

1.5   who is impartial

1.6   who has no authority to make any decisions with regard to their issues

1.7　which may relate to separation, divorce, children's issues, property and financial questions or any other issues they may raise

1.8　but who helps them reach their own informed decisions

1.9　by negotiated agreement

1.10　without adjudication.

The jargon

First, any potential confusion about the terms that are used here needs dispelling. Although 'mediation' is now the most popular term for describing the process of couples settling their disputes with the aid of an impartial, skilled person, 'conciliation', the term most often used in the past, is still occasionally used nowadays. For some people the term 'conciliation' is interchangeable now with 'mediation' but there is an important difference. 'Conciliation' is the term used to describe the court-based process of trying to make parties to a court dispute – usually over the children – settle their differences. The conciliator involved (usually a court welfare officer) may have to report to the court about the outcome of the discussions, so that conciliation is not entirely confidential and may involve a degree of coercion which mediation proper should not. However, there is also another potential confusion which can arise. Although the term 'conciliation' sounds like 'reconciliation', the two words mean quite different processes.

'Reconciliation' means getting couples back together again so is something quite different. The purpose of mediation (still sometimes termed 'conciliation'), on the other hand, is to enable couples to create their own tailor-made solutions to the issues which inevitably need sorting out in the wake of a separation or divorce. Although a few couples may decide to get back together when they are in mediation – and if there is a real prospect of reconciliation the likelihood of that happening will be greater in mediation than in the traditional legal process – for most couples the focus will be on current and future arrangements with each living apart, rather than looking back over the marriage.

Some mediation services deal only with problems relating to the children ('children only mediation'), whereas others deal with all issues (termed 'comprehensive' or 'all-issues' mediation, AIM) – whether or not to separate, the children, money, the home, family businesses, pensions and so on. You may therefore need to check what ranges of issues different local services are able to deal with.

Most mediation services will deal with unmarried couples who decide to split up. Here the legal issues are different – unmarried fathers have no automatic legal rights over their children, for example, and there can be no claims for maintenance for an ex-partner in her own right – but the process is pretty much the same.

In this chapter, we look at voluntary or out-of-court mediation (or conciliation). There is also a stage in the court process in contested disputes about the children called *conciliation*, or a *conciliation appointment*, which is explained more fully in Chapter 8. Most in-court conciliation is undertaken by a welfare officer from the civil division of the local Probation Service. Courts without their own conciliation service – and occasionally even those which have it – may suggest a referral to a local mediation agency. If this happens, remember that the decision about whether or not to go is still entirely up to you and that what happens in the sessions will be confidential.

Types of mediation

If you opt for mediation, you will need to decide whether to choose on the one hand a family mediator with a therapeutic or mental health background (a 'family mediator') or on the other a family mediator with a legal background (a 'lawyer mediator'). The former are, generally, mediators who have a background in social work or mental health (like therapists, counsellors, family court welfare officers, or social workers) and are therefore experienced in family problems. The latter are mediators who are experienced family lawyers; their particular skill and expertise is knowing what the law is with regard to family matters and how the courts are likely to deal with cases in divorce. Some services offer co-mediation where a family mediator and lawyer mediator work together. You should check what experience a mediator has before going to him or her. Advice on how to find a mediator is given later in this chapter.

Mediators with a therapeutic background (family mediators) have historically been cheaper than lawyer mediators. Most family mediation services are linked to NFM, and many of them charge fees based on a couple's income or even offer free sessions. Lawyer mediators will almost certainly charge more than family mediators, although some operate discretionary lower rates for low-income families. (See, however, page 90 on how you may be able to get free mediation under the pilot mediation scheme.) Because lawyer mediators offer more by way of legal information than mediators with a therapeutic background are usually able to do, it is more meaningful to compare their costs with those incurred by each spouse instructing a solicitor and both solicitors running up heavy costs. Lawyer mediators usually charge similar rates whether they are acting as traditional solicitors for one spouse or as mediators for both together – thus a husband and wife can potentially, by using a lawyer mediator rather than a solicitor, cut their legal costs considerably. Note that each spouse should still get independent legal advice, but because a couple is more likely to reach an agreement faster through a mediator than through separate solicitors, further costs savings will be achieved.

There are advantages in having a skilled lawyer assisting in the mediation process: although lawyer mediators do not advise either party individually, they draw on their own experience of family law cases in first of all piecing together an accurate picture of the family's finances and then in helping the couple work out realistic (and legally acceptable) solutions. Although mediators cannot offer advice, they can give the couple correct, up-to-date information on the rapidly changing law – such as changes on pensions and child support, and in procedure – so their clients can make well-informed choices during mediation. Family mediators often have an arrangement with a local solicitor who will check over the terms of an agreement towards the end of the mediation, but this may be rather late in the day to correct any wrong turnings made in the mediation process. However, an increasing number of NFM services are now using lawyer mediators too, so check with your local service.

The type of mediation service where a pair of mediators – a family mediator and a lawyer mediator – work together, known as co-mediation, was pioneered by the FMA, and is now used in many NFM services as well.

The mediation process

For mediation to work, both partners need to attend. It can be a daunting prospect to face your soon-to-be ex-spouse over a meeting table to discuss what future arrangements should be made, but a skilled mediator, who will always be impartial, will help by managing the process so that both parties can make their views clear. It is the mediator's responsibility to be even-handed, to create a balance between the parties so that they can both negotiate properly over conflicts. Even where a couple are very much in conflict with one another, addressing conflict is common in mediation and the right solutions can often be found. Mediation is very often the most appropriate forum for conflicts to be resolved.

A mediator will not impose his or her own views but will try to help a couple find common ground so that together they can craft arrangements which will work for each of them individually and the family as a whole. Sometimes this process can necessitate a mediator encouraging the more passive partner to put his or her own views forward and ensuring that the more dominant partner stays less verbal. The mediator will establish ground rules, to create a more positive framework for working things out. The agreement to mediate, which forms the basis of the terms on which a mediator will act in a mediation, will set out what the partners agree to in the mediation.

Mediation works by setting agendas covering the issues each party wants to discuss – it is up to each of the couple to decide what they need to talk about. The process of mediation is likely to take around five to six sessions, although more or fewer may be necessary. The agenda for the first session could cover, for example, the decision to separate, arrangements for the time being over the children, and payment of bills. Mediations are usually relatively informal, with first names being used. At the first session the mediator will explain what the process of mediation is all about and the terms of the mediation agreement.

As part and parcel of the agreement, in all-issues mediation both spouses must consent to give full disclosure over their finances. Each spouse will fill out a comprehensive form giving details about what he or she earns and any other income, savings, debts, pensions, the home, family business and so on, and supply back-up documents if need be. The forms are then sent to the mediator (usually by at least the third session), who will make a copy for the other partner.

To ensure that both partners are fully aware of the whole picture of the family's finances, the mediator will often put up the figures on a flipchart. Getting things up on the flipchart in this way helps to identify where more information is needed and clarify which money matters are issues between the couple. The lengthy (and costly) process of 'disclosure' in court cases is short-circuited by this method, because a spouse can often quickly identify if the other is holding back information and ensure that the figures are corrected. Often, various alternative arrangements or options are written up on the flipchart. Each spouse can put forward his or her own options. If he or she gets stuck, the mediator can help out, so more creative solutions to vexed problems can be worked through and tested as to how well they will work in reality.

As and when an agreement is reached, the mediator will prepare a summary of the agreement for each spouse and his or her solicitors. The summary contains 'open' information about money matters, but any agreement reached is 'without prejudice' – i.e. it cannot be made known to the court at a full hearing if the agreement subsequently breaks down. The agreement can then be translated by the solicitors into court documents – the divorce and a consent order over finances, for example.

Are solicitors still necessary?

Even if you have gone in for mediation it is still a good idea for you individually to get legal advice about what rights and responsibilities you have (so that you can negotiate on an informed basis) and also to double-check the terms of any agreement made during mediation. You can check whether the agreement will be watertight, whether anything has been missed out and whether you are giving away something you should not. Having your own solicitor also means you have legal back-up in case any urgent legal action needs to be taken – to prevent a spouse from disposing of assets, for example – or if the mediation does not result in an agreement (in which case you will probably still have to go to court or your solicitors may be able to negotiate on your behalf). Thus legal advice is complementary to the mediation process. But by using a skilled and knowledgeable mediator you could save thousands of pounds in legal fees by avoiding a full-blown legal battle.

Mediation and the children

Mediation takes a family-based approach, rather than the adversarial approach adopted in the family courts, where a husband and wife have to be on opposite sides, which is a distinct drawback when it comes to dealing with the children. Parents need to try to work together to sort out how the children will be looked after when the family separates, and the family-based approach of mediation can often help parents cooperate in planning for their children's and their own futures. If the dispute is only over the children, mediation by a family mediator may well be the best option. If problems over arrangements for the children are just a part of broader difficulties over finance generally, mediation involving a lawyer mediator would be a better bet. Try to ensure that comprehensive, or 'all-issues', mediation is available.

The emphasis in mediation is on allowing parents to create solutions which enable both of them to remain parents in as full a sense as possible. By meeting in a neutral environment in the presence of a non-partisan, experienced professional (or sometimes two professionals) trained in assisting couples to come to realistic agreements, both partners may find that they can at least (and perhaps at last) communicate directly rather than talking at each other or entirely missing each other's points. With the agreement of the parents, the children themselves may occasionally be invited to the mediation, but they should attend only if by being there they will themselves be helped in coping with the divorce.

Is mediation appropriate for you?
The potential benefits of mediation are numerous:

- control over the outcome: you and your spouse create your own tailor-made solutions to problems involved in the divorce or separation – arrangements which will suit your family, not ones imposed on you by the courts. Solutions worked out in mediation can indeed cover aspects where the court would have no power to make court orders
- speed and cost-effectiveness: the process is speedier – disputes can be resolved in weeks, not months and years – and much more cost-effective. Costs are likely to be measured in at most hundreds, not thousands, of pounds; you may get mediation for free
- respect for the family: members of the family can come to value others more. The mediation process can help improve communication between the couple and aid cooperation over the children. The process of divorce can be made more dignified
- confidentiality: the whole discussion in mediation is private and confidential. If you want to ensure privacy and confidentiality

over how you and your partner work things out, mediation will be right for you.

Mediation is not necessarily suitable for all couples. A study carried out in 1996 by the SFLA of its clients' views showed that around 30 to 40 per cent of divorcing couples felt mediation could be right for them: others preferred to rely on lawyers acting in the traditional way. The uptake may increase further as people become more aware of the benefits of mediation. The former Lord Chancellor who was behind the Family Law Act 1996 was, however, more optimistic – he seemed to believe that mediation will become the way in which most divorce disputes are resolved. Couples who have successfully resolved their disputes cost-effectively, efficiently and wisely through mediation certainly need no convincing of its benefits in comparison to a costly time-consuming antagonistic litigation process where there are only pyrrhic victories.

Critics of mediation have argued that it is biased against women, in that a wife may be too eager to agree in mediation to a settlement which gives her less financially than a court would, for the sake of a quiet life. Other studies have refuted this and have demonstrated that couples using all-issues mediation were glad they had used it, that they felt mediation had helped them end the marriage more amicably, were more content with childcare arrangements, and that their agreements had survived the test of time.

Together with the mediator, you and your partner can decide whether mediation will be right for you as a couple. You should be able to feel safe during mediation, so being scared of a violent partner, say, would make the exercise unworkable. Overall, as a rule of thumb, consider whether you feel that, with expert help, you would be able to negotiate with your spouse with respect for yourself and him or her. If you feel you would too easily give in, or on the other hand if you would definitely try to dominate the process and would refuse to listen, then mediation may not be right for you. However, remember that all sorts of conflicts can be dealt with satisfactorily in mediation – even if you cannot see how there can be a way out of your conflict a mediator may very well still be able to help you.

If you would like to give it a go, you could always arrange a first appointment with a mediator, go along and then decide whether mediation might work before committing yourself fully to the process. Some mediators offer a free half-hour introduction to mediation for you to have an opportunity to test the water. It is important that you trust the integrity and impartiality of a mediator, so an introductory session could reassure you whether mediation, and in particular this mediator, would offer the right way forward.

One-stop divorce centres

For most divorcing couples, getting help in their divorce may involve visits to several different services. However, the progressive Cambridge Family and Divorce Centre (CFADC)★ may be indicative of the shape of things to come.

The CFADC (which was set up in 1982) offers at a one-stop venue a range of services to couples facing the breakdown of their relationship. The service begins with a form of diagnostic interview, at which a husband or wife separating from his or her partner is assisted in finding out exactly what help is needed. Referrals can then be made to solicitors (with special Law Society permission the CFADC even offers joint information by giving appointments to couples together so both partners do not have to find their own separate solicitor), to one of the Centre's mediators, or to counselling services. Part-time child counsellors are also employed. Where the services identified as needed are not available in-house, referrals can be made to outside agencies.

There are currently plans to offer forms of service similar to the pioneering CFADC in other parts of the country, but at this stage the CFADC is probably unique. The recently established Family Law Consortium★ in London may also be a trend setter. Three experienced family lawyers who are also mediators have teamed up with two other mediators and counsellors to offer a range of different services – legal, mediation and counselling – under one roof. As the Family Law Act 1996 makes significant changes to the different services available, choices should continue to improve.

Where to find a mediation service

The first choice to make is whether you want to opt for a mediator with a family law background (a lawyer mediator) or a mediator with a therapeutic background (a family mediator).

If you decide to go for a mediator with a family law background, you could contact any of a number of organisations involved in training and recommending lawyer mediators. The best known of these nationwide is the SFLA, whose trained mediators will all be experienced family lawyers who have been practising for at least five years. If you send a stamped addressed envelope to its administrative secretary, you will get a list of lawyer mediators near you.

Other lawyer mediator referral networks are the British Association of Lawyer Mediators (BALM),★ Resolve★ and LawGroup UK ★ The longest established in the field is the FMA.

Solicitors in some areas are combining forces to make the availability of their mediation services more widely known. You may find local advertising appearing about such a group, but otherwise it is not always easy to find out locally about a mediation service. The heading 'Mediation' has recently started to appear in *Yellow Pages*, although the entries may be restricted or may include cross-references to 'Counselling' or 'Arbitration' (unfortunately nothing ever appears under the heading 'Divorce'.)

A national UK College of Family Mediators has more recently been set up by three organisations, the FMA, NFM and Family Mediation Scotland.★ Its purpose is to accredit mediation training and set professional standards, and to provide a register of accredited mediators. It published the *UK College of Family Mediators Directory and Handbook* in 1997 and a further edition is due out after spring 1998. This is a useful handbook, giving not only up-to-date information on how to get hold of a mediator and details of mediation services but also reference material on the mediation process, taxation and benefits, and changes under the Family Law Act 1996 for example.

As an alternative, your local Citizens Advice Bureau (CAB) should also be able to give you the address of your nearest service, or your solicitor can refer you to one.

As with all professional services, it is a good idea to ask for recommendations from trusted friends or acquaintances who may have used a mediator. Bear in mind, however, that as the concept is still relatively little known in the UK, you may not know anyone who has been to mediation already.

How much does mediation cost?

This depends on how long it takes and what type of mediation you opt for. The more sessions you have, the more it will cost. Six sessions are typical where there are a number of issues to resolve, fewer sessions are likely if the dispute involves a single issue.

Mediators with a legal background ('lawyer mediators')

Fees for a lawyer mediator are likely to vary regionally (usually £40 to £60 per person per hour, plus VAT, and more in London). Some mediators have a discretion to reduce fees. Rates charged by FMA co-mediators are similar, and the summary of the agreement reached (or mediation report) may be paid for by the Legal Aid Board (see below).

Mediators with a therapeutic background ('family mediators')

Here costs vary. The underlying principle has historically been that such services should be available to all regardless of income. Some schemes charge fees (of around £15 per session), some ask for a contribution dependent on income and others are free. If you are receiving advice from your solicitor under the green form scheme (see Chapter 1), the cost of the mediation report may be met by the Legal Aid Board up to a certain limit – check with your solicitor.

Free mediation under the Legal Aid Board's mediation pilot scheme

If you and your partner might qualify for legal aid and you also live in one of the areas in the Legal Aid Board's mediation pilot (see box for

---

Legal Aid Board's mediation pilot scheme

The following areas are covered in Phase I of the Pilot Mediation Franchising Scheme. The pilots, which ran from May 1997, covered London, Bromley, Cambridge, Peterborough, Bristol, Cardiff, Birmingham, Coventry, Northampton, Greater Manchester, Newcastle, Durham and Middlesbrough. An initial list of 28 mediation providers was established in those areas.

The pilots formed the first phase in the LAB's approach to mediation, announced in February 1997. Under a rolling programme, Phase II is due to last for a 12-month period starting from spring 1998 and it is planned to extend the pilot to other areas and providers.

---

details of the franchised mediation services in Phase I of the pilot), you may well be able to get free mediation from one of the franchised services in your area. The free sessions should not be restricted in number. Phase II of the pilot will extend the piloted areas, but as we go to press the new areas have not yet been identified. Check with your solicitor or CAB to find out more.

Court of Appeal mediation pilot

You may also find you are offered free or reduced-rate mediation if you are appealing your case up to the Court of Appeal under another pilot scheme still in the planning stages as we go to press. This is being organised through the Court of Appeal's administration structure. No finalised information is currently available.

Mediation and the impact of the Family Law Act 1996

The process of mediation is being given a boost by the Family Law Act 1996, which, when implemented around 1999, will provide a framework to make mediation more widely available – and better used by couples going through divorce. The new Act provides for an information meeting, when the addresses of local mediation services will be given to the couple. Under the new law, mediation will be available for those on legal aid, on the same basis as for legal representation, but the cost of mediation will be covered by a legal aid certificate only if both parties, not just one, are eligible for legal aid. The new Act also gives the courts power to direct the parties to attend a meeting with a mediator for an 'explanation of the availability and benefits of mediation', which in effect means a degree of coercion – the antithesis of the voluntary nature of mediation.

The government's explanation of the change reads:

'Many couples will see mediation as a preferable alternative to negotiating at arm's length through two separate lawyers or litigating through the courts. But it is not the intention of the Act to force people into mediation. Mediation only works if it is attempted on a voluntary basis. In cases where mediation is not suitable (e.g. in cases of domestic violence) legal representation will be available.'

As pointed out above, couples who have a history of domestic violence do not have to attend mediation. As an additional safeguard, mediators will be required to have a code of practice which ensures that cases where either party may be influenced by fear of violence or harm are identified as soon as possible. It is hard to see how this will work in practice successfully – if a victim of domestic violence is determined, through shame or embarrassment, to hide the fact that she (or, more rarely, he) has suffered domestic violence, it would be difficult for a mediator to root this out into the open. However, the deliberate raising of the issue in the Family Law Act to a more conscious level is an improvement.

Chapter 5

Using the Child Support Agency

Ever since the Child Support Agency (CSA)* began its operations on 5 April 1993 its activities have hit the headlines. Most reports have been highly critical. The CSA has been lobbied in particular by 'absent' parents shocked at unexpectedly large leaps in child support payments and sometimes too by parents looking after children who have found themselves pushed into applying for maintenance from ex-partners whom they want nothing to do with. Lawyers have been voicing their unhappiness about the loss of the courts' flexibility in family matters and quick to point out the CSA's (numerous) short-comings. In addition, a large number of people have quietly hoped for a fairer and speedier way of getting regular and realistic financial support for their children.

In January 1995, shortly after a public apology from the CSA for its deficiencies, the government introduced a package of reforms geared to counter absent parents' most vociferous criticisms. Some of the pro-blems in the formula which attracted the most complaints – the failure to take into account previous clean-break settlements and all the housing costs of a second family, for example – were addressed in the Child Support Act 1995. In December 1996 a new 'departure system' was introduced, designed to ameliorate the harshest effects of the rigidity of the child support formula.

A continuing challenge to the CSA is the massive scale of its opera-tions. The amount of maintenance collected directly in 1995/96 was £301 million. Inaccuracy of assessments has been a continuing bugbear, although a social security minister announced in December 1996 that the Agency, having improved its performance and intro-duced new systems, would be 'likely' to achieve an accuracy rate of 85 per cent by March 1997. Sadly in mid-1997 an independent audit by

National Audit investigators showed that 85 per cent of its assessments were still inaccurate. More worryingly still, errors of over £1,000 occurred in one in six cases.

So problems still remain. The Agency has been notoriously slow in processing claims. Although it says it is getting quicker, in 50 per cent of its cases it has taken over six months to complete assessments. It remains to be seen whether the extra money the CSA has received to help clear the backlog will enable it to achieve the fair, quick and effective service needed for the majority. The chief problem continues to be the inherently rigid yet horrendously complex formula – to which this book can provide only a brief introduction. For more detailed information, refer to the Child Poverty Action Group's* *Child Support Handbook*. You can also get excellent information and help from the National Council for One Parent Families.*

What is the CSA?

The CSA is a governmental Agency which comes under the umbrella of the Department of Social Security (DSS). The CSA was set up by the Child Support Act 1991 to take over responsibility for child support applications, which can no longer be made to the courts (except in unusual circumstances: see opposite). The Agency's main tasks are to assess child maintenance payments according to a special formula, and then to collect and enforce those payments from the parent who is no longer living with the children.

The CSA also has special powers to trace parents who have gone missing – it has access to DSS benefit records and Inland Revenue records. Moreover, where there is a difficulty in obtaining information the CSA may use inspectors as a last resort. It is an offence to fail to cooperate with CSA inspectors (whose task is to collect information about liable persons). The inspectors can enter business premises, such as the place of work of a liable person, and make any examination and enquiry that they consider appropriate.

Terminology
Under the Child Support Act, the terminology refers to 'the absent parent' and 'the parent (or person) with care'. The 'absent parent' is defined as someone who no longer lives in the same household as the

child and the 'parent (or person) with care' as the person who usually provides the day-to-day care of the child.

Who can apply?

Applications can be made to the CSA as soon as parents separate – they do not have to wait for the divorce to start. Either parent can apply; most applications are, however, made by the parent looking after the children full-time.

The CSA can be used for child support claims only for natural or adopted children; claims for stepchildren against stepparents still need to go through the courts. Moreover, the Agency can deal only with maintenance, not claims for lump sum payments or property transfers for children. If paternity is disputed, that dispute must be resolved before the Agency can act further.

There are other conditions which must first be met:

- the child must be a 'qualifying child', i.e. he or she must be under 16, or under 19 and still in full-time, non-advanced, education
- the child and both parents must all be habitually resident within the UK. So if a parent works – and therefore lives – abroad, no application to the CSA can be made (although an application can still be made to court).

In addition, there must (in most cases) be no maintenance agreement or court order made before 5 April 1993 – called 'pre-existing cases'.

When the Child Support Act was first implemented, it was due to be phased in over a four-year period from April 1993 to April 1997. The phasing-in period has now been postponed, so that older cases not already brought into the CSA's remit may well be excluded for ever.

If a couple have newly separated (and do not have a court order or written maintenance agreement pre-dating 5 April 1993) then either spouse can apply to the Agency for an assessment. (But see below for the differences in the way the Agency treats non-welfare claimants and certain welfare claimants.)

Making the application to the CSA

Applications are made on a lengthy maintenance application form (MAF), not unlike a tax return, which asks for full details of your income, assets, and so on. After receiving this, the Agency will send out a maintenance enquiry form to the payer-to-be, who will also be asked to reveal his or her financial position in full. If the maintenance enquiry form is sent back promptly, properly completed by the absent parent, he or she is given an eight-week holiday from paying maintenance, worked out from the date the MAF was first received. However, if he or she delays, an interim maintenance assessment can be levied, often at punitive rates, to 'encourage' the absent parent to return the form.

Originally the CSA was going to deal with child support applications only for those on benefit. Although its remit has been extended to everyone, differences remain in the way it deals with certain welfare claimants and others.

Welfare claimants

Parents with care who claim one of the three welfare benefits – income support (IS), family credit (FC) or disability working allowance (DWA) – have to use the Agency. More recently the new job-seeker's allowance (JSA), the income-based non-contributory version, has been added to this list. When a claim for IS is made, claimants who are looking after children will be referred automatically to the Agency and asked to complete an MAF. When signing the form, applicants will also be asked to authorise the Secretary of State to take steps to act on their behalf – namely to recover maintenance. Failure to complete the form as fully as possible or to authorise the Secretary of State to act can be termed 'failure to cooperate' and unless an applicant has 'good cause' can result in a reduced benefit direction (RBD). In October 1996, the RBD was made even harsher than before, so that RBDs issued after 6 October 1996 will last for three years and will knock the equivalent of 40 per cent off the IS personal allowance for an adult aged 25 or over, even where the parent is under this age. For 1997/98, the reduction in benefit is £19.66 per week. When benefit rates are increased at an April uprating, the amount of the reduction will also increase. There are plans to extend the three-year RBD period further if the parent with care still refuses to cooperate. However, if the parent decides to cooperate at any time and give the authorisation or information required, then the RBD terminates on the last day of the benefit week within which she (or he) complies.

To show 'good cause' for not providing information or authorisation an applicant has to prove that she (or he) or a child living with her (or him) would suffer harm or undue distress. Where a woman has fled to a refuge because of violence or abuse and is applying for income support from there, she should be taken to have good cause if she chooses not to go ahead with a maintenance claim against the abuser. The CSA says that it will act as a buffer between the applicant and the payer, and is under a duty to keep personal details (like addresses) confidential. If you are in any doubt about whether the good cause exemption might apply, seek advice from a Benefits Agency as soon as you can.

People not claiming welfare benefits

People who do not claim IS, FC, income-based JSA or DWA have the option of either using the Agency or making a private, voluntary agreement. They cannot go to court over disputed child maintenance unless the Agency has no jurisdiction to act in their particular case – say if the absent parent is abroad, for example. (The courts nowadays act as a safety net for all cases which fall outside the jurisdiction of the CSA.) The courts can, however, make a court order in the same terms as a written agreement if both parties wish this.

Private agreements will in normal circumstances last only as long as they remain real agreements. If either parent is unhappy about the level of payments, he or she can go to the CSA and ask it to take over the child support case. This is a strong argument for making sure that any agreed amount of maintenance matches the amount of child support worked out according to the CSA's formula. The CSA will not, however, be able to collect and enforce child support payments made under an agreement. One advantage of coming to such an agreement over using the Agency is that an agreement can, in theory, be worked out quickly, whereas an application to the Agency can take several months.

Fees?

The Agency waived payment of its fees for a two-year period up to April 1997, recently extended up to April 1999. Thereafter something like previous levels of fees (£34 for assessment and £44 for collection and enforcement payable by each parent) might be reinstated – if fees are reintroduced.

The CSA and 'pre-existing cases'

If a couple are classified as a 'pre-existing case' (i.e. they have a court order or written maintenance agreement pre-dating 5 April 1993), the key to whether or not they would have been brought within the Agency system depends on whether the parent with care claimed one of four trigger benefits. As explained earlier, these are IS, FC, income-based JSA and DWA.

- If any one of these benefits was claimed, then at some point the case is likely to have been brought under the Agency's jurisdiction. Such a case will continue to be dealt with by the CSA. As mentioned earlier, the Agency has, however, postponed taking on any more pre-existing cases.
- If none of these benefits was claimed, as the Agency has now indefinitely postponed the take-on of such cases, the case will not ordinarily be brought within the system unless the ground rules are changed once more.

If you have an existing court order pre-dating 5 April 1993, it may still be possible to bring forward the time when the CSA can take over the case, by applying to revoke the original court order and thereafter submitting an application to the Agency. This approach, however, should be taken only after getting proper legal advice. In a 1993 case the judge ruled it 'inappropriate' for a parent with care to try this strategy, saying: 'It seems to me that an assessment from the Agency is not necessarily in the best interests of the children. It might produce a higher figure, but it may be that other matters outweigh the purely financial'. Here the old court order was reinstated, and the parent with care advised that she should reapply for a variation of the old order.

Another problem is that because the CSA has built up such a backlog of cases it may not be able to offer a swift solution to the problem of getting an increase in maintenance, so an application to court for a variation of the old order may get a quicker response.

The CSA and clean-break orders

One particular matter which has received much adverse publicity is the issue of clean-break orders. Previously divorced couples who had opted for a clean break, whereby the absent parent (usually the husband) agreed to settle a lump sum on the wife and children or transfer the home to the wife in return for no maintenance claims being made against him, found that the CSA had the right to re-open the case and ask for future maintenance payments for the children.

A case in 1993 confirmed that while in some cases courts encourage clean breaks to end wives' rights to maintenance, they would never sanction a clean break ending a father's obligation to pay maintenance to his children. The courts have confirmed that they would not re-open 'old' clean-break cases decided before the Child Support Act came into effect on 5 April 1993. However, in another change introduced in the package of reforms in 1995, absent parents were given the right to claim an extra compensatory allowance to take into account transfers of the family home as a clean break if the transfer was made subsequent to a court order or written agreement pre-dating 5 April 1993.

In essence, the absent parent will usually be given credit for half the net value transferred (i.e. the value of the home at the time of the transfer less the mortgage) and then will be given an extra allowance in his exempt income to reduce the child support assessment. The allowance given is worked out on a band scale, so that if, for example, the value transferred was between £5,000 and £9,999, he will be allowed to keep an extra £20 per week. In some cases this allowance can be given if what was transferred was cash or, say, an endowment policy. This change is actually fairly restrictive: the new departure system may be a better bet for taking into account the financial cost of an old (i.e. pre-April 1993) clean-break order. However, note that only old clean-break orders will benefit from the flexibility – for cases since April 1993 there can be no departure from the formula (if it applies) if a clean break is agreed.

The 'departure system'

In a further, limited, move away from the rigidity of the CSA's formula, since 2 December 1996 for all parts of England and Wales a new 'departure system' gives a small amount of discretion to alter child support payments. The system allows for parents to request reductions as well as increases in child support payments; overall the applicant must prove that it is just and equitable to depart from the formula.

Applications for a departure from the formula could be made on any (or a combination) of the following grounds.

Special expenses

- high travel to work costs
- high travel costs for maintaining contact with children
- costs arising from the disability of the applicant or a dependant
- debts incurred while the family was together
- pre-April 1993 financial commitments from which it is impossible or unreasonable to withdraw
- costs of supporting stepchildren, where responsibilities were taken on before April 1993.

Property and capital

- pre-April 1993 'clean-break' property or capital orders
- diversion of income or assets capable of producing income, or higher income (say, if one parent takes out a large amount of savings from an income-producing account and puts them into a current account where no interest would be earned)
- inconsistent lifestyles (e.g. a parent drives an expensive car and goes regularly on foreign holidays but says he – or she – has no income from a business).

Additional cases

- housing costs included in the formula assessment are unreasonably high, or a new partner is capable of contributing to them
- travel to work costs in the formula assessment are unreasonably high, or the parent can afford them.

Because of the complexities of the formula, any extra expenses sought to be deducted under a departure direction, for example, will not be knocked off pound for pound against the formula but instead will be added to the absent parent's exempt income. So if an absent parent wishes to claim special expenses of £25, this will result in a reduction of only around £10.

When the departure system was piloted, 'inconsistent lifestyle' was the most often cited ground for an application for a departure direction, although it also usually turned out to be unsuccessful – 90 per cent of these applications were dismissed at an early stage as being 'unsubstantiated'. The onus will be on the applicant to provide (probably documentary) evidence, which may not be easy to obtain. An application is made on a special form, available from the CSA, and further information can be requested by the Agency. (Those applications deemed to be 'hopeless' will be weeded out at an early stage.) After the other parent has been invited to make representations, a Child Support Officer will make a decision. There is no fee payable but legal aid is not available. The CSA predicts that it will take ten weeks to carry out a departure assessment (but it has been overly optimistic in the past about how long it will take to process applications).

So far, the information shows that very few departure system applications have been successful. In a pilot where 6 per cent of those invited to apply did so, only 10 to 15 per cent of applications were likely to be successful, leading to the conclusion either that the departure gateways are far too narrow or that the basic formula may be less harsh than some commentators think.

Getting advice about the CSA

Solicitors and Citizens Advice Bureaux (CABx) should be able to offer advice and help about getting or paying child support through the CSA. However, there are restrictions on legal advice and assistance (the green form), and legal aid for problems concerning the Agency. Solicitors will usually not be allowed under the green form scheme to help a client fill in an MAF or a maintenance enquiry form; green form advice is available only where there are particular legal problems – say over paternity or whether the absent parent lives in the UK – and where, according to the Legal Aid Board, it would be *reasonable* for the solicitor to do the work.

Legal aid is not available for applications to challenge a CSA assessment through most of the initial appeal stages – e.g. to review an assessment, or for appeals to the Child Support Appeals Tribunal or to the Child Support Commissioner. However, if there is an appeal against a Child Support Commissioner's decision – which can be on a point only of law, not of fact – then legal aid can be applied for. If you need help in challenging an Agency assessment or decision, your solicitor may, however, be able to advise you under the green form and then act as a 'McKenzie friend' – an advocate/assistant – on your behalf at a Tribunal hearing (see *Challenging a CSA assessment*, at the end of this chapter). Legal aid is available for taking a case about paternity to the courts.

There is a Child Support Agency* enquiry line which anyone can telephone for advice and help. It can be difficult to get through on this helpline, so patience may be called for.

Calculating child support

Calculating child support is the task of the CSA, which must use a formula laid down by special regulations. The regulations (some of which have been based on social security regulations) are complex and very detailed, and are designed to cover a wide variety of individual cases. The following is only a summary of the way the formula works – you may well need to get more information to find out exactly how it applies to you (see the summary later in the chapter).

In very broad terms, the main change that the formula has made is to increase child support payments quite significantly. On average, payments more than doubled in the first years of the Agency's operation – from around £20 to £50 weekly. Figures produced by the Agency showed that an absent parent might expect to pay somewhere between 18 per cent and 35 per cent of net income, although in 1995 a 30 per cent 'cap' on maintenance payments was introduced (see *Protected income*, page 106). The precise amount depends largely on the income of the absent parent, although the income of the parent with care is relevant too, as both parents are viewed as being financially responsible for their children. There are minimum (set at 5 per cent of the adult personal allowance of income support, which is £5 at the standard rate in 1997/98) and maximum levels set for payments. The maximum sets the ceiling for child support which can be assessed by the CSA, and again in 1995 this ceiling was brought lower. In very high income families, if child support is sought over and above this level, a court application will be required; the court will also be able to order additional amounts of maintenance to cover school fees and extra costs incurred because of a child's disability (again, by and large in wealthy families).

Once the child support level has been set, it will be reviewed every two years (not every year as in the Agency's early days). As the formula is based on IS rates (which are increased annually), the amount of child support will usually be increased every two years to take account of rises in inflation. The review takes the form of a complete reassessment, so if either parent's financial circumstances have changed, those changes will be taken into account. Parents can also request a review during the two years if one is needed, for example if one of them loses a job, although a minimum change in the amount payable will be necessary before a review will be put in train.

Using the formula

The formula is applied by using five different sums (*a.* to *e.*) set out below. Examples have been used to show the different stages of its workings. They should be treated as illustrations only.

a. Maintenance requirement

This represents the day-to-day expenses of looking after children, based on IS rates, adding together sums calculated for the parent looking after the children as well as for the children.

- **The adult personal allowance** for those aged 25 or over is paid in full when all the children are under 11. Added to this is the family premium (lone-parent rate) if the children are living with a lone parent (£15.75 in 1997/98). The maintenance requirement is always based on the adult personal allowance rate for a single person aged 25 or over (£49.15 per week in 1997/98), whether or not the parent with care is younger than that or lives with a partner. Adjustments have to be made to the personal allowance element of the maintenance requirement where the parent with care is looking after children of whom the youngest is 11 or over. For example, the £49.15 rate would go down to £36.86 where the youngest child cared for was between 11 and 13, and to £24.58 where the youngest child is at least 14.

- **The personal allowances for children** vary according to the age bands the children fall into. For 1997/98, the rates per week are:

under 11	£16.90	16 to 18	£29.60
11 to 15	£24.75		

Although the maintenance is payable for the children, the maintenance requirement includes the adult personal allowance for the parent looking after the children as a carer allowance. It is the core calculation for child support but it is very unlikely that the amount of child support paid will be the same as the maintenance requirement. The actual amount will be adjusted downwards depending on the other factors below. Child benefit is deducted from the amount of the maintenance requirement.

The maintenance requirement does not limit the amount that the absent parent pays. Where the absent parent is well off, he (or, more rarely, she) is expected to make maintenance payments over and above that maximum. The regulations lay down an extra percentage payment of up to 25 per cent of assessable income, once the maintenance requirement has been met, if the absent parent's circumstances allow for this (see *d.* below).

b. Exempt income

Exempt income applies to both parents' separate incomes and represents what is allowed for each parent's own personal essential expenses, including:

- a personal allowance to cover both parents' day-to-day living expenses *plus* (if any new partner is not working or otherwise is deemed not to be able to contribute financially to the children's upkeep) the costs of caring for their natural and adopted children who are living with them, assessed on IS rates
- reasonable housing costs
- some travel to work costs.

Housing costs are included only where they are 'reasonable'. Costs which are under the limit of £80 per week, or half a parent's net weekly income (whichever is higher), are automatically assumed to be reasonable. There are some other special cases where housing costs are taken to be reasonable – for example, where the parent who has left the home has had to take on a high mortgage because he has not yet taken out his financial share of the family home.

Housing costs include rent or mortgage repayments (both interest and capital, unlike income support) and repayments made for a loan taken out for some eligible repairs or improvements to the home. Payments of an endowment premium or Personal Equity Plan (PEP) policy are also included as long as the mortgage is £60,000 or under. They do not cover insurance premiums for buildings and contents cover.

Since April 1995 an allowance towards travel costs has been introduced into exempt income for parents who have to travel long distances to get to work. This is based on the straight-line (i.e. as the crow flies) distance between work and home. If the distance is more than 15 miles each way, i.e. more than 150 miles each week ($15 \times 2 \times 5$) then 10 pence is included for each mile over 150. The allowance does not apply to the self-employed or if the employer provides certain help towards travel costs.

Exempt income does not include other outgoings like childcare costs or debts; parents who have high payments on any of these may find themselves being treated very harshly by the Agency as it will ignore these actual outgoings before assessing what an absent parent can afford to pay. Repayments of debts built up while the family was together could, however, be taken into account now for an application under the new departure system.

Parents on low incomes do get some extra help from the 'protected income' calculation (see *e.* below).

c. Assessable income

Assessable income is the part of a parent's income used for calculating his maintenance obligation. This is worked out by taking his net income (i.e. the amount of income after payment of tax, National Insurance contributions and usually half the pension contributions) and then deducting from that the *exempt income*.

There are special rules for the self-employed, childminders and some other cases. While not all sources of income count (for example, social fund payments and attendance allowances are disregarded), the Agency can assume a notional amount of income if a parent deliberately deprives himself of a source of income or, in some circumstances, performs services without pay.

d. Deduction rate

Assessable income will be shared 50/50 between the children and the absent parent until the *maintenance requirement* is paid. Once that has been paid, if there is any remaining assessable income, further child maintenance at a lower rate of deduction, up to 25 per cent of the excess of income, is payable. The 25 per cent rate is payable only if there are three or more children eligible for maintenance: the deduction rate drops to 20 per cent if there are two children and 15 per cent if there is only one child. There is a cap or ceiling to the maximum amount of maintenance which can be paid.

e. Protected income

The protected income is designed to prevent the liable parent's income being pushed down to IS levels or below by the amount of child support which he is obliged to pay. For absent parents on low incomes, there is a special formula which gives a margin over and above income support rates and this protected level of income is guaranteed. For all absent parents (since 1995) there is a cap of 30 per cent of net income placed on the level of child support, so that if net weekly income is £300, the maximum child support payable under the formula is £90.

Examples

CASE 1: Where the parent caring for the children is not working

Mark and Sally have separated and Sally is looking after the children. They have two children, Fiona and Brad, aged 12 and 5.

1. Calculating the maintenance requirement

Using April 1997/98 rates, the maintenance requirement is:

Child allowance:	Fiona	£24.75
	Brad	£16.90
Family premium (lone-parent rate)		£15.75
Adult personal allowance ('parent as carer')		£49.15
Sub-total		£106.55
Less: Child benefit: Fiona		£11.05
	Brad	£9.00
TOTAL MAINTENANCE REQUIREMENT:		**£86.50**

2. Calculating the exempt income

Calculations about how much an absent parent may have to pay begin with calculating his net income.

Gross income

less

(Tax, National Insurance contributions and usually 50 per cent pension contributions)

equals

Net income

For the purpose of this example, Mark's net income per week will be taken to be £172.

Exempt income is supposed to cover a parent's own personal essential living expenses which must be met first. These do not, however, include all actual living expenses, but those specified in the Child Support Act and its regulations. In most cases this includes only housing costs and the adult personal allowance for IS. It can also include:

- the costs of caring for the parent's own natural or adopted children if they live with her (the children's personal income support plus family premium if appropriate)
- an amount equal to the IS disability premium if the parent is disabled
- the carer premium if the parent is caring for a disabled person.

Mark is living alone in rented accommodation costing £55 per week and his travel costs are worked out at 200 miles per week. His exempt income is:

Personal allowance	£49.15
Housing costs	£55.00
Travel to work costs (50 miles @ 10p)	£5.00
TOTAL EXEMPT INCOME:	**£109.15**

3. Calculating the assessable income
Assessable income, the amount from which maintenance will be paid, is calculated as net income *less* exempt income. So Mark's assessable income is:

Net income	£172.00
Less:	
Exempt income	£109.15
TOTAL ASSESSABLE INCOME:	**£62.85**

4. Calculating the deduction rate
Fifty per cent of the assessable income is paid towards the child maintenance requirement, so Mark should pay £31.43 (50 per cent of £62.85) child maintenance. Double-check that this is below 30 per cent of Mark's net income (£172 × 30% = £51.60). Mark will pay £31.43 in child support.

CASE 2: Where both parents are working

Sally has now got a job as Brad has started going to school. She receives a total net income of £160 per week. Mark has just been given a pay rise and receives a net income of £200 per week. Sally's housing costs are £70 per week and Mark is still in his flat paying £55 per week.

1. Calculating the maintenance requirement

The children are still the same ages as before, so the maintenance requirement calculation is the same, i.e. £86.50

2. Calculating the exempt incomes

Mark's exempt income is the same as before, namely £109.15. Sally's exempt income will also need to be worked out:

Personal allowance	£49.15
Child allowance: Fiona	£24.75
Brad	£16.90
Family premium (lone-parent rate)	£15.75
Housing costs	£70.00
TOTAL EXEMPT INCOME:	**£176.55**

As Sally's actual net income is less than her exempt income, her income will be ignored when working out how much Mark will have to pay. Her net income would have to exceed her exempt income before the amount that Mark paid would be reduced.

3. Calculating the assessable income

Mark's assessable income is now £90.85 (£200 less £109.15), of which he is liable to pay half, i.e. £45.43, towards the maintenance requirement. Again double-check that this is below 30 per cent of net income (£200 × 30% = £60) so the original calculation is confirmed.

If there is a shortfall in the maintenance requirement, as in this example, it will not automatically be made up by the CSA or any other body. The formula simply works out a notional amount of maintenance for the children. (An application for welfare benefits could be made if required.)

CASE 3: Where parents have high incomes

Under the Child Support Act framework, both parents are deemed financially responsible for their children. In practice, as the parent with care is meeting the costs of looking after the children anyway, her income is often ignored when working out how much the absent parent has to pay as parents with care have to earn quite a significant amount to get above their exempt income (most lone parents, who tend to work part-time, are on fairly low incomes). However, for families with higher incomes, the income of the parent with care does more often directly have an impact on the amount the absent parent pays. However, the calculation is complex.

Rupert and Georgina have just separated. Their four children (all under 11) live with Georgina, who is not working.

1. Calculating the maintenance requirement

Child allowance: (children – all under 11		
	4 × £16.90)	£67.60
Family premium (lone-parent rate)		£15.75
Adult personal allowance		£49.15
Sub-total		£132.50
Less: Child benefit (1 × £11.05 + 3 × £9)		£38.05
TOTAL MAINTENANCE REQUIREMENT:		**£94.45**

2. Calculating maintenance at the higher level

For the purpose of this example, Rupert's assessable income (net income less exempt income) is £570 per week. As 50 per cent of this (£285) exceeds the maintenance requirement (£94.45), Rupert will have to pay a further slice of child support calculated using the 'additional element' which here is 25 per cent (as he has more than three children).

To work out how much of his income is used up at the basic deduction rate of 50 per cent, the formula doubles up the maintenance requirement to find out how much assessable income at the basic rate of 50 per cent will be paid.

Basic assessable income (£94.45 × 2)	£188.90
Additional assessable income (£570 − £188.90)	£381.10
Additional element maintenance (£381.10 × 25%)	£95.28
PROVISIONAL MAINTENANCE PAYABLE:	
(£94.45 + £95.28) =	**£189.73**

Double-check. Is this less than 30 per cent of Rupert's net income ($£570 \times 30\% = £171$)? No. Thus the maximum Rupert will pay is £171 per week.

Say Georgina were to get a job. Her assessable income (i.e. net income less exempt income) for the purpose of illustration is £80 per week. Rupert's assessable income is still £570 per week, and the maintenance requirement is still £94.45 per week. Their joint assessable income is $£570 + £80 = £650$.

Again, Rupert will still be paying an extra slice of child support of 25 per cent.

To work out how much maintenance Rupert will now pay:

$£94.45 \times \frac{£570}{£650} = £82.82$ (rounding down to the nearest penny)	
Basic rate assessable income ($£82.82 \times 2$)	£165.64
Additional assessable income ($£570.00 - £165.64$)	£404.36
Additional element maintenance ($£404.36 \times 25\%$)	£101.09
PROVISIONAL MAINTENANCE PAYABLE:	
($£82.82 + £101.09$) = £183.91	

This would in theory be a reduction of £5.82 from the amount Rupert was originally assessed to pay. However, this new provisional maintenance payable is still more than the 30 per cent cap on Rupert's maintenance so he will still pay only £171 weekly.

For families on very high incomes there is a ceiling or maximum amount of maintenance which can be assessed under the formula, though an application to court can be made for a top-up.

Effect of child support on welfare benefits

As the MAF is worked out on the basis of income you are currently receiving, it may be sensible to delay making an application for family credit (if you intend to do so) until after you have applied to the Agency. When your FC is reassessed in six months' time, it should be based on the child support you will then be receiving (if any) but you may be able to delay having FC taken into account until the assessment is reviewed in two years' time.

Family credit
The first £15 of income from maintenance is ignored when calculating a lone parent's entitlement to FC, housing benefit, DWA and

council tax benefit. This £15 provision is referred to as a 'maintenance disregard'; it can be an incentive for the payer, who can see a direct financial benefit for the family (as opposed to a simple reduction of payments made by the state).

One problem experienced in the early days of the Agency was that while FC or DWA were calculated on a six-monthly basis, taking into account the maintenance due, no allowance was made if the maintenance payments were reduced. Given that recent changes may have led to a reduction in maintenance, compensation will now be given equal to half the amount of the reduction in the maintenance assessment until the benefit is reassessed. Any queries about these compensation payments can be made to the Family Credit Unit* or the Disability Working Allowance Unit.*

Income support and jobseeker's allowance

No maintenance disregard currently applies to IS (nor to income-based JSA), where the amount of maintenance reduces the state benefits pound for pound. However, since April 1997, a new maintenance bonus scheme has been introduced, whereby a parent with care who is on IS or income-based (non-contributory) jobseeker's allowance will be able to 'save' a credit amount of up to £5 per week (to a maximum of £1,000) which will be payable when they start work of 16 hours or more per week. To gain the maximum, maintenance of at least £5 must have been paid for 200 weeks – i.e. around four years' worth.

No flexibility

The amount of child support paid can sometimes float the recipient off IS if it is the same as or more than the amount of the maintenance requirement. This can have the knock-on effect of disentitling the recipient to the 'passported' benefits that are available to IS payees, such as mortgage repayments and free school meals, which can cause real hardship to a family. Because the CSA has to apply the formula rigidly, there is no flexibility to provide any financial protection for such families – the parent looking after the children may have to try to find work to help support the family. For working parents, child support can provide real help as a cushion to provide, or help towards providing, for the extra costs of going to work (like childminding fees and travel). Child support payments will be reduced only if the parent looking after the children increases her income to more than the amount of her exempt income.

Summary of steps required to work out the formula

1. Maintenance requirement

Using income support rates, ADD together:

> Child allowances
> + Family premium (lone-parent rate)
> + Adult personal allowance [reduced if youngest child over 11]

then DEDUCT child benefit for each child to work out the weekly maintenance requirement.

2. Exempt income

Using income support rates, ADD together:

> Adult personal allowance
> [+ Child allowances, if natural or adopted children living in]
> [+ Family premium (lone-parent rate) if applicable]
> + Housing costs
> [+ Travel to work costs, if travelling is over 150 miles per week]

If the children are older – i.e. the youngest is at least 11 – then the adult personal allowance element will be reduced.

3. Assessable income

Work out first the weekly amount of net income, i.e. gross income less tax, National Insurance contributions and usually 50 per cent pension contributions. Then DEDUCT exempt income from net income to get assessable income.

4. Deduction rate

For calculating the maintenance requirement the basic deduction rate is 50 per cent of assessable income. If 50 per cent of assessable income equals or exceeds the maintenance requirement, then an extra proportion of assessable income (up to 25 per cent of the excess) may be payable.

5. *Protected income*

The protected income calculation is designed to prevent the absent parent's income falling below a certain level. For those on low incomes, a cushion above IS rates is given. For those on higher incomes, the cap of 30 per cent of the absent parent's net income will be more relevant. The aim is to provide an incentive to work.

Challenging a CSA assessment

If you feel that your assessment is wrong, you can seek to challenge it. The first stage in this process is an internal review, which will be carried out by a Child Support Officer who is different from the one who dealt with your case. If you are still dissatisfied, you can appeal to a Child Support Appeal Tribunal, and thereafter to a Child Support Commissioner; if you feel the decision was still wrong in law, you can appeal further to the Court of Appeal. All this will cost time and probably money – legal aid is not available until an appeal has been made to the Court of Appeal. If you are on a low income you may, however, be able to ask someone from your local Welfare Rights Advice Agency to come with you to the Appeal tribunal and help you prepare your case.

Chapter 6

Getting money from the court before divorce

Even before the divorce begins, one partner can apply to court for an order for financial provision from the spouse if he or she is not providing proper maintenance. However, nowadays in most divorce cases (where children are involved), the first step in getting maintenance before a divorce will be via the Child Support Agency (CSA),* as the courts have lost virtually all their powers to make court orders for child support in a disputed case.

The courts can still act if the Agency cannot take on a case, say if a parent wishes to make a claim for a stepchild or if one parent lives abroad. However, it is useful to get legal advice about whether it will be worthwhile going to court, i.e. whether the costs involved are worth it in view of the maintenance payments that might result.

As an alternative, if you and your spouse agree on the terms of separation, you can together enter into a separation agreement which will deal with financial issues (although you may still be required to use the CSA for child support if you are claiming benefits). If you can agree interim financial arrangements, getting a court order based on your agreement may still be useful or even necessary to ensure that the agreement is watertight. You can ask for a 'consent order' to be made in your agreed terms and this can include an order for maintenance for the children on the basis that the order is in the same terms as a written agreement. Generally, an order is easier to enforce than a simple separation agreement.

Court orders: through the county court
An application can be made to any Family Hearing Centre (a type of county court) for maintenance or a lump sum payment, even when no divorce is required or possible. The applicant only has to satisfy the

court that his or her spouse has failed to provide reasonable maintenance while being in a position to do so.

The application needs to be submitted in duplicate, together with a
statement in support, providing evidence of the applicant's financial
resources and needs. The court fees, which have to be paid at the time
of submitting the application, are £30.

The respondent (that is, the other spouse) is required to file with the
court a statement in answer within 14 days of receiving the application
from the court. The court will set a hearing date usually some weeks
off; the county court district judge normally hears the application in
chambers (i.e., in private, in the same way as an application for maintenance in divorce proceedings).

Unless there are any special reasons why an application should be
made to a county court, it is unlikely that a legal aid certificate will be
available for such an application. Because the solicitors' costs in a
Family Proceedings Panel (within the magistrates' court) tend to be
less, the Legal Aid Board★ will generally only sanction applications
for that court.

Court orders: through the magistrates' court

A magistrates' court can make orders for periodical payments for any
amount and for lump sums of up to £1,000 each for the applicant and
any children. An application can be made, for example, for a lump
sum to repay expenses reasonably incurred in maintaining the applicant for the period before the order was made. The initial limit is
£1,000, but there appears to be no limit on the number of applications
that can be made: thus a spouse can apply, if the need arises, for lump
sums on more than one occasion.

The procedure for applying for a maintenance order in a magistrates' court costs relatively little; no affidavits are required. The application can be made to any magistrates' court in the area where either
spouse lives, or where the couple last lived together. Legal aid (or
approval for 'assistance by way of representation' under the green
form scheme) can be applied for to make or defend such an application.

Proceedings are started by a written or oral 'complaint'. The applicant must be able to prove to the court that the spouse:

• has failed to provide reasonable maintenance for him or her or made a proper financial contribution towards the children (if this is a child support case which can still be dealt with by the courts), or

- has deserted him or her or has behaved in such a way that the applicant cannot reasonably be expected to live with the spouse (this could include adultery). Note, however, that this ground will be removed by the Family Law Act 1996 once it is brought into force.

If it seems that the applicant has a case, the court will issue a summons for the spouse to appear before the court on a given day.

If both parties have agreed about maintenance, they can go to the magistrates' court and ask for an agreed order to be made along those lines, provided the court has no reason to think it would be unjust. (There is no upper limit on lump sums in 'agreed' orders.)

If the order contains provision for a child (where the court has jurisdiction), the court has a specific duty to check that as far as possible adequate payment is ordered to be made towards the child's needs.

Both the applicant and the respondent will be asked to provide evidence to the court about their income and expenditure, and assets. Before making any order, the magistrates' court will take into account all the circumstances of the case, giving first consideration to the welfare of any child of the family.

Other factors are income and earning capacities, obligations and responsibilities, age, any physical or mental disabilities, duration of the marriage, previous standard of living, the contribution each spouse has made to the family, and the conduct of each of them if it would be unfair not to take it into account.

The interval between applying to the magistrates' court and the date fixed for the hearing varies from court to court; it is likely to be between one and two months.

In a case of urgent need, a court can be asked for an expedited hearing, or for an interim order to tide the applicant over until such time as the case can be heard fully. An interim maintenance order lasts for a maximum of three months but may be extended for a further three months.

If subsequently there is a petition for divorce, details of any magistrates' court order for maintenance have to be given on it, where information is asked about 'other proceedings in any court'.

Because the magistrates' courts tend to deal with people on a low income, and because there used in the past to be a very low upper limit to maintenance orders, the tendency to set low levels has stuck. The amounts of maintenance and lump sums ordered by the magistrates' court may therefore be lower than those ordered by either the county court or the divorce court. In practice, little use is now made of these provisions anyway since the Child Support Agency took over responsibility for child maintenance.

Court orders: through the divorce court

Once a petition for divorce (or for judicial separation) has been lodged at the divorce county court, a spouse should apply there for an order for 'financial relief'. (If an order has been obtained for maintenance at the magistrates' court or county court, this will remain in force until there is an order in the divorce county court.)

Maintenance pending suit

A long-term order for maintenance or an order for a capital sum cannot be made until decree nisi and will not take effect until the decree has been made absolute. However, the court has power to order temporary maintenance payments for a spouse until the decree absolute. This is known as 'maintenance pending suit' (MPS). The main point of the MPS order is to keep the spouse seeking maintenance going until the court can make an order after fuller examination of his or her financial position. For children's maintenance applications, the court's powers are now much restricted. Applications can be made for children who fall outside the jurisdiction of the CSA, for example stepchildren, although the courts will usually expect the parent with care to try to get the other natural parent to pay before making an order against a stepparent.

An application for MPS can be made as soon as the petition for divorce is filed. The court fee for an application for financial relief (the legal term is 'ancillary relief') was increased in January 1997 to £50. The following information will not apply to courts operating the new ancillary relief pilot scheme; see pages 217–19 for an explanation.

It takes between three and six weeks (often longer) for the application for MPS to be heard and for the district judge to make an order. The applicant will have to give the fullest possible information about his or her needs and provide an affidavit of means (a sworn statement of earnings and other resources, and what he or she owns, owes and needs), as should the respondent.

If the respondent fails to file an affidavit of means, the district judge may make the order for quite a high amount in order to force him or her to bring his or her financial affairs into the open – if the respondent claims that the order is too high to manage, he or she will have to disclose his or her finances to substantiate it.

An MPS order comes into effect straight away and may be backdated to the date of the petition. It lasts at most until decree absolute. Its purpose is to tide the applicant over until there is a full inquiry into all the financial facts; this is generally reflected in the level of payment ordered, which will simply cover the applicant's immediate needs.

An interim lump sum?

In a couple of recent cases, the courts have hinted that they might, in effect, order an interim lump sum to meet immediate needs, for example, to provide a deposit for a house. The issue as to whether the courts actually have this power is hotly debated in legal circles; so far the courts have exercised it only where there has been a lot of capital available. Accepted wisdom at present is that the divorce court can make only one lump sum order – which it usually does once there has been a full inquiry into the financial facts. However, once the Family Law Act 1996 is fully implemented, the courts will have powers to make interim lump sum orders

Financial applications and domestic violence

Since Part IV of the Family Law Act 1996 was introduced on 1 October 1997, it is possible to ask the court to make an order to cover payment of outgoings – like rent or mortgage payments – at the same time as making an occupation order (the new term for an exclusion order: see Chapter 12). This short-circuits the previous necessity of having to make a separate application to the court for financial support to cover basic running costs for the home.

Financial applications for children

As well as reforming the legal framework of the relationships between parents and children, the Children Act 1989 codified the law about financial applications for children. It also enables children over 18 to apply for periodical payments or a lump sum. Since the Child

Support Act 1991 came into force on 5 April 1993, most claims for child maintenance are made through the CSA, although the courts retain their powers for stepchildren and any other children for whom the Agency cannot act. This would include children whose absent parent was working – and was thus habitually resident – abroad. Even if the Agency has jurisdiction over maintenance, however, capital sums or even property orders can be sought for the children.

To make an application under the Children Act 1989, a parent, guardian or anyone with a residence order for a child can apply to court for an order that either parent (or both) pays:

- periodical payments (maintenance) – these can be secured and apply only if the Agency has no jurisdiction
- a lump sum
- a settlement of property
- a transfer of property to the applicant for the benefit of the child or directly to the child (a transfer of property could cover a transfer of a tenancy too).

Applications can be made to either a magistrates' court (Family Proceedings Panel), the county court (Family Hearing Centre) or the High Court, although the magistrates' court has power to order only periodical payments or a lump sum.

The court must look at all the circumstances, including the income, earning capacity of the parties (and the financial position of the child), their needs and obligations, any physical or mental disability of the child and the way in which the child was (or expects to be) educated or trained (this approach is often summed up as 'needs and resources').

See also Chapter 5 about applying for child support under the Child Support Act 1991.

Applications by sons or daughters over 18

A son or daughter over 18 can apply for periodical payments (like weekly or monthly payments) or a lump sum if he or she is in full-time education or training (although this would also cover situations where the son or daughter was working in the evenings to supplement his or her income while in continuing education). The courts will take the approach as outlined above.

There are, however, some restrictions on applications: they can be made only if the parents (whether married or not) are no longer living together in the same household and there was no previous maintenance order in existence before the child's sixteenth birthday. In other words, this provision is intended primarily for sons or daughters who plan to go on to further education and whose parents have comparatively recently split up and where the parental part of the grant (for example) is not being paid. Instead of the parent being forced to go to court to chase up maintenance payments, the son or daughter can make his or her own application. Such children can also apply if they are not covered by the CSA, i.e. they are 19 or over.

Chapter 7
Getting a divorce

There is only one ground for obtaining a divorce in England or Wales, namely that the marriage has irretrievably broken down. Under current law, i.e. before the Family Law Act 1996 changes the law (unlikely to be earlier than 1999), the court requires proof of one or more of 'five facts', which are set out below. Once the Family Law Act 1996 is implemented, proof of irretrievable breakdown will instead be time-based – spouses will have to wait for a period of 'consideration and reflection' before their divorce will be granted. In most cases, it will take much longer to get a divorce, especially if there are children. The new law will also alter the way in which people get divorced. For example, mediation is likely to play a greater role and husbands and wives must sort out future arrangements over children and money before they can get a divorce – a change from the present law under which it is quite possible to get a divorce without resolving money problems. An outline of the key points of the new law is included at the end of this chapter. The law as it stands is set out below.

The five facts to prove irretrievable breakdown are, in essence:

Fact 1: adultery and intolerability
Fact 2: unreasonable behaviour
Fact 3: desertion for a period of two years
Fact 4: separation for a period of two years with consent of the other party
Fact 5: separation for a period of five years.

The full wording of the facts which have to be proved, and explanations, are set out later in this chapter.

A petition for divorce cannot be presented until a year after the marriage took place, whatever the circumstances. But you do not have to start off divorce proceedings to apply to the court about problems over the children (for details see Chapter 8). Applications for a residence or contact order, for example, can be made at any time. Similarly, you don't have to start a divorce to ask the Child Support Agency (CSA)* for maintenance for the children (or the court for maintenance for yourself). So there is no need to begin an application for a divorce until you have finally made up your mind that that is what you want.

Even if you can establish the facts for going for a divorce now, you might want to consider whether to make a separation agreement with your spouse now and then apply for a divorce on the 'no fault' ground (Fact 4) later. Applying for a divorce when you have lived separately from your spouse for at least two years and where you both consent to the divorce going ahead can help to remove some of the bitterness and difficulties often associated with divorce.

Jurisdiction

Where you got married is not relevant in determining if you can get a divorce in England and Wales – i.e. whether an English court has jurisdiction to hear your petition. What matters is that either you or your spouse must be 'domiciled' in England or Wales or have been resident there for at least one year before the date of presenting the petition. Short absences (for example holidays) can be ignored. It is advisable to consult a solicitor straight away in connection with any proposed divorce where there is doubt about domicile or where neither of the couple lives in England or Wales.

The law in Scotland and the procedure in Northern Ireland are different and are dealt with in Chapters 15 and 16. Domicile or residence in Scotland, Northern Ireland, the Channel Islands or the Isle of Man is not sufficient to enable you to get divorced in an English or Welsh court.

Where to apply

Divorce proceedings are usually started in a divorce county court or a county court which is classed as a Family Hearing Centre (see the chart on page 289). Not all county courts deal with divorce proceedings, so telephone first to check. Although you do not have to start proceedings in a court that is local to you – choosing a court in another part of

England and Wales could be useful in sensitive cases or if you want to avoid publicity – it makes sense to go to the one that is most convenient for you (and your spouse).

Your case may be transferred to the High Court if the divorce proceedings become defended or, in a very small number of cases, where the financial proceedings or the proceedings relating to the children are extremely complex. In London, the Divorce Registry acts as both a county court and High Court.

Judicial separation

Judicial separation proceedings can be used where a spouse does not accept that the marriage has irretrievably broken down, or does not want to divorce, for example for religious reasons. The facts that have to be proved are the same as for divorce.

The effect of a decree of judicial separation is that the husband and wife are technically relieved of the obligation to reside with each other. But they remain married, in law, so that neither can marry anyone else, and on the death of one spouse, the other would be his or her widow or widower. This can be particularly important in the case of an elderly couple, because a wife would lose substantial widow's pension benefits if the couple divorced. The decree does, however, affect inheritance rights: if either spouse dies without making a will, they are considered as if they were divorced.

A decree of judicial separation does not preclude a divorce later, and the facts relied on to obtain the judicial separation decree (except for desertion, which formally ends on a decree of judicial separation) may be used in divorce proceedings later. The procedure for obtaining a judicial separation is similar to divorce, but there is only one decree, with no interim stage. Applications for judicial separation are made much less frequently than applications for divorce: if ultimately what you want is a divorce, applying for judicial separation in the meantime can double your costs.

Separation and the new law

Under the new law to be introduced by the Family Law Act 1996 (likely to be sometime in 1999), a 'separation order' can be applied for, which is not dissimilar to judicial separation. The effect on inheritance rights of a separation order is the same as that of judicial separation – i.e. if either spouse dies without leaving a will, the survivor is dealt with as if the couple had been divorced. This 'separation order' will meet more neatly people's expectations of being able to get a 'legal separation' – an improvement on the present law under which getting a judicial separation decree is usually too cumbersome and costly whereas drawing up a separation agreement is frequently perceived to be 'not legal enough'.

Embarking on a divorce

The spouse who formally starts off the divorce process is called the petitioner; the other becomes the respondent. Under current law, it is not possible to file a joint petition, but see the end of this chapter for changes under the new law. Try to agree between yourselves who is going to file the petition and on what facts. Some people find offensive the idea of being the respondent and admitting adultery or unreasonable behaviour. But being the respondent will very rarely affect how a court decides related issues to do with money or the children. The only circumstances in which the court will be influenced by anyone's conduct, when considering money or children matters in the divorce, is if the conduct of either spouse, in legal terms, is proved to be so 'gross and obvious' that it would be wrong for the court to disregard it – for example, where a husband attacked his wife causing such severe injury that she would be unlikely to remarry or perhaps even work again.

There is a practical advantage in being the petitioner because it is he or she who is in the driving seat and who can, to some extent, control the pace of the divorce. In certain cases, it is possible for a respondent to file a cross-petition. However, this merely adds to the expense and is rarely worthwhile. There is also no exemption from fees for those who would otherwise qualify for legal aid for a defended divorce (e.g. income support recipients) and the court fee for filing a cross-petition or answer to the divorce petition is an offputting £100 – added to which must of course be any extra legal costs.

In an undefended case, a solicitor is not a prerequisite for the actual procedure of getting divorced. However, advice from a solicitor before embarking on proceedings is often very helpful and should ensure that you don't unwarily fall into any misunderstandings, like thinking that getting a divorce means an automatic end to your financial obligations to your ex-spouse – it doesn't. You may want to check whether there is a basis for divorce in your case and that you understand what has to be done, by whom and when, and what the implications are of the questions you will be required to answer on the various forms that have to be completed and submitted to the court.

If you have children, it would be wise to discuss with your solicitor the arrangements that you propose to make for them. Under a procedure brought in by the Children Act 1989, the petitioner must try to agree the contents of the form called 'statement of arrangements for the children' with the respondent before the divorce proceedings start. You may want some advice about how to complete the form and what approach to take with your spouse. It is also useful to get some advice on financial matters at an early stage.

Undefended divorce – the 'special procedure'

Undefended divorces are dealt with by what is known inaptly as the 'special procedure'. The divorce process is carried out on the basis of paperwork and neither husband nor wife will have to attend any hearing in respect of the divorce petition itself – although they may still have to go to court if there are problems over children or money.

The facts in the petition (and the subsequent affidavit) are considered by the district judge of the divorce court without either spouse being present. If there are children, the district judge will also review the arrangements for them. He or she must then decide whether or not any order should be made about the children. If he or she is satisfied that no court order needs to be made, then again the divorce will proceed just on the paperwork and the couple will not be asked to go to court. If the district judge has doubts or problems, he or she can ask for further evidence, which may require personal attendance at court. In practice, the vast majority of divorces will not have any order made about the children, leaving it up to the parents to make their own arrangements. A court order about the children will be made only if there are disputes or if in some other way it will be better for the children.

The cost of a divorce

Chapter 1 included information on a solicitor's fees for a divorce. Following a significant hike in January 1997, the court fees (sometimes called 'disbursements' by lawyers) will need to be reckoned with too.

Unless a petitioner is in receipt of income support, family credit, jobseeker's allowance or advice under the legal aid green form, the basic out-of-pocket expenses for an undefended divorce will come to £177 (the petition fee, £150, plus affidavit fees, £7, plus the cost of an application for decree absolute, £20). If the petitioner does claim income support or family credit or gets advice under the green form, then he or she will be exempted from fees but will still have to pay the affidavit fee of £7.

These costs can easily be increased further. For those who cannot claim any reductions, for example, if there are disputes over the children, an application under the Children Act 1989 will cost a further £30 by way of the court application fee. If the dispute is resolved by consent, a further £20 should be added for the fee for an application for a consent order. Disputes over finances will cost £50 for making an application for ancillary relief and could cost a further £20 for an application for a consent order if matters are settled. Assuming that in an initially straightforward divorce there are applications over children and money both resolved by consent, a minimum of £297 in court fees (excluding the cost of swearing further affidavits) would have to be stumped up. If the battles last longer, a further court fee of £20 for a request for directions for trial and affidavit fees will be added. In addition to the court fees, of course, are solicitors' costs too, if they are acting in the case.

Although those on income support, family credit, jobseeker's allowance or receiving advice under the green form are exempted from fees, the fee exemption applies only to undefended divorces or judicial separations: anyone wanting to defend a divorce will have to pay the full fee of £100 for filing an answer or cross-petition. A fee exemption form (Form EX160) will need to be completed and handed in with the other documents, at the start of a divorce. If you are in receipt of welfare benefits, you will need to provide evidence that you are receiving that benefit – e.g. a letter from the Benefits Agency or a photocopy of your current benefit book. Others on low incomes can apply for remission of their fees in cases of 'hardship'. There is no definition of 'hardship' in place, and in practice the way fee remission applications are dealt with varies from court to court. Requests for remission of fees have to be made to the court at each stage that fees are due and it is up to the court to decide whether or not an individual's fees will be reduced. Ask your solicitor or Citizens Advice Bureau for more details.

Documents needed

To start off divorce proceedings, the petitioner needs to send to his or her chosen divorce county court or the Divorce Registry★ in London:

- the completed form of petition for divorce, with a copy for the other spouse (the respondent) plus an extra copy in an adultery case where the other person involved (the co-respondent) is named
- the marriage certificate or a certified copy of it. A photocopy of the marriage certificate is not acceptable. A certified copy can be obtained from either the registration district in which the marriage took place or by going in person to the Family Records Centre★ in London, both of which will provide a certified copy for a fee of £6.50. The Family Records Centre also has a priority service which takes 24 hours and costs £22.50. Alternatively, you can write to the Office for National Statistics,★ which will provide a certified copy in 28 days, for a fee of £12; its telephone priority service costs £28. (The marriage certificate will not be returned after the divorce.) If the marriage certificate is in a foreign language, the petitioner will also need a formal notarised translation of it.

In addition the petitioner needs to send:

- a fee of £150 or a completed fee exemption form
- a statement of the proposed arrangements for any relevant children (see page 133) with a copy for the spouse. The petitioner should try to get this completed form agreed in advance with the spouse and countersigned by him or her.

If a solicitor is filing the divorce petition for the petitioner, he or she will also need to file a 'certificate of reconciliation' stating whether any advice has been given about reconciliation.

Blank forms for the petition and the statement of arrangements for the children are available from divorce court offices and the Divorce Registry, without charge, as are a series of free booklets to give you some basic advice about the divorce and legal processes. There is a standard printed form of petition for each of the five facts which prove that the marriage has irretrievably broken down. Sometimes, the court supplies notes for guidance which need careful reading before the petition is completed. In some courts, the staff will help to complete the forms but they are not allowed to give legal advice. If the petitioner is dealing with the divorce proceedings him- or herself, he or she should always keep a copy of any documents supplied to the court and/or to the spouse.

The court will send the petitioner a letter confirming that the divorce proceedings have been lodged, that states the reference number allocated to the petition. This must be quoted on all communications to the court.

The petition

In the petition, you (the pronoun 'you' is used to refer to the petitioner in this chapter) must give your full name and that of your spouse; the date and place of the marriage (copied from the marriage certificate); the address at which you and your spouse last lived together and until when, and the present address(es); your occupation and that of your spouse; the full names of children and dates of birth if they are not adults; and details of any previous court proceedings relating to the marriage or property.

The form assumes that you are domiciled in England or Wales; if you are not, you must make it clear that you are relying on your spouse's domicile or the fact that you or your spouse have been habitually resident in England or Wales, which means at least one year's residence ending with the date on which the petition is presented.

You must set out one or more of the five facts on which you rely to show that the marriage has irretrievably broken down. Later in the proceedings you will have to swear on oath that the facts that you have alleged are true. If you have any doubts about or difficulties with completing the petition form, which the court office is unable to help you with, you should consult a solicitor.

Fact 1
That the respondent has committed adultery and the petitioner finds it intolerable to live with the respondent
In the petition, no more need be said than that the respondent has committed adultery with the co-respondent, who need not be named. The petitioner must, in addition, state that he or she finds it intolerable to live with the spouse – what this means in practice is that you must be living apart, even if under the same roof.

If you know the name and address of the co-respondent, you can include these, although you do not have to. Also, if you do not know the co-respondent's identity, you can state, for example, that the respondent 'has committed adultery with [a man or a woman] whose name and identity are unknown to the petitioner'.

You are asked to say when and where adultery has taken place, so far as you know. You can ask the respondent to provide a 'confession statement' admitting adultery at a specific time and place with a person (stating the co-respondent's name and address or stating that the respondent refuses to disclose the identity). Such a statement can be admitted as evidence and you can copy the details given on to the petition.

If the co-respondent is named, you will need to send to the court an extra set of papers for serving on him or her too.

If your spouse refuses to admit to adultery and you have no proof of it, there is a risk that the divorce will become defended (with all the expenditure of money and time that this necessitates), so another of the 'facts' on which to base the divorce may be more sensible.

Fact 2
That the respondent has behaved in such a way that the petitioner cannot reasonably be expected to live with the respondent

There is no simple definition of unreasonable behaviour. Violence or serious threats of violence to the petitioner or to the children, alcohol- ism, persistent nagging, refusal to have sexual intercourse or refusal to have children knowing that the other spouse wishes to have them, financial irresponsibility such as gambling to excess – these are some serious examples of what can amount to unreasonable behaviour. But many less grave matters are sufficient.

The test is whether the court feels that between a particular husband and wife the behaviour complained of is sufficiently serious to make it unreasonable to expect the petitioner to carry on living with the respondent. Usually, there will have been a number of incidents to evidence the breakdown of the marriage but one very serious incident (such as severe violence) can be enough. Mere incompatibility is not enough unless it has driven one or both partners to behave unreason- ably – for example by showing no sexual interest or affection, being abusive and derogatory, and so on. If the behaviour of one of the spouses has forced the other to leave home, this would be evidence of the unreasonableness of the behaviour.

In the petition, you should give as precise details as you can. You can allege in general terms the types of behaviour but then you should insert specific incidents, giving details with the approximate dates and places, preferably in date order. But be concise – a few short paragraphs giving the bare bones of the allegations will usually be enough.

If you continue to live under the same roof, it is particularly important that instances of unreasonable behaviour within the last six months are included in the petition. You will have to prove that the marriage has broken down, so if you are living under the same roof then you will, at the very least, need to be sleeping and eating separately: there must, in effect, be two separate households. Further evidence of unreasonable behaviour can, if necessary, be given in the affidavit that follows the petition.

Fact 3
That the respondent has deserted the petitioner for a continuous period of at least two years immediately preceding the presentation of the petition

Desertion as the basis for divorce means a period of separation of at least two years brought about by a husband or wife leaving the other against the deserted party's wishes. You have to state the circumstances, the date on which he or she left and that it was without your consent. This fact is used relatively infrequently these days.

Fact 4
Separation with consent: that the parties have lived apart for a continuous period of at least two years immediately preceding the presentation of the petition and that the respondent consents to a decree being granted or,

Fact 5
Separation without consent: that the parties have lived apart for a continuous period of at least five years immediately preceding the presentation of the petition (even if the respondent does not consent)

In order to establish separation as proof of the breakdown of a marriage, a couple must have lived apart for at least two years if the respondent consents to a divorce, or for five years if there is no consent. If you are still living under the same roof as your spouse but in separate households, you may be required to give evidence of details of your separation later in the proceedings. In order to be considered to be living apart, you have to be sleeping separately, eating separately and not carrying out any domestic tasks (like cooking or cleaning) for each other.

The date of the separation should be stated accurately in the petition. If the separation has been for more than two but less than five years, the respondent's positive consent to being divorced – not just lack of objection – is necessary. The respondent confirms his or her consent by completing the acknowledgement of service form (see *Service of the petition*, page 136). If there is a real risk that the respondent may withdraw consent after the divorce papers have been served, it might be worthwhile considering filing for a divorce based on another fact, if appropriate.

After five or more years' separation, the respondent's consent is not required (but there is provision for opposing the divorce on the grounds that it would cause grave financial or other hardship).

In all separation cases, the respondent may request that his or her future financial position be considered by the court before the decree is made final (absolute). This will then be closely scrutinised and, in order to obtain a decree, the petitioner may have to safeguard it.

Time for attempted reconciliation

On the affidavit that has to follow the petition, there are questions about times when husband and wife have lived in the same household. To allow for attempts at reconciliation, you can have gone on living together for a period of up to six months, or several short periods which together add up to less than six months, without affecting the facts on which the petition is based.

Six months for attempted reconciliation after adultery: After a petitioner became aware of the spouse's adultery, a period of living together which exceeds six months would prevent a decree. Time begins to run from the date that you knew of the actual adultery which is referred to in the petition. Knowledge does not mean mere suspicion. For example, if you had suspected your spouse for some time but only properly found out about the adultery after you had confronted him or her about it, the six-month period would start to run only from the date of your confrontation. If the adultery is still continuing, you can rely on the latest incident, rather than the date you first knew about it.

Six months for attempted reconciliation after unreasonable behaviour: Where unreasonable behaviour is alleged in the petition, the period of living together is counted from the last act of unreasonable behaviour referred to in the petition and will be taken into account in deciding whether the petitioner can reasonably be expected to live with the respondent. Living together for more than six months would not necessarily prevent a decree being granted, but the court would require a detailed explanation and might well conclude that the respondent's behaviour was not unreasonable.

Six months for attempted reconciliation after separation: Although periods of living together (up to a total of six months since separation or desertion) will not invalidate the divorce petition, any such period does not count as part of the two- or five-year threshold. For instance, if you lived together for three months in an attempt at reconciliation and then parted again, the petition cannot be filed until two years, three months and one day have elapsed since the original separation.

The prayer

The last page of the petition asks the court for various things:

- a prayer (request) for the marriage to be dissolved (ended)
- an order for costs to be made against the respondent and/or co-respondent; in the case of a petition for adultery, unreasonable behaviour or desertion, it is usual to ask the court to make an order for costs against the respondent
- under the heading of 'ancillary relief', orders for maintenance (called periodical payments), lump sum payments and property adjustment; such applications are made in general terms at this stage, so you do not need to specify any actual amounts
- any orders sought for the children (for example, a residence or contact order).

Under the Children Act procedures, you should only include the application for an order about the children if you really want an order to be made.

Do not cross off the claim for financial relief because it may be complicated or even impossible to apply for it later: you would have to make a special application to the court for leave (permission) to apply later for any required order. Such an application is not certain to be granted if it is made after a long time lapse or if, for example, the respondent says that he or she decided not to defend the petition only because of the absence of any request for ancillary relief. So, even if you have agreed with your spouse that no financial claims will be made, you should nevertheless include them in the petition so that they can be formally dismissed by the court (only if claims have been made can they be dismissed and a full and final settlement order be made). But to avoid misunderstanding when your spouse receives the petition, explain to him or her that the claims are being included only so that they can be dismissed by the court later.

Similarly, you can include a prayer for costs even though you may agree or decide not to follow this request through. What you are claiming here is costs only in respect of the divorce itself (not ancillary issues such as finance or claims about the children). These will be comparatively low, as they are worked out on a standard, limited basis, and are unlikely to cover the full costs of your solicitor.

In the case of a divorce based on periods of separation, the petitioner and respondent often agree that costs will be divided between them, so the petitioner would seek an order for only half the costs to be paid by the respondent. It is possible to seek costs against a co-respondent, but it would be wise to discuss this with a solicitor.

The last page of the petition should be signed by you if acting in person or by your solicitor if he or she is acting for you. You should also include the names and addresses of the respondent (and co-respondent) for service of the petition, and your address. Home addresses can be used, but if solicitors are acting for either or both of you, their address(es) should be inserted instead here.

Statement of arrangements for children
All 'children of the family', whatever their ages, have to be named in the petition. Children of the family are, in broad terms, those who are:

- children of both husband and wife
- children adopted by them both
- stepchildren

- other children who have been treated by both at any time during the marriage as part of the family, but not foster children.

'Relevant' children are those under the age of 16, or under the age of 18 and still in full-time education or undergoing training for a trade, profession or vocation (even if the child is also earning). If your child is over 16 and under 18 but is in full-time employment or is unemployed (i.e. no longer in the education system), it is important to say so because he or she is no longer a 'relevant' child.

A statement about the present and proposed arrangements for relevant children must be prepared by the petitioner. (A blank printed form of statement is available from the court office: the other spouse will need a copy of the completed form.) The petitioner should try to agree its contents with the respondent in advance of starting the divorce, and get his or her counter-signature if possible. If the respondent refuses to cooperate, the petitioner can file his or her own statement of arrangements and the respondent will have the opportunity of producing his or her own statement of arrangements later. If the respondent has not signed the statement of arrangements, some courts will want the petitioner to confirm that he or she has tried to obtain the former's signature.

The statement of arrangements form is eight pages long and requires detailed information about the children of the family. Although it is long, it is fairly jargon-free. The petitioner will need to set out details about the home where the children currently live, their education or training, any childcare arrangements, amounts of support payable for the children and whether a claim has been made to the CSA, contact (access), their health and if there are any other court proceedings about them. If he or she does not agree with the current arrangements, any proposed changes should be set out. At the end of the form the petitioner will be asked whether he or she would agree to attend conciliation (mediation) with the spouse if arrangements are not agreed. The petitioner has to sign the form.

The aim of making the form so comprehensive is to get parents to look in depth at the realities of how their children's lifestyles will change as a result of separation and or divorce. As the courts will not be able to ask the parents in person about the children (most divorces now proceed on the basis of paperwork alone), they want to have as complete a picture as possible of arrangements for the children. If your

Agreed arrangements for children: a quick guide

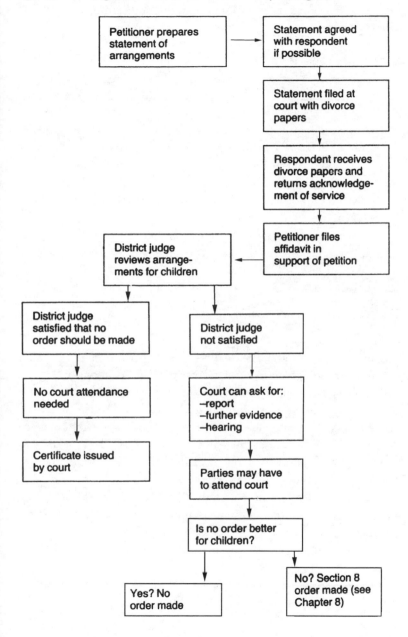

future is uncertain, it may be difficult to complete the form fully; if so, just include as much information as you can, indicating where necessary what arrangements have yet to be decided upon.

Service of the petition

The court posts to the respondent, at the address given in the petition, one copy of the petition and of the statement of the arrangements for any children.

The court also sends an 'acknowledgement of service' form, which the respondent has to complete and return to the court within eight days (although this time limit is, in practice, not always adhered to). If adultery is alleged and a co-respondent is named, a copy of the petition is also sent to him or her, again with an acknowledgement of service form to be returned to the court.

The court has to be satisfied that the respondent (and co-respondent) has received the divorce papers or that all reasonable steps have been taken to serve the documents on him or her. The return of the acknowledgement of service form to the court is normally taken as proof of service. If, however, the acknowledgement of service form is not returned, the petitioner can apply to the court for a fresh set of documents and arrange for 'personal service'.

The petitioner cannot personally serve the petition, but any other person over the age of 16 can effect service by delivering the set of papers to the respondent personally and then completing an affidavit of service and taking or sending it to the court. If the petitioner has had difficulty in serving the papers, he or she can apply to the court for the petition to be served by the bailiff of the county court for the area in which the respondent lives, or can employ an enquiry agent (a private detective) to act as process server.

If the respondent (or co-respondent) fails to return the acknowledgement of service form but has acted in a way which makes it clear that he or she has received the petition, an application can be made by the petitioner for service of the petition to be deemed to have been effected.

If service turns out, in practice, not to be possible, the petitioner may be able to get an order dispensing with service.

The respondent's response

With the documents sent to the respondent are explanatory notes called 'notice of proceedings' telling the respondent about the implications of the answers he or she may give on the acknowledgement of service form.

The acknowledgement of service form does not serve merely as an acknowledgement that the petition has been received; it also includes questions about the respondent's intentions, namely:

- **whether he or she consents to the divorce proceedings**

In an adultery case, the respondent is asked to indicate if he or she admits adultery, and must sign the acknowledgement of service even if a solicitor is also signing. In most other cases, if the respondent has instructed a solicitor, the latter's signature suffices.

In a separation case, the respondent has to reply to the question on the acknowledgement of service form as to whether he or she intends to apply to the court to consider the financial position as it will be after the divorce.

Where the divorce petition is based on separation with consent, the respondent has to confirm that consent by writing 'yes' and also putting his or her signature on the form.

- **whether he or she objects to a claim for costs; if so, why**

If a prayer for costs has been made in the petition, the respondent is asked whether he or she objects to paying the petitioner's costs and, if so, why. The respondent may, for example, have agreed with the petitioner that no order for costs will be pursued against him or her, and a comment to this effect on the acknowledgement of service form should remind the petitioner to delete that request in the affidavit following the petition.

- **whether he or she wishes to make his or her own application for an order about the children**

If the respondent does not agree with the proposed arrangements, he or she should first make sure that what he or she is objecting to are actual proposals and not mere intentions, and should try to discuss them with the spouse. If there is underlying disagreement, the respondent should send to the court his or her counter-proposals by filing his or her own statement of arrangements.

All financial matters and any disputes about the children are dealt with as separate issues, irrespective of whether the divorce itself is defended or undefended.

The respondent has to sign the acknowledgement personally where there are children and a statement of arrangements has been filed.

Cross-petitioning

As an alternative to a fully defended divorce petition, the respondent can file an 'answer' not necessarily denying the allegations but seeking a divorce on other facts (a cross-petition). Since January 1997 a new court fee of £100 has been introduced for filing an answer or cross-petition. No fee exemptions are available.

A respondent might want to cross-petition if he or she felt that the facts in the petition did not represent the true picture and needed some breathing space while negotiating with the spouse. Such a tactic could, however, backfire and increase costs in the long term. The new court fee is in any event a disincentive to cross-petition.

If the petitioner does not dispute the cross-petition, the divorce will proceed on the respondent's petition and the special procedure (see page 125) will again be adopted. It is also possible (but unusual and expensive) to obtain cross-decrees, whereby the petitioner obtains a decree on the basis of the petition and the respondent on the basis of the answer.

After an answer has been filed by the respondent, the petitioner may file a reply. Once these divorce documents have all been sent to the court, either party can apply to the district judge for directions for trial. Courts go out of their way to discourage defended petitions and the district judge will try to see if there is any way of avoiding a defended divorce. Only if these efforts fail will the district judge allow the case to go forward to a hearing of the divorce. In practice there are only a tiny number of defended divorces which proceed to a full hearing.

The full divorce hearing will be in open court before a judge. Each party should instruct his or her own solicitor who may in turn instruct a barrister for representation in court.

Getting back together

Some couples find that there is a chance of saving the marriage when the divorce procedure is well under way but feel that they are bound to continue with the court action until the end. This is not necessary. If you feel at any stage that you and your spouse might like to give the marriage another try, you are quite free to do so; it is best to tell the solicitor and the court what is happening if your spouse wants to give the marriage another try too. You can apply to the court to dismiss the petition when you feel the reconciliation is working. It is particularly important to tell the court if you have obtained an order to get or keep your spouse out of the house and/or not to molest you. Such an order will automatically lapse once you start living together again.

Recent studies of divorced couples suggest that not only did some of them regret the decision to get divorced, but also that many started to feel uneasy about the process long before getting the decree but felt unable to halt it once it had gained momentum. Remember that it is you who must make decisions, not your solicitor. If you are not sure about wanting to go ahead with a divorce you can always call a halt (if you are the petitioner) as long as you do so before decree nisi.

You may want to consider whether some or all of the differences with your spouse can be resolved with outside, non-legal, help. A fresh viewpoint can often be useful. Such help can, for example, be obtained from a marriage guidance counsellor (such as RELATE);* see also Chapter 4.

Continuing proceedings

The next stage in getting an undefended divorce is to apply to the court for a date for the decree nisi to be pronounced, by completing the 'request for directions for trial (special procedure)' form.

The petitioner can make this application only if he or she can prove that the respondent and any co-respondent have been served with the petition and have had the opportunity to defend it. Usually, proof of service is provided by the respondent's filing the acknowledgement of service. The court then sends a copy of this to the petitioner, usually together with a blank form of 'request for directions for trial' and a blank form of affidavit.

The petitioner must complete the 'request' and affidavit and lodge them with the court. In the 'request' form, the petitioner should fill in only the top part by inserting the name of the court, the number assigned to the petition, the names of the petitioner and respondent, and then date and sign it. The rest of the form is completed by the district judge and court staff.

Affidavits

The 'special procedure' affidavit is a fairly straightforward document, mostly in the form of a questionnaire. The questions refer to the petition, asking for confirmation that its contents are true and for any alterations or additions. (Knowingly giving false information is perjury, which is a criminal offence.) The petitioner also has to state whether he or she is going to pursue any requests for costs made in the prayer of the petition.

There is a slightly different form of affidavit for each of the five facts on which a divorce can be based.

Except where the respondent has failed to file one, the acknowledgement of service is referred to and sworn with the affidavit as an 'exhibit'. Where there are children, the petitioner will also be asked if he or she has read the statement and if he or she wishes to change anything on it. He or she will also have to identify the counter-signature at the bottom of the statement as that of the respondent. A swearing fee of £5 plus £2 per exhibit will have to be paid.

Affidavit where the 'fact' is adultery

The petitioner must insert the facts on which he or she bases the allegation of adultery. He or she must refer to the relevant numbered paragraphs on the petition and state that the allegations are true to the best of his or her knowledge and belief. If the respondent has admitted the adultery on the acknowledgement of service form or by making a written confession statement, the petitioner should identify the respondent's signature on the document (and similarly if the co-respondent has supplied a confession statement). A co-respondent does not need to have admitted the adultery for the divorce to go through, provided that the respondent has made the admission or that the petitioner can prove the adultery.

If the adultery has not been admitted by the respondent (and provided that the petitioner can prove service of the petition on the respondent and co-respondent), the petitioner should give all the first-hand information available, such as the date of confession of adultery or details of circumstances to show that the respondent has committed adultery.

'Hearsay' evidence, that is, indirect information from somebody else, is not usually acceptable: the petitioner may need to supply further affidavits by people who can give first-hand information to back up the allegation. In the past, an enquiry agent's report often provided additional evidence, but this form of investigation is used less often now.

The petitioner also has to confirm in the affidavit that he or she finds it intolerable to live with the respondent.

Affidavit where the 'fact' is unreasonable behaviour

Further evidence to substantiate any allegations made in the petition may be given, but it is not necessary. There is no need for a blow-by-blow account of every incident, provided that the respondent's conduct has been adequately set out in the petition. If the district judge is not satisfied with the information given, he or she will call for further evidence to be supplied, which could be outside evidence too, such as a medical report or a witness's affidavit.

In order to clarify whether, and for how long, you have gone on living with the respondent, you are specifically asked whether the behaviour described in the petition is continuing and, if not, when the last incident took place. You then have to say whether you have lived at the same address for more than six months since then; if so, you have to describe what arrangements you have for sharing the accommodation. This involves giving details of sleeping, cooking and cleaning arrangements and so on.

Affidavit where the 'fact' is desertion

The date on which desertion began has to be given, and you must state that you did not agree to the separation and that the respondent did not offer to return.

Affidavit where the 'fact' is separation

Where you and your spouse have been living in separate households for the whole of the period apart, the relevant dates and separate addresses should be given and details of when and why you decided that the marriage was at an end. Merely living apart is not always

Undefended divorce by Special Procedure: the steps

Time stage	Who acts	Action required and documents involved
1 –	spouse wanting divorce (petitioner)	–may go to solicitor for advice on grounds for divorce and for help with completing petition –gets appropriate form of petition and, if relevant, statement of arrangements for children, from divorce county court office or Divorce Registry –completes statement of arrangements and tries to agree its contents in advance with the other spouse (respondent) if possible; if respondent agrees, he or she countersigns the form
2 any time after 1 year from date of marriage	petitioner	–lodges at court office: i) completed petition plus copy for respondent (and named co-respondent, if petition based on adultery) ii) certified copy of marriage certificate iii) two copies of completed statement as to arrangements for children, where relevant –pays fee of £150 to court office (limited fee exemptions or remissions – fee exemption form needs to be filled in)

3	court office	within a few days of (2) depending on the court's workload	sends to respondent copy of petition, statement of arrangements for children, notice of proceedings, and acknowledgement of service for completion (in adultery case, all documents except statement about children also sent to co-respondent, if named)
4	respondent (and co-respondent)	within 8 days of receiving documents in (3) (longer if respondent living outside England and Wales)	must return acknowledgement of service to court, plus, if desired, any counter-proposals about arrangements for children
5a	court office	if acknowledgement(s) of service not returned	notifies petitioner and gives information about alternative methods of service
b	court office	once acknowledgement(s) of service returned	sends copy of acknowledgement(s) of service to petitioner, plus form of request for directions for trial and form of appropriate affidavit in support of petition, to be completed

[continued]

	Time stage	Who acts	Action required and documents involved
6	after 8 days from service of petition if respondent (or co-respondent) has not indicated intention to defend on acknowledgement of service **or** after 21 days from filing acknowledgement of service if respondent (or co-respondent) indicated intention to defend but no answer has been filed	petitioner	–completes affidavit in support of petition, takes it to a solicitor or court for swearing, plus copy of statement of arrangements (if there are children) and acknowledgement of service, identifying respondent's signature (and, in adultery case, any confession statement from respondent) –completes request for directions for trial (sent at 5b by court office) and takes/sends it to court with i) completed affidavit with any relevant supporting documents ii) copy of any previous court orders relating to the marriage or the children
7	when request for directions for trial received	district judge	reads and considers the documents

8a	if all in order	i) district judge	—enters case in special procedure list —certifies entitlement to decree (and to any costs claimed, if appropriate) —certifies there are no children or that the court need not exercise its powers over the children
		ii) court office	fixes date for pronouncement of decree and issues certificate of satisfaction about arrangements for children; sends notification of date to petitioner and respondent and co-respondent
b	if district judge not satisfied	i) district judge	requests further evidence or information
		ii) petitioner	has to supply required evidence or information to court
		iii) district judge	—considers further evidence or information supplied —grants certificate as in 8a(i)
c	if district judge then satisfied	i) district judge	fixes date for pronouncement of decree by judge
		ii) court office	sends notification of date to petitioner and respondent
d	if district judge still not satisfied	i) district judge	removes case from special procedure list
		ii) court office	informs petitioner and respondent
9	on date given in 8a(ii) or 8c(ii)	i) judge	pronounces decree nisi (petitioner and respondent need not be present)
		ii) court office	sends copy of decree to petitioner and respondent

[continued]

	Time stage	Who acts	Action required and documents involved
10	six weeks and one day after (9) (provided certificate of satisfaction about children issued)	petitioner	applies to court (on form available from court office) for decree to be made absolute; pays fee of £20 to court office (or completes form to get remission from fee); if petitioner fails to do this, respondent must wait a further three months before applying for decree absolute
11	when application (10) received	court office	–checks court records that there is no reason why decree should not be made absolute –issues certificate making decree nisi absolute –sends copy of decree absolute to ex-husband and ex-wife

sufficient; separation starts from the time you considered the marriage had actually broken down.

You are asked to say when you came to the conclusion that the marriage was at an end – not when you decided to get divorced, which could well have been at a later date.

You may have had to continue living at the same address because it was impossible or impracticable to live completely apart, even though the marriage was at an end. You may not consider that you have been 'living together' if you have merely been under the same roof and, for example, sleeping separately, not having sexual intercourse, and barely communicating; but a court could hold that you have in fact been living together in one unhappy household and would need to be convinced that there were, to all intents and purposes, two households. You will therefore have to give the fullest possible information about the separateness of the households. (If the space provided in the standard affidavit form is inadequate, attach an extra sheet dealing with this point.)

If the district judge is still in doubt about the circumstances, he or she may remove the case from the special procedure list, to be heard in open court so that fuller evidence can be given. If this happens, you should consult a solicitor; if your financial position makes you eligible, you can apply for legal aid to be represented at the hearing.

Completing the affidavit

When lodging the affidavit, you must return the copy of the respondent's acknowledgement of service form sent by the court. If the respondent has signed it personally, you must identify the signature on it as being that of the respondent by inserting the respondent's name exactly as he or she has signed the acknowledgement of service.

If the respondent's acknowledgement of service has been signed by his or her solicitors alone, you cannot identify the signature and therefore must delete the relevant sentence in the affidavit.

An affidavit can be sworn in front of a solicitor (other than the one acting for you), a commissioner for oaths or the court office. Most solicitors' firms are very willing to offer this service and you can go to a firm convenient for you. A solicitor or commissioner for oaths makes a small charge (£5 plus £2 per exhibit, i.e., any document attached). Since January 1997 court officials at the county courts will charge the same fee for an affidavit.

The completed affidavit, signed and sworn, has to be sent or taken to the court with the application form requesting directions for trial.

District judge giving directions

About the divorce

Provided that the district judge is satisfied as to the service of the petition on everybody concerned, that an opportunity for defending has been given and, in a consent case, that the respondent's consent has been confirmed, and that all the paperwork is correct, he or she will give directions for the case to be entered in the special procedure list.

If the district judge is not satisfied with the information in the affidavit, the petitioner (or a witness) may be asked to lodge a further affidavit or give additional information on the points of concern.

If the district judge still does not accept that there is sufficient evidence for a divorce, he or she may direct that the petition be removed from the special procedure list. A fresh application then has to be made for directions and for a date to be fixed for a hearing in open court before a judge.

When the district judge is satisfied that there is sufficient evidence to support the petition, he or she will certify that the petitioner is entitled to a decree nisi of divorce (or decree of judicial separation). The court will then fix a date for the judge to pronounce the decree nisi.

About the children

At the same time that the district judge looks at the divorce papers, he or she must also consider the arrangements for the children and whether *no* order is better for the children. If so, a certificate of satisfaction will be issued to this effect and the decree nisi pronouncement will go ahead.

If, however, the district judge has doubts or concerns about proposals for the children, or if there is a clear dispute between the parents, then further evidence will usually be called for. The judge can ask for the parents to attend a special appointment at court, or for affidavits or a welfare report to be filed. In that case the decree nisi will usually be postponed until the district judge is again satisfied that no court order needs to be made, or that a residence and/or contact order will be made where appropriate.

Decree nisi and decree absolute (final decree)

The decree nisi is a provisional decree and does not end the marriage. It entitles the petitioner to apply to the court for the decree to be made absolute after a period of six weeks and one day have elapsed. Until this is done, you are still legally married.

A decree can be made absolute earlier than the six weeks if the petitioner applies for this when the decree nisi is pronounced and attends to explain to the judge in person the reason for the application. The respondent must be given notice of the application by the petitioner. An application will be granted only in urgent circumstances, for example to enable one of the couple to marry again before a child is born.

The procedure for applying for a decree absolute is simple. The form 'application for decree absolute' (obtainable from the court office) is completed by the petitioner by inserting the date of the decree nisi, the date of the application and his or her signature and lodging this form, together with a fee (in January 1997 raised to £20), at the court office. A certificate of decree absolute will then be issued by the court and sent to the petitioner and respondent (and co-respondent).

If the petitioner does not apply for the decree nisi to be made absolute when the time comes, after a further three months have elapsed (i.e. six weeks and one day plus three calendar months after decree nisi), the respondent may apply to the district judge for the decree to be made absolute, with an affidavit setting out the reasons why it is he or she who is applying rather than the petitioner.

If decree absolute has not been applied for within 12 months of the decree nisi, the delay must be explained when the application for decree absolute is lodged, giving the reason for the delay and stating whether the couple have cohabited since decree nisi and whether the wife has borne any more children. A district judge may require further explanation or even affidavit evidence before the decree is made absolute.

It is important to keep your certificate of decree absolute in a safe place. You would, for example, need to produce it for the registrar or priest if you wanted to marry again.

Defended divorce

A divorce petition becomes a defended divorce if the respondent states on the acknowledgement of service form that he or she intends to defend the petition. He or she must also file at court an 'answer' to the petition within 29 days of service of the petition (court fee £100). The answer can consist of a simple denial of the facts contained in the petition or can go into more detail by including facts which the respondent claims refute the allegations in the petition. The petitioner then has the opportunity of filing a 'reply' 14 days after receiving the respondent's answer if he or she wants to dispute allegations made in the reply.

The court will then usually fix an appointment for a pre-trial review, at which it will state whether any further evidence needs to be filed. The case will usually be transferred up to the High Court at this stage. The court may try to find out if a settlement can be reached before a full hearing.

Defended divorces are costly not least because they culminate in a full hearing before the court, which both parties (and any witnesses) plus their legal representatives (usually solicitors *and* barristers) must attend. Some sort of compromise (perhaps by the petitioner agreeing to amend some of the more hurtful allegations in the petition, for which a new court fee of £50 is payable) can usually be made (and should be wherever possible). Defended divorces which come to a full hearing in court are indeed very rare – only 50 or so a year in England and Wales.

Divorce reform: the Family Law Act 1996

The Family Law Act 1996, which will revolutionise the experience of divorce, was passed by Parliament in July 1996. The changes it will bring about necessitate the setting up of a new infrastructure – consisting of more mediation and increased marriage support services, for example – which is why it will be at least 1999 before the new law will be brought in across England and Wales. Some of the detail of how the new law will actually affect the process of divorce – what an 'information meeting' at the start of a divorce is like, who will run it, whether other couples will attend too – is yet to be finalised.

However, the broad details are known, and pilot schemes are being implemented to test out which arrangements will work best.

On the basis that readers may be considering delaying their divorces so that the new law, rather than the old one, applies, set out below are some key changes in the divorce process, together with a short explanation of the transition period when the old and new law will run alongside each other. A key overall change will be that future (i.e. after the divorce) arrangements about the children, maintenance and the home for example will have to be worked out before a divorce order is granted under the new system. If you wish to read further, guides to the new Act (which currently are primarily geared to professionals such as lawyers) are available, such as *Blackstone's Guide to the Family Law Act 1996* by T. Bond *et al*, *Divorce: The New Law. The Family Law Act 1996* by Stephen Cretney and Roger Bird, and *Divorce Reform: A Guide for Lawyers and Mediators* by Bishop *et al* (of the Family Law Consortium). The Lord Chancellor's Department★ also produces a free booklet *Marriage and the Family Law Act 1996: The new legislation explained.*

The old law and the new law: transition period

If you are newly separated and are considering which fact you should use to start off a divorce, then if you think that the divorce will be based on adultery or behaviour, no problem arises and the Family Law Act 1996 does not have any effect on any current decision to divorce, as long as you are starting the divorce process before the implementation date of the new Act. But if you are actively considering a 'no-fault' divorce petition (i.e. a separation petition based on two years' separation with consent), then the question arises about whether you would be caught by the provisions of the new Act and thereby have to wait for a much longer period before being able to get your divorce than just the two years of separation. You should still be able to opt for an old-style divorce as long as you start off divorce proceedings within a two-year transitional period when both the old and the new law systems will run side by side. This would enable you to avoid having to wait for an extra 12 months (or more) before being able to get a divorce.

Here is an example. Say Mrs Jones and her husband separated in July 1997 and the new Act's provisions on divorce are to be implemented in April 1999. Mr and Mrs Jones will still be able to have an 'old-style' type of divorce founded on two years' separation with consent – as long as one of them starts off divorce proceedings before April 2001, i.e. within the two-year transitional period to run from (say) April 1999. They can of course divorce earlier than this, still under the old law: if they wait until they have been separated for two years, i.e. until July 1999, they will be able to start off an 'old-style' divorce at that time. However, if they so choose, they can alternatively opt for a new-style divorce, i.e. a time-based petition on a specified period of reflection and consideration under the Family Law Act, but they will then have to wait for a time-based divorce (see below).

In essence, as long as a couple separate before the Family Law Act is implemented they will still have open to them the possibility of opting for an old-style petition based on a two-year separation with consent. However, the likelihood of a petitioner being able to opt for an old-style divorce based on five years' separation is rapidly diminishing. Such a couple would need to have clocked up at least three years' separation before Part II of the Act is implemented and the two-year transitional period starts to run.

Time-based, not fault-based, divorce

Under the new law, the concept of fault will no longer apply: the rationale for this is that if divorcing couples stop focusing on who was responsible for the marriage going wrong, the divorce itself is likely to be less bitter. If, instead (the theory goes), couples are given time to consider and reflect on what has happened and what arrangements should be made for the future, divorces may become less hostile and more positive. The 'period of consideration and reflection' will probably turn out to be the most obvious change. Divorces will by and large take longer to achieve, but at least when a divorce is finalised, so too should be arrangements over children and money.

The first stage in the new-style divorce will be an information meeting. The process of divorce and the services available – marriage guidance counselling, mediation and legal services – will be explained.

Pilots of these information meetings have been running since June 1997 for Phase I. The pilots will run alongside the existing divorce process – so attendance will not be compulsory, but it will be free. Phase II was launched on 13 October 1997 in the North East including Northumberland and Cleveland, and a second tranche of this phase began in early 1998 in Manchester and South London.

The timetable under the new law: a summary

- All divorcing couples must wait three months after attending an information meeting before starting divorce (or separation) proceedings by filing a statement of marital breakdown at court. Fourteen days afterwards the statement is deemed to have been served on the other spouse.
- A nine-month period of consideration and reflection then follows. This could be extended to 15 months, if one of the couple requests the extra six months, or if there are children under 16.
- Couples can have an additional 12 months at the end of the period, if they require it, to decide on future arrangements. However, the application for a separation order or divorce order must be made within 12 months of the end of the period of consideration and reflection – otherwise the whole process is likely to have to start again.
- (Couples will be able to suspend the period for reflection and consideration for up to 18 months to attempt reconciliation.)
- One month after an application for a separation order or divorce order has been made is the likely time scale for the court to make the final order if all the arrangements are satisfactorily in place.

In Phase III the Lord Chancellor's Department (LCD) plans to test alternative methods of providing divorce information, looking specifically at provision of information via interactive CD-ROMs and videos. The intention was to establish pilot projects in two areas – first the south coast/Solent area (from Chichester to Weymouth, Winchester and the Isle of Wight) and second Merseyside and North Wales, to include the area from Southport to Caernarfon including the area South of Wrexham. This phase commenced in early 1998 and will last for nine months or until 1,000 individuals have received divorce information.

During the pilot, the LCD is to test different types of meetings, with interested parties being allocated to different types of meetings at random:

- an individual meeting of up to one hour (for one or both spouses)

- an individual meeting of up to half an hour and the opportunity to attend a group meeting lasting up to one hour
- a group meeting aimed at those who have children but who are either unmarried or not intending to divorce. For this pilot, unmarried people can get information about separation too, although their legal rights are quite different. It seems likely that they will not be included once the pilot period is completed.

The group meetings in the pilots will be conducted by two presenters comprising either a lawyer, a mediator or a court welfare officer (there was also some suggestion that the LCD wishes to involve judges as presenters at the group meetings). A variety of different venues were also to be tested – accessibility obviously being a key issue – with the LCD requesting that at least one neutral venue would be specified. During the first phase, dedicated premises were to be used both for the individual and group meetings.

As we go to press it is not known which form of offering the information meetings was to be preferred.

Three months after that meeting, one spouse (or both together) can file a 'statement of marital breakdown', which starts time running for the divorce – this is called the 'period of reflection and consideration'. A minimum of nine months after that, if all the financial arrangements have been agreed and are to the satisfaction of the court and there are no children under 16, one or both can apply for a 'divorce order'. If there are children under 16, the couple will usually have to wait for a further six months before being able to apply; their new arrangements over the children must also be finalised to the satisfaction of the court. The new law provides a waiver of this extra waiting period if there is a court order in force involving domestic violence. However, as another time extension either spouse can apply on his or her own for a six-month extension if desired.

There are new provisions so couples can postpone the divorce or even stop it altogether. If both partners want to make a go of their relationship again, they can file a notice with the court saying that they are attempting reconciliation, and the time stops running. The period can be extended for a further 12 months, if couples require it. It is also possible that if arrangements are not finalised within a year after the end of the period of consideration and reflection, the original statement will normally lapse, so that the spouses have to start all over again with a new statement of marital breakdown – if they still want a divorce. Another change is that a hardship bar can be applied for in the meantime, preventing divorce. Such a bar will be made only if the court is satisfied that substantial financial or other hardship would be caused to the applicant or to the children of the family by divorce.

Extra consideration for children's views

The views of the children on divorce will in future be taken into account when the court has to decide whether or not to exercise its powers under the Children Act 1989. Extra factors will need to be considered by the court before it makes a divorce order. They are:

- the wishes and feelings of the child
- the conduct of the parties in relation to the bringing up of the child
- the general principle that a child's welfare is best served by having regular contact with those who have responsibility for him or her and with other members of the family, and 'the maintenance of as good a continuing relationship with his or her parents as possible'
- any risk to the child arising from the arrangements for his or her care and upbringing.

The court would be able to postpone a divorce order and in 'exceptional circumstances' could make a special direction to take into account children's views on the divorce of their parents. As we go to press, it is not clear how this will work out in practice, except that a child will not be able to apply to stop the parents' divorce.

Support of marriage

It seems odd that a new Act to reform divorce should contain suggestions on how to support marriage, but the government hopes that the Act will help achieve this end. Marriage counselling – one session at least – will be provided for free on a voluntary basis to spouses who both qualify for legal aid.

Mediation services

The availability of local mediation services and the process of mediation must be explained in the initial information meeting, and spouses will in effect be encouraged to attend mediation. The courts can make a direction that proceedings be adjourned so that the parties can attend a meeting at which mediation facilities will be explained to them, thereby 'providing an opportunity for each party to take advantage of those facilities'. Mediation will be available free to anyone eligible for legal aid, but others will have to pay a fee. Legal services should still be available while mediation continues. See Chapter 4 for more information on the pilot scheme being run by the Legal Aid Board to test out mediation services, under which you may already be able to get free mediation if you qualify financially and live in one of the pilot scheme areas.

Chapter 8

Children and divorce

Divorce is a decision reached by adults and often comes as a great shock to children, even when the strains in the marriage have become only too clear to their parents. The instinctive reaction of a child may be similar to your own or your spouse's reaction – disbelief, denial and a frantic attempt to make it not happen. It is important that you find time to allay a child's fears by explaining what is happening and by providing reassurance. This can be far from easy when you yourself are in a state of emotional turmoil and stress.

When you are trying to put the past behind you and start a new life, it may be difficult to accept that your children's needs are different from yours and that they may even conflict with yours to some extent. For example, children often say very little about wanting to see the parent who has left home because they are aware that this may upset the person they are living with. Their silence does not mean that they are not missing the other parent. Both parents need to reassure the children that they do not have to choose one and reject the other, and that their separation is in no way the children's fault. Children will need endless reassurance that both their parents still love them and that the fact that their Mum and Dad don't feel they can live together any more does not mean that either of them will disappear out of the children's lives.

Your status as a husband or wife will finally be over when the decree is made absolute, but not your status as a parent. Your children will always have two parents and your link with your former spouse will continue as long as you have children. This enduring bond is indeed now legally acknowledged by the Children Act 1989, which states that both parents (if they were married to each other when the children were born or married later) will continue to have 'parental responsibility' for their children even after the break-up of the marriage.

As parents, you are related to each other by blood through your children and you need to shift the focus of your relationship from that of husband and wife to that of parents.

A fundamental issue is how the children are going to keep in touch with the parent with whom they are not living day to day. Working out arrangements for contact (formerly known as 'access') that both parents can cope with takes a lot of effort. Bear in mind that your former spouse is likely to behave in the same kind of irritating way that he or she did while you were married (and that the same is probably true of you), so you will both need to behave with greater consideration than before. Be careful not to play out, in the guise of disputes over contact, what are really matrimonial disputes.

Sorting out arrangements concerning the children will be a continuing process, but it is one that gets increasingly easier – as emotions die down, as the children get older and as routines become established. Initially, you may find great difficulty even in discussing proposed arrangements with your former spouse. This is a time to consider the possibility of mediation with professional help (see Chapter 4).

It is worthwhile persevering with setting up sound and workable arrangements for the children to see each parent. While the most important factor affecting how well the children cope with divorce is the emotional and psychological health of the parent who looks after them, another key factor is the maintenance of strong links with *both* parents. Studies have shown that children of separating parents who see the 'absent parent' regularly are able to cope better with the emotional stresses of divorce. This is particularly true in the period just after the separation, which is most traumatic for the children. Although it may be tempting to wait for a 'cooling off' period before the parent who has left home sees the children again, this would be storing up trouble for later. The emotional needs of the children are greatest just after the separation, and seeing regularly the parent who has left can help them adjust gradually to the fact of the family break-up.

There is a financial incentive in this, too. Other studies have shown that fathers who have contact with their children are more likely to pay maintenance on a regular basis.

There are other ways in which you can help your children. Psychologists have identified the effects of 'secondary' divorces suffered by all who go through divorce, but particularly by children (through moving house, school, leaving grandparents behind, for example). If you can keep the family home, so as to provide the children with the security of a known base, this will help them considerably. Maintaining their links with their school friends and grandparents also can help them to cope better.

Both you and your spouse need to affirm frequently your continuing love for the children and assure them that they are in no way to blame for the break-up. If you are able to, you should work together with, rather than against, your spouse in your approaches towards the children. Tell them jointly, if you can, about the separation and do not give the children any opportunity to play you off one against the other. It is better probably to tell your children during the day rather than last thing at night, however tempting it may be to use that special time just before bed to let them know. If you do tell them in the evening, they may soon feel abandoned and alone as their fears are made more terrifying by the darkness of the night. Remember especially that your children will, just like you, need time to come to terms with what has happened.

The focus of the advice contained within this book is practical and legal. There are many good books now on the market which give valuable advice for parents who want to help their children overcome the adverse effects of divorce, such as *Divorced Parenting: How to Make it Work* by Sol Goldstein.

Parental responsibility

Since the Children Act 1989 came into force in 1991, parents who were married to each other when children were born (or who married each other later) both automatically have 'parental responsibility', the new legal concept which defines the framework between parents and children (for information on unmarried parents see Chapter 14). As a major change from the old law, *both* parents will retain parental responsibility until their children are 18, even after marriage breakdown. So the continuing blood tie with the parent who will no longer be looking after the children on a day-to-day basis is formally acknowledged. He (or she) will keep the duty and right to have a continued involvement in a child's upbringing. The courts cannot take away parental responsibility from married parents unless an adoption order is made.

The fact that both spouses will always have parental responsibility is intended to encourage absent parents (usually fathers) to take an active interest in their children's welfare. Its aim is that fathers will lose out less on divorce (unlike under the old law, when they often lost custody).

In another major change, the Children Act 1989 also gives parents who want to cooperate with one another much greater flexibility to make their own arrangements for the children; courts will now make no court order unless 'it would be better for the children to do so'. Advocates for the change argued that as the courts never usually intervened to divide the children up between the parents during a marriage, why should a marriage breakdown automatically give them that right? Parents, they argued, are the best people to create their own tailor-made solutions to the problems arising on family breakdown. If the parents can work out answers to the problems by themselves, the courts should not interfere.

So, in reality, in most divorce cases nowadays, the courts will not make any orders about whom the children should live with, thus encouraging the parents to work out arrangements for the children. But if there is conflict between the parents which they cannot resolve by themselves or through negotiation (with the help of solicitors or mediators), either parent can apply under section 8 of the Act for a court order, such as a residence order or contact order (see opposite).

What it means in practice

Parental responsibility is defined as 'all the rights, duties, powers, responsibilities and authority which by law a parent of a child has in relation to the child and his property'.

In practice this means the responsibility (and right) to make choices over all the issues that are necessarily involved in bringing up a child, like:

- where a child will live
- where a child will go to school
- what religion a child will be brought up in
- what medical treatment a child will have.

If you have parental responsibility you are also able to apply for a passport for a child.

Having parental responsibility is not exactly the equivalent of being a parent, as unmarried fathers do not automatically have parental responsibility but must acquire it (either by making a formal agreement with the mother or by successfully applying to court).

In some more unusual circumstances, other people may acquire parental responsibility: anyone who has a residence order in their favour automatically acquires parental responsibility too if they do not already have it. So a grandmother who permanently looks after a grandchild could apply for a residence order although usually she will first have to ask the court's permission to make that application. If she is ultimately successful in getting a residence order, she will also have parental responsibility – in other words, the right and duty to make decisions about how the child is brought up. But the fact that the grandmother acquires parental responsibility does not mean that the parents lose it. Now three people have parental responsibility: the mother and father (if they were married) and the grandmother.

Orders the courts can make

All the following orders are made under section 8 of the Children Act 1989 and are thus referred to as 'section 8 orders'. They all restrict in some way the exercising of parental responsibility. They are intended to be more focused than the old court orders and easier to grasp. So, instead of the old confusion about (for example) whether 'custody' meant legal custody or care and control (physical custody), there is now a residence order.

Residence order

This settles the arrangements about with whom (and thus where) a child will live. In most cases it will be with one parent (usually the mother), but a residence order can allow for shared parenting, whereby children divide their time equally between their parents' homes. It could also be applied for by two people together, for example a parent and stepparent.

Contact order

This requires the person with whom the child lives to allow contact with the applicant (thus more clearly indicating who is responsible for making the order work – namely the parent looking after the child). It can be by way of visits or stop-overs, telephone calls or letters, or all or any of these.

Specific issue order

This gives directions for determining a specific question connected with parental responsibility, for example which school the child should go to.

Prohibited steps order

This has the effect of restraining in some way the actions of a person in relation to the child. No step stated in the order can be taken without the consent of the court. This could be used, for example, to stop one parent from changing a child's surname or from taking the child out of the country without the other parent's or the court's consent.

Both specific issue and prohibited steps orders have their origins in wardship proceedings, which are now much less likely to be used. Both types of order can be applied for in an emergency 'ex parte', in other words, without the other party having the opportunity of putting his or her side to the court.

The courts may attach conditions in certain circumstances to the new orders. For example, they could state that contact should take place only in the home of the parent who looks after the children or that another adult is present during the visit.

Who can apply for section 8 orders?

Either parent can apply for an order, if necessary even before the divorce itself has started. The new court orders can be used much more flexibly than before, and indeed other people, such as relatives or even the child him- or herself, may also be able to apply where appropriate (see *Applications by a child*, page 177, and Chapter 14).

The courts themselves can make a section 8 order in any family proceedings, thus widening their own powers. But the courts are supposed *not* to use such orders without proper consideration: court orders can be made only if it is better for the children. If the parents can decide between themselves about who should look after the children and when the other parent should see them, then it is likely that no formal court order will be made, and the situation will continue fluidly with both parents having parental responsibility and thus both deciding together about how the children will be brought up. In the vast majority of divorce cases, the end result is precisely that – both parents with parental responsibility and no court order.

Neither partner will be in a stronger position than the other, although in practice the parent having the day-to-day care of the children will be in more of a position of influence over choices made in their upbringing. Parental responsibility can be exercised independently, so that each parent can make up his or her mind about issues relating to the children (though effective co-parenting needs a measure of cooperation between the parents). The fact of independent rights and responsibilities can be useful in an emergency: if the child were in an accident, then one parent could sign the necessary consent form for medical treatment without having to consult the other parent. Nevertheless, if in future the parents reached stalemate about any particular issue involving the children, a section 8 order (say a specific issue order) could be applied for.

The role of the court

No divorce decree can be made absolute without the court having considered the arrangements for the children of the family. The court has to look at the arrangements and decide whether it is satisfied that a court order need not be made. In the vast majority of cases no formal court order will be made – there is nowadays an in-built presumption that no court order should be made unless it would be better for the children. By and large the court will leave it up to the parents to sort out arrangements between themselves. This will also mean that no attendance at court will be necessary, so that unless there are financial applications which have to be heard by the court, the whole divorce can go ahead on paperwork only.

'Children of the family' means the couple's own children (including adopted children and those made legitimate) and any child treated by them as one of the family, so arrangements made for a stepchild will also have to be put before the court.

Normally, only arrangements for children under 16 have to be set out for the court. Although parental responsibility lasts during the children's minority (until they are 18), court orders (i.e. section 8 orders) will be made for children over 16 only in exceptional circumstances. What 'exceptional circumstances' means has not been defined by the Act, but the courts may feel it is appropriate to make a section 8 order if, for instance, a child is disabled and dependent on an adult and a full court order is needed.

Applications for maintenance for the children will now usually be dealt with by the Child Support Agency* (CSA, see Chapter 5). Other applications (such as for capital lump sums for the children) can still be made to the court under the Children Act 1989 (see Chapter 10).

Agreed arrangements

1. Where the parents are in agreement about arrangements for the children, the petitioner (the spouse starting divorce proceedings) should prepare a statement of arrangements for the children in advance and try to get its contents agreed with the respondent (the other spouse) and countersigned by him or her if possible. (If they cannot agree, the respondent can file his or her own statement of arrangements later, but this is more likely to mean that the court will ask for further evidence and that personal attendance at court will be required.)

2. After the divorce papers have been served, the respondent has filed an acknowledgement of service and the petitioner has filed a statement in support of the petition, the papers go before a district judge for consideration.

3. If there are 'children of the family', the district judge has to consider whether the court needs to exercise its powers to make an order under section 8. If the district judge decides that the court does not need to make a section 8 order, he or she issues a certificate to this effect (called a section 41 certificate). A date for decree nisi is fixed and neither party need attend a court hearing about the children.

4. If, however, there are problems (for instance, if there is an application for a section 8 order, or there is some dispute, or the district judge otherwise considers that the arrangements might not comply with the overriding principle that the welfare of the child be paramount), the judge can ask for:

   - further evidence
   - a welfare report to be prepared
   - the parties to attend a court hearing.

5. Once that direction has been complied with, the district judge

either issues a certificate saying that no court order needs to be made or makes one.

Sometimes, one spouse may want a section 8 order to be made even if the arrangements are otherwise agreed – say, for example, the local authority is insisting on the production of a residence order before re-housing (although strictly it is not authorised to do so). In this situation it will be up to the applicant to persuade the court that a court order should be made and that it is better from the children's viewpoint to do so. It would be sensible to obtain legal advice about what approach should be taken.

Contested arrangements

In any case involving disputes over children, it is wise to consult a solicitor and obtain further legal advice. Court disputes are costly, both financially and in emotional terms. There is rarely any winner in battles over who will have primary care of the children on a day-to-day basis.

Wherever possible, you should try to negotiate with your spouse either directly, or through a mediator or solicitors, to avoid a full-blown battle over the children. In such battles, you are forced to lay bare your private family life and will accuse your spouse of not being fit to be awarded the day-to-day upbringing of the child or even to have contact with the child. A bitterly fought court case can make it harder to establish a decent parenting relationship with the other parent later. In all cases, consider carefully whether, from the child's viewpoint, it is best for you to go ahead with an application to the court.

If repeated and, in the courts' eyes, vexatious applications are made to the court by an adult, the court can make a special order under section 91(14) of the Children Act 1989, preventing a named parent from making further applications to the court without the court's prior permission. The aim of such an order is to prevent further unhappiness being caused for the children. This order is, however, used only sparingly. The criteria for using it are fairly tight. It will not be enough that there is deep bitterness between the parties, for example: the parent on whom the order is served must be shown to have gone beyond what is reasonable.

The procedure

An application for a residence or contact order (or other section 8 order) is triggered off when you apply for one to the court, stating clearly what order you are seeking. Since January 1997 a new court fee of £30 is payable.

Since the Children Act was implemented, the need to make the 'right application' is not absolute, as the court has the power to make an appropriate section 8 order even where the wrong order was sought. No evidence should be filed at this stage. If your court has set up a system of 'in-court conciliation', as most have, it will fix a conciliation appointment before the district judge for you, your spouse and any legal representatives; a court welfare officer will also be in attendance. The children may also be asked by the court to come, depending on their ages – not if they are less than about ten years old.

The aim of the conciliation appointment is to help the parents reach a solution acceptable to both in a supportive, relatively informal, private setting. The court welfare officer or other appointed conciliator will talk with both parents and will be concerned to try to defuse the parents' competition to 'win' the children. If a settlement is achievable but cannot be reached in one session, the courts can fix other appointments to allow the conciliation process to continue.

If the conciliation process is not successful, or in courts where conciliation processes have not yet been set up, the district judge will make an order for directions concerning the evidence to be filed. This usually consists of the original application, the answer and witness statements. All of these are similar to statements but they are not sworn.

The district judge will also order that a court welfare officer (not the same one who assisted in the conciliation process) should prepare a report. Time limits will be set which must be strictly complied with (the Children Act specifically recognises that delay may be harmfully prejudicial in a children application). In practice, however, you may find that due to the workload of the court welfare service, the welfare report may take several weeks to be filed. You should also be told the 'return date' – in other words, when the case will next come to court.

In your evidence, try to confine yourself to setting out the facts, rather than inserting emotional arguments. 'The facts' can extend in children cases to hearsay evidence (information you learned secondhand), but the courts are far more influenced by clear, concise, factual and accurate information than they are by gossip.

The welfare officer will usually interview both parents and the children. The older the children are, the more weight their views will carry. The welfare officer may also make enquiries of the children's schools, and other relevant parties – for example, a child's grandmother, if it is proposed that she will be looking after the child while her son or daughter (the child's parent) is at work. The welfare officer will prepare a report which sets out the facts and circumstances and his or her impressions, and occasionally a recommendation to which the court will pay great attention (although will not necessarily follow).

A copy of the welfare officer's report will be sent to the parties directly or through their solicitors, if appointed. It must not be shown to any third parties without prior permission of the court. Before a final hearing the court may have set a date for an interim hearing to try to resolve which issues are in dispute. Again at this stage the date for a final hearing will be fixed.

Using a McKenzie friend

With the erosion of the numbers of people eligible for legal aid, it is increasingly likely that someone who feels that he or she cannot afford full legal advice may have a helper in court to give support and advice – in legal terms a 'McKenzie friend'. The notion of a McKenzie friend (sometimes known as a 'McKenzie man') dates back only to 1970, to a Court of Appeal case involving a Mr McKenzie, which confirmed the right of a lay person to have a helper in court. The friend cannot, however, address the court or examine the witnesses. A 1997 case confirmed that someone handling his or her own case should not be deprived of the presence and assistance of a McKenzie friend, even when a hearing is in chambers (i.e. not open to the public) because it concerns a child.

The court's considerations

The overriding principle is that 'the child's welfare shall be the court's paramount consideration'. In applying this welfare principle, the court has a checklist of matters it must look at in particular:

- the ascertainable wishes and feelings of the child (in the light of the child's age and understanding)

- the child's physical, emotional and educational needs
- the likely effect on the child of any change in circumstances
- the child's age, sex and background, and any characteristics the court considers relevant
- any harm the child has suffered or is at risk of suffering
- the ability of each of the child's parents, and of any other person in relation to whom the court considers the question to be relevant, to meet the child's needs
- the range of powers available to the court.

The checklist is neither exhaustive nor exclusive, but one which lays out simply what the court *must* consider. The court *may* of course consider that other factors are important in an individual case. For example, the parents' wishes and feelings, although not listed, may often have an important bearing on the eventual outcome of a case.

The wishes and feelings of the child

The fact that the child's wishes and feelings have been placed at the top of the checklist highlights the child–centred approach of the Children Act: children should, wherever possible, be put first. At a hearing, the judge may ask to see the children in private in chambers, without parents or legal advisers present, to talk to them and ask them what they want. If so, the court will ask the parents to bring the children along to court (usually this applies only to children of about ten or over). Far more often children's wishes and feelings will be explored by the court welfare officer when preparing the report.

As mentioned above, the older the child, the more persuasive will be his or her views. Teenage children in any event often 'vote with their feet' over where they want to live, whereas younger children may find it very difficult to put what they want into words. In practice, the child's wishes are extremely influential. The views of mature, articulate children from around ten upwards, who have sound reasons for choosing a particular outcome, will often be the decisive factor. But if the court suspects that children have been coached by one or other parent, 'their' opinions will carry little weight. Although children's views will be respected, they should not be forced to choose unwillingly between two people both of whom they love. Ultimately, especially for younger children, it is up to adults to make decisions.

The child's physical, emotional and educational needs

If the child is very young or sickly or otherwise especially needs a mother's care, a residence order is more likely to be made in favour of the mother. In the past the courts have usually decided that a child's welfare is best protected by being with the mother rather than with the father. One case decided since the implementation of the Children Act confirmed the presumption that a baby would stay with his or her mother. There is thus an in-built bias in favour of mothers, although that bias becomes less strong as the child gets older. It is not unusual, for example, for a court order to provide for older boys to live with their fathers. The courts will always look at each individual family: whichever parent has primarily looked after the children and with whom the children have the closer bond is likely to have a residence order made in her or his favour.

The effect of change

The courts have long recognised that changing the status quo can compound the difficulties of a child adjusting to the parents' separation. So a parent who is already looking after the children usually has a much stronger claim. This, however, does not apply if the children have been snatched from their usual home environment: the courts can act quickly to return children to the parent best able to care for them.

Likewise, splitting the family is almost always regarded as undesirable, so that wherever possible siblings (sometimes even half-brothers and -sisters) should be kept together.

The child's age, sex and background

The inclusion of this factor in the Children Act is an attempt to get away from a stereotypical view of the family which does not 'fit' an individual family unit. So if, for example, it is the cultural norm that the parents go off to work while the grandmother cares for their children, the court might well feel it is best for the children to continue to be cared for by the grandmother. Each case will be decided on its own merits.

Harm or risk of harm

Alcoholism or violence (whether towards a partner or the children) will prejudice a parent's case. Also, if there is a real risk of sexual abuse by a parent, that parent would definitely not get a residence order. A contact order might be given, but only if it would be in the child's best interests (for example, if there were a strong bond between parent and child, if the parent were seeking treatment and if the contact were supervised properly). In the past the courts have been prejudiced against homosexual parents to the extent that they have overlooked that parent's capacity to bring up his or her own child. A case decided in 1991 stated that while a parent's homosexuality will now be a factor taken into account it will not necessarily be decisive (unless the court thinks the children will be adversely affected).

It is still sensible for a homosexual parent to obtain professional advice from a solicitor experienced in this area. There are several organisations concerned with lesbian and gay parenting; for most of them the first point of contact would be the London Lesbian and Gay Switchboard,* where someone can make a referral if necessary.

It there is a real and significant risk of harm to the children – like sexual abuse for example – the local authority's social services department may become involved and may apply for an order that the children be taken into care in really extreme cases. Such a case would then become a 'public law' case (i.e. where the state, here the local authority, gets involved) instead of just a 'private law' case (i.e. just between individual people) and is likely to be heard in a different court. It will be important to have a solicitor acting for you who is experienced in public law cases and is (ideally) on the Law Society's Children Panel (whose members have been specially trained in dealing with children cases).

Since Part IV of the Family Law Act came into force in October 1997, the courts also have new powers to make court orders excluding suspected abusers from a child's home – where the local authority wants to take emergency protective action to protect the children. Interim care orders and emergency protection orders are also now available, and if domestic violence occurs, children as well as adults can be protected by court orders.

Capability of the parents

This can range from practicalities, such as whether a parent works outside the home, to an ability to respond to the child's needs. Overall it is a matter of trying to assess which parent will be better able to look after the children during the week (contact orders may be made for the children to see the other parent during the week, at weekends and/ or holidays); sometimes the claims of both will be equal. Note that this factor does not refer to the parents' conduct as individuals, and a distinction must be drawn between a person's behaviour as a parent (which will be looked at) and as a partner (which will often be ignored unless it has directly affected the children).

A parent who can offer a stable home life (perhaps particularly if remarrying) will usually have a stronger claim than an unreliable and unpredictable parent. A parent who abandons the children and puts the interests of a lover first is likely to be at a disadvantage when applying for a residence order.

Where relatives or other people (like childminders or full-time nannies) are involved in bringing up the children, their capabilities too may be explored.

The courts' powers

As the courts' powers under the Children Act are wider and more flexible than before, they might be able to come up with more creative solutions than in the past. For example, residence orders could be split between both parents: if both parents were equally capable and the children wanted to share their time with each parent, the court could make a residence order specifying that the children would spend two weeks with the father and then two with the mother so that the parents had the opportunity of sharing the care of the children. But the parents would have to tailor their own lifestyles to suit the children's needs (for example, both would have to live near to the children's schools) and the children must usually also really want to spend equal time with each parent to convince the court that such unusual arrangements were really in their best interests.

Residence orders and financial applications

A case in 1995 appears to have added to the above list of factors the fact that when the court decides on a residence order application, it is entitled to look at any financial disadvantage resulting from the child living with the mother and the CSA's assessment of child support to be paid by the father.

In that particular case it was decided that a three-year-old child should live with the father during the week and the mother most weekends. The case proved controversial but it may well be that financial considerations, including the probable consequences of a mother giving up employment and drawing state benefits if she looks after the children full-time, will also be taken into account in applications for a residence order.

A child's right to contact

The chief principle is that it is the right of every child to have contact with both parents. The proven advantages of regular contact with both parents are undeniable – if the parent who is looking after the children wants to deny the other having contact then she (or he) will have an uphill battle in doing so.

In very rare cases, where the parent looking after the children can show an 'exceptional and cogent reason' why the other parent should be denied contact, the courts may accept that for the time being contact should not be ordered. The courts have described the process in making such a Solomon's judgment as follows:

> The court must ask whether the fundamental emotional need of every child to have an enduring emotional relationship with both parents is outweighed by the depth of harm which the child would be at risk of suffering by virtue of a contact order.

Factors such as actual or potential abuse of a child obviously counteract the in-built presumption towards contact. But where a father has, say, a history of criminal conduct and lacks control over his aggression he may be denied contact in any form. In very exceptional cases a mother's (or even sometimes a stepfather's) implacable hostility to a father having contact has been enough to stop him from having contact, but the court has often insisted that he should have indirect contact via letters or telephone calls. In an unusual 1996 case where a father wanted to apply to re-establish contact after some time, the court ordered that he make videos for the children, which were previewed by the mother, to help prepare them for meeting him face to face. However, if a father is extremely violent, abusive, abuses drugs and/or alcohol or in other ways will have a profoundly negative effect on the children, the negative effects are likely to outweigh the in-built balance towards contact.

If an order for contact is made and the parent looking after the children disobeys it, the ultimate sanction is imprisonment – although the courts are very reluctant to resort to such extreme action.

Appeals

Successful appeals against decisions made by the trial judge (the one who originally hears the case) are extremely rare. The judge has a wide discretion, and appeals will be allowed only if the first decision can be shown to be 'plainly wrong'. This is so even if the appeal court feels it would have come to another decision itself. But if further important evidence comes to light, then an appeal might work. If you do go to the Court of Appeal, you may be offered a mediation session to see whether the problem can be resolved out of court.

An appeal against a decision of either the county court (for family cases this is now called a Family Hearing Centre) or the Family Proceedings Panel within a magistrates' court will go straight to the High Court. From the High Court an appeal will go to the Court of Appeal.

Challenging an old order

If a parent wishes to vary or change an old court order made before the Children Act 1989 came into force (14 October 1991), the application will usually be made under the Children Act 1989. Although an application to reopen an old decision has a better chance of success than an appeal, the situation would have to have changed fundamentally before it would be worthwhile going to court again.

Before the Children Act

Prior to the Children Act's implementation there were three different legal concepts applicable to children: custody, care and control, and access. The legal usage of some of the words was (and is) different from ordinary English usage. Because these terms are still popularly used even though they no longer apply, it is useful to be aware of what they mean. (You may also have an old court order which uses these concepts.)

Custody

This meant the bundle of responsibilities that parents have towards their children, for example, the right and duty to make major decisions concerning their upbringing, their religion and education.

There were two different court orders for custody: sole custody (for one parent) or joint custody (for both). Joint custody was the court order that resembled most closely the pre-divorce role towards the children. In a sense, the effect of a joint custody order was primarily psychological, because it confirmed for the parent who did not look after the children the fact that he or she had a recognised role to play towards his or her children. ('Parental responsibility' now fulfils this function.)

Care and control

This meant the actual physical 'possession' of the child. Orders were made only for sole care and control: an order for care and control could not be split (unlike the new residence orders). Care and control is what most people meant when they talked about custody.

An order for care and control was granted to the parent with whom the children were living on a regular basis. Even in the unusual cases where children divided their time equally between their parents, one parent used to have to have an order for care and control.

Access

This meant the visiting periods for the parent who did not have care and control. This could have been 'staying access' (when the child stayed with the non-custodial parent) or 'visiting access' (when the non-custodial parent simply visited or took the child out for the day).

Where parents were able to agree, the courts usually made an order for 'reasonable access' which left the terms of the access visits, or periods of staying access, up to the parents to agree between themselves. Where the parents could not agree, the court may have made an order for defined access, determining when the child would visit the non-custodial parent, sometimes specifying the time when the child should be collected and brought home again.

Other issues

Changing a child's surname

If a child is to be brought up in a new family, a parent (usually the mother) may want to change the child's surname to that of her new partner when or after she remarries. Whether there is anything in the law preventing her from doing so depends on whether there is a residence order (or an old custody/care and control order) in force.

If there is such an order, there will automatically be a provision stating that the child's surname cannot be changed without the consent of the other parent or the court. But if no such order exists, the mother can in theory change the child's surname, as she has parental responsibility which she can exercise independently. However, in practice, where two parents both have parental responsibility, the parent who wants a name change should apply to court for permission if the other parent objects. A parent who objects can in any event apply to the court for a specific issue order. The court application will be decided by the principles that the child's welfare is of paramount consideration and that no court order will be made unless one is better for the child.

It is likely that the courts will be influenced by the old case law which broadly disapproved of changes of surname. The courts usually took the line that the link between a child and his or her natural parent, as symbolised by the surname, should not be broken, so changes of surname were usually refused.

However, a mature child him- or herself may apply for a change of surname by way of a specific issue order. If the child has strong feelings about wanting to be included in the new family and sound reasons for making the application, the court may be persuaded to make an order for a change, given that the child's wishes and feelings rank number one on the welfare checklist.

Taking a child abroad for a holiday

If there is a residence order, the usual rule is that a parent who wants to take a child abroad (this includes going from England or Wales to Scotland) should obtain the other parent's written consent first. This is because it is a criminal offence to remove a child from the country without the written consent of both parents or the consent of the court.

Where a parent simply wants to take the child on holiday and has a residence order in his or her favour, he or she can take the child abroad for a period of up to a month. If the other parent objects, an application can be made to court for its permission by way of a section 8 order. (See also Chapter 13 on child abduction.)

If there is no residence order, the civil law says nothing either to permit or prevent a parent from taking a child abroad. Again, if parents are in dispute, one or other should apply for a section 8 order.

But whether or not a residence order exists, the criminal law still applies.

Applications by grandparents and others

When a marriage ends, sometimes the contact between children and one set of the grandparents ends too, as families divide into opposing camps. This is rarely good for the children: often they can be helped to cope with their distress by grandparents (or other close relatives or friends, say, perhaps a godparent), who can give a helping hand to guide the children through their trauma.

Grandparents (or for that matter any other interested relative or family friend) can now apply to the court for a contact order or other section 8 order. They do not have to wait until divorce or other proceedings have been started (as under the old law). Children Act applications are not limited to new cases either: if an old order is already in existence, an application can still be made for a section 8 order under the new law.

Before such an application can proceed, the court's permission may first have to be sought. The Children Act gives some categories of people the automatic right to make an application. So, if the potential applicant has had the child living with him or her for three years or more *or* has the consent of the person with a residence order in his or her favour, *or* has the consent of everyone with parental responsibility (or that of the local authority if the child is in care), he or she can apply as of right to the court for a contact order or other section 8 order. Otherwise, the court's permission must be obtained before the application will be given the go-ahead. The court will then take into consideration:

- the nature of the proposed application
- the applicant's connection with the child
- the risk of harmful disruption to the child's life.

(The local authority's care plan for the child would also be a factor if the child is being looked after by the local authority.)

If applicants, for example grandparents, have lost contact with the children over many years and formerly had a bad influence on them, it is possible that their application for permission to apply to court will fail. The legal test is whether a grandparent can show that he or she has a 'good arguable case' and that there is a serious issue to try. Usually the court will grant permission to apply and leave a full investigation of the facts to a proper court hearing involving all sides.

Applications for contact by grandparents will more likely than not be granted unless there is deep bitterness between the families which would be exacerbated by making a contact order. Contact orders can be in the form of letters, cards and telephone calls, so the court may make an order for contact in stages, building up contact from letters and telephone calls before a face-to-face meeting, especially if the last time that the grandparents met their grandchildren was some time ago.

Applications for residence orders by grandparents may be unlikely to succeed unless the natural parents (or the local authority if the child is in care) are fully in support and the child has established a pattern of living with a grandparent.

Legal representation for children

In some cases where the parents are presenting opinions of the children which are totally at odds with one another, it may be helpful to ask the court for the child to have separate representation – in other words, to have his or her own advocate at court.

In public law cases (where the local authority is concerned), children are usually represented by a 'guardian ad litem', a person skilled and experienced in dealing with children, who will put the arguments for what is in the child's best interests. Occasionally the courts have taken the step of appointing a guardian ad litem in private law proceedings (i.e. those involving disputes between private individuals). In other cases the courts have asked the Official Solicitor (a public official who is a lawyer and acts for children and others who do not have full legal capacity) to intervene and present the case from the child's viewpoint. Appointing the Official Solicitor is still a relatively unusual step and costs can be a problem: the courts will need to be sure that the costs are met from some source (which may be a costs order against one of the parents). Solicitors have also been instructed to act for a child directly.

Applications by a child

The Children Act also allows children themselves to make an application for an order under section 8: the extra hurdle that the child has to overcome is to show that he or she is of 'sufficient understanding' before an application will be allowed to proceed.

The first stage in seeking independent legal representation for a child is for the child him- or herself to approach a family law solicitor to give instructions. The solicitor will have to decide whether the child is mature enough to make an application to court – whether he or she sufficiently understands the consequences. The legal test is often termed 'Gillick competency', after a case involving a Mrs Gillick and one of her daughters, namely 'the attainment by a child of an age of sufficient discretion to enable him or her to exercise a wise choice in his or her own interests'. A solicitor must first assess whether a child passes this test, and then the Legal Aid Board has to be convinced too. Legal aid will be available on the grounds of financial eligibility (assessed on the basis of the child's own resources, if any) and merits.

Although applications by children in their own right are still relatively rare, a lot of publicity has been given to the handful of cases where, according to the media, children have applied to 'divorce' their parents. In law, to use the term 'divorce' in this context is incorrect. Children cannot actually divorce their parents: parents will still continue to have parental responsibility and thus be legally connected to their children. The courts have endeavoured (not always with success) to protect the privacy of children who have made their own court applications, on the basis that conducting family battles in the full glare of the media is not conducive to resolving family problems calmly and reasonably. More often than not the cases brought by children have been sorted out without a full court battle: the much-publicised case in the early 1990s of a teenage girl who wanted to live with her boyfriend and his parents eventually ended amicably, with the teenager agreeing to go back home to her mother.

It is still relatively early days since the Children Act was implemented, and so far the new right of children to make their own court applications has not yet been fully tested. Cases have been brought by children to ask the court for a residence order that they live somewhere else or for a contact order that the parent who has left the home be made to see them (sometimes against that parent's will). In many cases the disputes have been resolved by the family themselves eventually.

In general, remember that court applications by children must cross three hurdles. First, a child will have to convince a solicitor to act for him or her (and the solicitor must usually get legal aid). Second, the courts must be asked permission for a child's application to go ahead; the child will have to show that he or she has got sufficient understanding. Only if that stage is passed will the courts go on to the third stage, which is to look at the merits of the case. The courts need to be convinced that the child making the application is mature and has sound reasons for asking the court for help, and is not just making the application on impulse because of a row with a parent.

Once the second hurdle is crossed, the courts may sometimes appoint the Official Solicitor to act for the child in place of an ordinary solicitor. If a child wants to ask the courts for help, care should be taken to get the advice of a solicitor experienced in dealing with children cases. Contact the Solicitors Family Law Association* or the Children's Legal Centre.* The law may not be the best remedy for sorting out children's problems – also consider mediation or a form of therapeutic help.

Changes under the Family Law Act 1996

The Family Law Act 1996, when all of it is implemented (expected to be in 1999), will not change the basic legal framework for parents and children as outlined in this chapter. The courts will still need to consider whether they need to exercise any of their powers under the Children Act and whether they are satisfied that no order needs to be made for the children. A divorce or separation order cannot be made by the court until requirements about the children have been met – in essence, arrangements over the children, as well as finance, must be worked out in the period of reflection and consideration before the divorce or separation is finalised.

Extra duties on the courts to consider the children's needs will also be in place. So the court must consider the wishes and feelings of the child in the light of his or her age and understanding and the circumstances in which those wishes were expressed; the conduct of the parents in the child's upbringing; the general principle that (save for contrary evidence) the child's welfare will best be served by having regular contact with family members and maintaining good continuing relationships with both parents. Evaluation of risk to the child must also be undertaken. Some commentators on the new law (although remember it has not yet come into force as we go to press) have pointed out that this may necessitate the children being seen by a judge or district judge at court – because on the limited information otherwise available to the courts how could they satisfy themselves on these points? How the new law will work in practice is certainly not yet clear. What is, however, clear is that children's needs, wishes and concerns will be brought more firmly into the spotlight in the new-style divorce.

Chapter 9

The family home

Lawyers often refer to the family home as the 'matrimonial home'. This term is used in the context of divorce to refer to the home – house or flat – acquired by husband, or wife, or both, to be lived in by the family during their time together. However, the term is an awkward one, and by and large the more familiar term of 'family home' is used throughout this book except where legal terminology necessitates its use.

Before the divorce

The spouse who does not legally own the family home – that is, whose name is not on the title deeds – has certain rights of occupation:

- the right not to be evicted without a court order if he or she is in occupation
- the right (if the court thinks fit) to return to the home if he or she has left it
- the right (if the court thinks fit) to exclude the owner spouse from occupying the home for a period (usually only when violence has occurred).

The same occupation rights apply if the home is rented.

These rights were formerly termed 'rights of occupation', but since the Family Law Act 1996 has been partly implemented, are nowadays called 'matrimonial home rights'. The new terminology has left the old system more or less unchanged. However, one key innovation is that matrimonial home rights are now also available for a property which a married couple intended to use as their home but which they never actually occupied.

Matrimonial home rights are in essence short-term rights which exist while the marriage lasts (until decree absolute is granted). The long-term decisions about the rights to live in the home or to get a share of the proceeds if it is sold will have to be made as part of the divorce financial settlement. If violence has been threatened or used against you, making it unsafe for you to live in the family home, you can apply to the court to protect yourself (as described in Chapter 12) and sometimes gain an occupation order which can exclude your spouse or allow you to re-enter the home. The courts will also be able to make an occupation order overriding one spouse's matrimonial home rights.

Registering matrimonial home rights: owner-occupied homes

If you are a joint owner of the family home, you do not need to register your matrimonial home rights separately. Third parties (for example, a potential buyer or mortgagee) will become aware of your interest when they carry out a search of the property title, so your spouse cannot try to sell or mortgage the property without your consent.

If, however, your spouse, not you, is the sole owner of the family home, you must register your matrimonial home rights to ensure that they are protected against third parties.

How you register your matrimonial home rights depends on whether the title to the family home is 'registered' or 'unregistered'. 'Registered' here means registered at the Land Registry. Most homes will have titles registered at the Land Registry as the whole of England and Wales is now subject to compulsory registration of title, but if your home was, until recently, in an area of voluntary registration, and you bought it some time ago, the title to your home may not yet have been registered.

If you do not know whether the title to your home is registered or not, you may be able to find out from your bank or building society (if the home is mortgaged). If the bank or building society has a 'Charge Certificate' (a Land Registry document), the home is registered. If there is no mortgage and your spouse has a Land Certificate, then again the title is registered.

As an alternative, if you do not wish to ask a solicitor to register your rights of occupation, you can carry out an 'Index Map Search' at

HM Land Registry* (usually no fee) to find out whether the title to the home is registered and, if so, what the title number is.

If the title is registered

The district Land Registry for your area will advise you how to register your matrimonial home rights and should provide the various forms and tell you about the procedure. HM Land Registry in London can advise you which is your local Land Registry. There is a form to help called *Protecting Matrimonial Home Rights under the Family Law Act 1996*.

If the title is unregistered

A 'class F' land charge should be registered at the Land Charges Department.* The form to be used, K2, is available from law stationers' shops and the fee for registration is £1 per name.

The information required includes the full name in which the property-owning spouse bought or acquired the property. If you are unsure of the precise name shown on the conveyance, register the charge against all possible permutations: for example – John Smith, J Smith, John Peter Smith, J P Smith. The charge is ineffective unless it is in exactly the right name. If you are in any doubt, or time is short, apply to register at both the Land Registry and the Land Charges Department until you have sorted out the position. If you find that the title is registered you should cancel the charge at the Land Charges Department.

The green form scheme allows for a solicitor to deal with registration of a land charge or a notice if you are financially eligible.

All Citizens Advice Bureaux (CABx) can help with filling in the forms to register matrimonial home rights and some have a supply of the necessary forms.

The effect of registering a charge or notice

Anyone buying the property or granting a mortgage on it would, as a matter of routine, check the appropriate registry and discover your notice or charge protecting your rights. (Even if a buyer or mortgagee does not actually search the register or has no knowledge of the registration, the effect of registering a land charge or notice amounts in law to notice of a non-owning spouse's matrimonial home rights.) If the house is then bought or mortgaged, this is done subject to your matrimonial home rights and the buyer or mortgagee cannot turn you out unless you have agreed to give up your rights.

The effect of registration normally ceases once a decree of divorce is made absolute. If the question of the family home has not been settled by then, the non-owning spouse should ask the court, before the decree is made absolute, for the registration of the class F land charge or the notice to be renewed after the decree absolute. Alternatively, if you are making a claim for a share of a property, you should register a 'pending action' claim, which similarly puts third parties on notice of your interest.

Finding out if your spouse owns a second home

Sometimes there may be good reason to suspect that your spouse has bought another home – say if she or he has moved in with a new partner in a newly bought home which she or he says belongs to the new partner. There is now an easy way of checking who legally owns the home, again via the Land Registry. As long as you have the postal address of the new home, you can ask the Land Registry to supply the name and address of the registered proprietor of land. The fee is £4.

If your suspicions are confirmed and your spouse is shown as a legal owner, once you have made financial claims in the divorce proceedings you may also be able to register a 'pending action' claim on the title of the second property if you think that your spouse may try to sell it to avoid paying money.

Moving out

If you hope eventually to have the home to live in permanently, it is tactically best to try to stay there, if possible. Even if you are not planning to remain in the long term but want to persuade your spouse to make other financial provisions for you, staying put may help you in your negotiations. However, the strategy of staying put can sometimes be counterproductive: remaining at close quarters with your spouse once the decision to separate has been made can give rise to tensions which may undermine the prospect of successful negotiations. It may be helpful to discuss with your solicitor the pros and cons of moving out, whether on a temporary or permanent basis.

It may be tempting, if the situation between you and your spouse has become very volatile, to lock your spouse out of the home while he or she is away. Remember, however, that your spouse has matrimonial home rights, being a right to occupy the home, at least while the marriage is in being, and can apply to the court for an order restoring to him or her the right to occupy the home.

Severing a joint tenancy

If you and your spouse own your home (or any other land or buildings) jointly, you need to check whether the ownership is held under a 'joint tenancy' or a 'tenancy in common'. Check the title deeds to ascertain this information (if you have a mortgage, ask the building society or bank).

Under a joint tenancy (the most popular method for spouses to hold the matrimonial home), a spouse's interest in the property is not determined: both partners own the whole of the house (or flat) jointly. When either partner dies, the whole property automatically passes to the survivor, irrespective of any provision the former may have made in a will. Under a tenancy in common, on the other hand, the interests of each spouse are fixed (usually on a 50:50 basis but it can be in any proportion) and separate, so that each partner can separately dispose of his or her share by will.

Some solicitors advise that you should end the joint tenancy and, pending a financial settlement or a court order, divide your respective interests in the property by becoming tenants in common. Either of you can do this by sending a 'notice of severance' to the other spouse at any time. The notice can simply take the form of a letter to your spouse, stating: 'please accept this letter as notice of my desire to sever as from this day the joint tenancy in our property known as [*insert address of property*] now held by us as joint tenants both at law and in equity so that henceforth the said property shall belong to us as tenants in common in equal shares'.

A notice of severance will convert your ownership into that of a tenancy in common. It does not affect your status as co-owners but, when one of you dies, the deceased's share of the property would be part of his or her estate and would be distributed under the terms of his or her will or according to the rules of intestacy. This in effect increases your control over a certain equal share in the property while money matters are being sorted out comprehensively in the divorce proceedings. However, there is also the risk that if your spouse were to die in the meantime, you would lose the chance that you would have had of inheriting his or her share of the home when it was held under a joint tenancy. In summary, you will have to weigh up the risks both for and against – there is no clearcut right or wrong course of action applicable to all. Whether it would be in your interest to sever the joint tenancy is something you might like to discuss with a solicitor.

During the divorce

The kinds of order that a divorce court can make are:

- for a sale, with division of the proceeds
- for outright transfer of one spouse's interest to the other
- for a transfer of one spouse's interest to the other with a lump sum adjustment
- for a postponed sale – usually until the children complete their education but sometimes beyond that, the house then to be sold and the proceeds divided in specified proportions.

There are no special rules about when and what order a court should make: the courts have a fairly wide discretion. A sale and 50:50 division of the proceeds is appropriate in some cases (especially where the marriage has been short and there are no children); in many others, this would operate unfairly against one or other of the parties. A court's decision in a particular case depends on whether or not there are children, the ages of husband, wife (and any children), the length of the marriage and whether the spouse who will move out has potentially secure accommodation.

Rented property

The courts have power to make a transfer order on divorce with regard to 'property', which includes some but not all rented property, under section 24 of the Matrimonial Causes Act 1973.

The Matrimonial Homes Act 1983 gave the courts power to transfer certain tenancies from one spouse to another on granting a decree of divorce or at any time after that. The power was contained in section 7 and schedule 1 to the 1983 Act, and covered:

- protected and statutory tenancies under the Rent Act 1977
- statutory tenancies under the Rent (Agriculture) Act 1976
- secure tenancies under the Housing Act 1985
- assured tenancies under the Housing Act 1988.

If a non-tenant spouse has been deserted by the tenant spouse it is important that he or she should ask the court for a transfer of tenancy order *before* the divorce decree is made absolute.

This is because the occupation of the accommodation by the non-tenant spouse is keeping alive the protected, statutory, secure or assured tenancy arising from the 'deemed occupation' rules contained in section 1 of the 1983 Act.

Once the marriage is ended on divorce (decree absolute), these rules no longer apply, and the tenancy will lose its protected, secure or assured status, or in the case of a statutory tenancy will simply cease to exist. If there is no longer a protected, statutory, secure or assured tenancy in existence, there is nothing for the court to transfer under the 1983 Act.

The general rule is that a transferee spouse cannot get better tenancy rights than the tenant spouse, so if the home is rented on a short-term basis the court will not be able to extend the term of the tenancy, and if rent payment debts have been built up then these would be passed on to the transferee. Some doubts have been raised about whether a statutory tenancy created, for example, under the Rent Act 1977 counts as property which can be transferred under the Housing Act 1983 – this point has not specifically been tested by the courts. However, a case decided in 1997 – *Newlon Housing Trust v Al-Sulaimen and Another* – confirmed that a contractual periodic tenancy is classified as a matrimonial asset and can thus be transferred by the courts as part of the financial arrangements on divorce. Similarly, an earlier case held that a council tenancy counts as 'property' and is thus transferable too.

Rented property: changes under the Family Law Act 1996

Under the Family Law Act 1996, the courts specifically have the power to transfer tenancies between spouses on divorce (or on a decree of judicial separation) and can also, in rare cases, compensate the transferring spouse by an order for compensation against the transferee. The types of tenancy covered are those specified above but also categorically include protected or statutory tenancies under the Rent Act 1977 (although it excludes shorthold tenancies or long leases). The new power extends to cohabitants and former cohabitants as well as former spouses.

Owner-occupied property

If the property is in joint names and expressed on the title deeds to be for the benefit of both parties equally, each technically has a half-share in the 'net equity' (or value) of the home. Occasionally, the deeds may express a different division of the property, say 60:40, but this is more common where two cohabitants buy a property. Where spouses buy a property together this is usually done on an equal basis.

Whatever the title deeds may say, the courts can act on their own discretion about how to divide up the equity of a home.

The courts need to assess what the financial interest of husband and wife is in the home, but in most cases this is only the first stage of the process by which the courts decide what is to happen. The courts have a fairly wide discretion and each individual case is decided on its own merits.

Whose name the house is actually in (husband's, wife's or both), who put up the deposit and who paid the mortgage are obviously important, but by no means the only factors when decisions are made. The longer the marriage, the less important who contributed what becomes.

Where the home has dropped in value

During the recession it was not uncommon for the value of the home to be less than the amount of the mortgage (i.e. to have 'negative equity'), especially if the original mortgage was for 100 per cent of the purchase price. Even now that house prices have been rising again, it may take a little time for the value of a property to rise to more than the amount of the mortgage. Remember also that for properties where the value is slightly higher than the unpaid mortgage, the added costs of selling the home, including legal and estate agents' fees, may mean that the home is worth nothing or even less than the mortgage.

Where your home in effect has negative equity, you will need to weigh up carefully what your best course of action might be. In favour of retaining the home and carrying on meeting the mortgage repayments would be the facts that a spouse and any children would keep a roof over their heads and that property prices may rise later to make the investment worthwhile. Sometimes estate agents may suggest a very low price for the home just to ensure a sale, but keeping the property until the market has improved can raise the price that the home would eventually fetch.

On the other hand, continuing the mortgage repayments if the home is unlikely to increase sufficiently in value to cover your indebtedness may only be throwing good money after bad, so it could be tempting to consider handing the keys in to the mortgagee (the bank or building society) and leaving it to them to sell. The drawback of this option is that the mortgagee may sell the property at a considerable loss and will look to you for the balance of what is owing under the mortgage at a later stage, plus interest which will still continue to run against you.

None of the options that you face may look attractive, and you may be forced into choosing the least unattractive, namely the one that costs you least. Ask several estate agents for a free valuation of the home and for their views on the property market. Although some of what you are told may be speculative rather than factual, you should get a clearer picture on which to base your decision. Talk to your bank or building society to see whether they offer any schemes to help out homeowners in your situation. Make sure that you also talk to your solicitor or CAB to discuss your options before finally making up your mind.

Where there are no children

Where there is a divorce after a short marriage, the courts may look mainly at what financial contributions relating to the house or flat had been made and decide that the person who put in the most should have the most out. The longer the marriage has gone on, the less the courts are interested in who put in what, in money terms, and the more they are prepared to recognise the other party's non-financial contribution. For instance, the wife's contribution in keeping the home going may count as much as the husband's financial contributions.

The main consideration is likely to be whether the net proceeds of sale of the house are sufficient to enable each spouse (with the aid of such mortgage loan as each might be able to obtain) to buy an adequate new home. If so, the courts may well order a sale of the house without delay. Even if one spouse wants to stay on, it may not be practicable or fair to the other because the latter would need his or her share of the value of the house in order to buy a new home. The house may have to be sold where the combined resources of husband and wife are insufficient to keep up the mortgage repayments on the existing home and to provide accommodation for the other spouse.

Where the home has been bought from the local authority under the 'right to buy' with a discount and is sold within three years of buying, the couple have to pay back to the local authority part of the discount they were allowed. This could be grounds for asking the court to defer a sale until the three-year period is up.

Division of proceeds

When determining how best to share out the money from the sale of the house (or flat), the courts will take into account direct financial contributions by the non-owning spouse towards the purchase (payment of part of the deposit or part of the mortgage repayments) or for the improvement of the house. They will also consider indirect financial contributions – for example, where the wife has worked for all or part of the marriage and has used her earnings to pay some of the household bills, food, or clothing or has paid her earnings into the couple's joint bank account.

If the wife's share would be insufficient to enable her to buy a new home, particularly if her earning capacity puts her into a less favourable position for getting a mortgage, the courts could order that the wife should get a greater share of the proceeds of sale. They may compensate the husband by ordering him to pay relatively low maintenance to the wife – or none at all.

Not selling

A sale of the family home may, however, not be the right solution. The expenses of selling, and of buying two other houses, will have to be met, and the net proceeds of sale may not be sufficient to enable either spouse to buy another home. (Moreover, if either was legally aided, the Legal Aid Board may have a statutory charge over the home to cover legal costs.) A court could order that the wife remain in the house:

- until she wants to move out, or marries again, or cohabits permanently (this is normally taken to be the case after, say, six months of living together, but preferably should be defined in the order) or she dies; *or*

- for a period of time specified by it.

After that, the house would be sold, and the net proceeds divided in the proportions decided by the court at the time of making the order (these cannot be varied later).

The wife might have to compensate the husband in the meantime by a (notional) payment of rent. In practice, this might be achieved by an appropriate reduction of his maintenance obligations to her.

An arrangement which leaves the wife with uncertainty as to her future home, and the husband having to wait a number of years before he receives his capital while he has to continue paying maintenance, can cause bitterness. The courts try to avoid some of these difficulties by arranging a 'clean break': for example, it might be fair for the house to be transferred outright to the wife, and for the husband to be compensated by dismissal of the wife's claims for maintenance for the present and the future. No clean break can, however, be made in respect of maintenance for the children – parents continue to be financially responsible after divorce. So the cost of child support will need to be weighed up to see if this option is affordable (see also Chapter 5).

If an order is made for the transfer of the whole of the home into one of the spouses' sole name or from one into the joint names, a transfer or conveyance will have to be drawn up. On the transfer of property by court order following the break-up of a marriage, no stamp duty is payable irrespective of the value of the property.

One spouse 'buying out' the other

An alternative clean-break arrangement is for the spouse who is going to remain in the house to buy out the departing spouse, by paying him or her a lump sum for his or her share in the house. If the spouse who remains has to borrow the money or raise an extra mortgage, there will be tax relief on the interest on the amount of mortgage up to £30,000 (which since 1995/96 has been restricted to 15 per cent).

If the person who has been bought out uses the money towards buying another house and borrows the rest on mortgage, he or she will get tax relief on the interest on a loan of up to £30,000. In other words, both ex-spouses can take advantage of the full amount of tax relief on mortgages for a house each.

Beware, however, the danger of a delay in the lump sum payment if the house market is volatile. In a case in 1989 (*Hope-Smith v Hope-*

Smith) the husband had been ordered to pay his wife a lump sum of £32,000 within 28 days; if he failed to do so, the matrimonial home was to be sold forthwith and £32,000 of the proceeds given to the wife. The husband unsuccessfully appealed against this order, but three years later the house was still unsold. His former wife then successfully appealed against the original order and the court substituted a larger payment to her because of the increase in house prices over the three years.

Wherever there is likely to be a delay in payment, it may be better to express the payment in percentage terms of the equity of the house, rather than as a fixed lump sum.

Where there are children

The courts' priority is that an adequate home should be provided for the children. Recent cases continue to stress that, while the courts have a number of matters to take into account, the interests of the children have priority over others.

The Child Support Acts have made a significant impact on the way the courts and lawyers deal with the home following a divorce where there are children. The full extent of the changes has not yet been fully tested in the courts. One thing, however, is clear – the fact that in general child support payments have increased substantially.

Because the spouse who has left the home (called the absent parent) is likely to end up having greater outgoings in the form of child support payments, one knock-on effect is that he (or, more rarely, she) may no longer be able to afford to transfer his share in the home to the parent remaining to look after the children. So the advice which follows here must be tempered by the consideration that there may not be enough money both to achieve proper child support payments and changes in ownership of the family home. As payments of child support are usually fixed, the absent parent may have to retain a share in the family home unless there are sufficient funds to meet both child support payments and the costs of his re-housing (see also Chapter 5 for more information).

Where there are sufficient funds to stretch to two homes, however, a 1997 case (*B v B*) highlighted that, where possible, each party needs a home, particularly when children are involved. The case is more important for families who are slightly above the financial position of only being able to afford one owner-occupied house – but where there is not a lot of extra capital. The judge in the case made it clear that the courts will expect families to try to make the financial effort to buy two homes.

Selling

It is unlikely that the courts would order a sale unless selling the home would bring in enough money to buy other adequate accommodation for the parent (usually the wife) who is going to have the children to live there with her.

The house would, however, have to be sold if the wife could not keep up the mortgage repayments with whatever assistance by way of maintenance the husband could finance. More economical accommodation would then have to be provided for her and the children out of the proceeds of selling the house.

Not selling immediately

In order to secure the house as a home for the children, the courts may order the husband to transfer it into joint names if it had been in his sole name. When a house is in joint names, it cannot normally be sold without the agreement of the joint owners, but either party can apply to the High Court for an order to enforce a sale. To prevent this, the divorce court normally directs that the house shall not be sold for a specific period while the wife and the children live there – usually until the youngest child reaches a particular age, usually tied to the time when he or she is expected to leave school.

A more usual alternative is to transfer the house into the wife's sole name, subject to a charge securing to the husband whatever sum or proportion of the net proceeds of (eventual) sale the courts think proper. A 'charge' over the property means that when it is sold, the charge (which is like a mortgage) comes into effect and the other spouse will get his or her money out of the proceeds. The husband does not have the right to intervene in respect of the property by virtue of such a charge – his position becomes just like that of a bank or building society to whom money is secured on the property. The husband may have to pay Capital Gains Tax (CGT) on the money he eventually receives. Normally, the provisions for inflation and his personal exemptions cover this but it may be worth bearing in mind if there is an anticipated gain, or if the husband is likely to use up his exemptions in some other ways.

In either case, the court specifies at what point the husband can realise his interest in the house. This is likely to be when the youngest child of the family comes of age or when any child undergoing full-time education ceases to remain normally resident in the home. The husband can then enforce the sale.

Selling later – pros and cons

A difficult consideration is whether the house should be kept as a home for the ex-wife even after the children have left home. The courts will take into account whether the wife's share of the proceeds, if the house were sold then, would enable her to buy another house, and also the husband's need for the capital. The courts can only gauge what the situation is likely to be at a time possibly 12 or 15 years ahead – how much the ex-wife would receive from the sale of the house, her likelihood of employment, and her earnings and mortgage capacity. Her share would need to be sufficient for her to buy a flat or a smaller house at an age when she may be unable to raise much by way of mortgage. Meanwhile, the husband will have been able to start afresh with another mortgage because of his lower age and possibly higher earnings at the time of the divorce.

Another disadvantage of delaying a final resolution of a division of the parties' capital assets is that, when the time eventually does come for a sale, the ex-wife may well be reluctant to move out, particularly if she sees her former husband doing comfortably in another property. In a sense, this type of order can prolong the agony of a divorce. But sometimes there is no alternative.

If it seems likely that the ex-wife will have insufficient funds to enable her to buy another house when the children are no longer dependent, a court may either award her a larger share of the value or defer the sale (or enforcement of the ex-husband's charge) for the remainder of her life (or until she remarries or cohabits). The court may not make such an order if, by not selling, the ex-husband's problems are likely to outweigh the ex-wife's.

Where either party was legally aided, the Legal Aid Board's statutory charge (if applicable) will not be levied until the house is sold. By then, the rise in house prices may have reduced the practical effect of the charge (but remember there will be accrued interest on the charge to be paid in addition).

When the house is eventually sold, liability for CGT may arise for an ex-spouse who is still a joint owner but who had moved out of the house.

If there is no mortgage to be paid off, the ex-wife will, in effect, be living in the house at the ex-husband's expense. The court therefore may make an order requiring her to pay the ex-husband an occupation rent from the time that the children cease to need the house as a home. If she is paying off the mortgage on the house, the ex-wife will be contributing to the value of the ex-husband's eventual share of the proceeds of sale.

If the house or flat is mortgaged

Mortgages cannot simply be transferred, and the court has no power to order the transfer of a mortgage, only the transfer of a property subject to a mortgage. The consent of the building society or other mortgagees is necessary, otherwise the mortgagor (usually the husband) remains liable for the mortgage even if the property is transferred. The mortgagees must be served with notice of an application to the court for a transfer of ownership and have the right to object.

It may well be the ex-wife who is going to be responsible for meeting the mortgage repayments in future, possibly out of an income (from maintenance payments) on the basis of which the building society or bank would not have agreed to make a mortgage loan. It is advisable for her to contact the mortgagees as soon as possible to discuss ways of making repayments if and when the house is transferred.

The building society or other mortgagee must agree before the transfer can take effect. If it does not, it may be necessary to try to pay off the mortgage and find a new mortgagee – if necessary through a mortgage broker (although remember that mortgage brokers usually charge fees at around 1 per cent of the amount borrowed).

It is not uncommon for building societies to ask a former husband to guarantee a mortgage that is being taken out by a woman whose income comes from his maintenance payments either in whole or in part. The ex-husband would have to meet the mortgage repayments only if his former wife defaulted. (He can ask her for an indemnity so that she is liable to compensate him if this does happen.) In practice, her default is likely to happen only if he defaults on the maintenance.

Where there is an endowment mortgage

A mortgage on an endowment basis is linked to an insurance policy that should pay out enough to repay the loan (with a surplus if it is a with-profits policy) at the end of the mortgage term or on the policy-holder's death. In the meantime, only the interest has to be paid on the loan, plus the premiums on the insurance policy. Doubts have recently been raised about whether in reality endowment policies will realise sufficient funds to cover the mortgage, especially if the policies were affected by the stock market crash in 1987. It may be worthwhile checking with your mortgagee or insurance company how financially healthy your particular endowment is.

The application for a property adjustment order where there is an endowment mortgage should include an application to transfer the husband's beneficial interest in the insurance policy to the wife (or vice versa). If this is not transferred, the ex-wife would be in a position of getting nothing under the policy and would have to pay off the whole mortgage loan out of the proceeds of sale of the house. When the mortgage term comes to an end, a decision has to be made regarding any bonuses on the policy over and above the amount required to repay the loan. This surplus could be ordered to go to the ex-husband to compensate for the loss of use of capital, or to the ex-wife, particularly if she has been paying the premiums for many years, or to be shared between them.

Capital Gains Tax

Capital Gains Tax is payable on gains arising on the 'disposal of assets'. Before the Finance Act 1988 capital gains were treated differently from income for tax purposes. For disposals made after 6 April 1988 the amount of a person's chargeable capital gains is added to his or her income. He or she is charged the appropriate income tax rate (in 1997/98 at 20, 23 or 40 per cent) calculated by treating the capital gain as the top slice of income.

A specified amount of gains in any one tax year is exempt. Husband and wife each have their own £6,500 annual exemption (1997/98 figures).

So long as a husband and wife are living together, and for the rest of the tax year after the separation, no chargeable gain results where one transfers his or her share of the house to the other. But when the asset is eventually transferred or is sold to someone else, the gain (or loss) is calculated over the whole period of ownership, not just since the date of transfer to the ex-spouse.

For the calculation of gain on disposals of property owned before 1982, the base cost is the market value of the asset on 31 March 1982 (subject to certain special rules mostly dealing with business). To calculate the inflation since that date, reference is made to the increases in the Retail Prices Index (RPI) based on the figure at March 1982.

On divorce or separation, the major areas where disposals are likely to arise are:

- household contents – antiques, for example
- other assets such as a car, a second home, stocks and shares, savings ('assets' means practically everything capable of being owned and sold or transferred)
- the home.

Most consumer goods decrease in value, so the question of 'gain' does not arise. Most chattels with a lifespan of less than 50 years are exempt from CGT, anyway.

Cash and cars are specifically exempt from CGT, and so are any sums received on the surrender of life insurance policies. So if, for one reason or another, you cash in an endowment policy which is linked to a mortgage, there is no question of liability to CGT. A sale of other assets, such as stocks and shares, can give rise to CGT.

The home and CGT

Any gain made on the sale of a person's principal private residence (PPR) is normally exempt from CGT. But CGT liability arises when the home is sold if you had stopped living there more than three years earlier.

On divorce, it is likely that you will do one or other of three things with the home:

- sell it and split the proceeds
- transfer it to your spouse outright
- put it into joint names (or leave it in joint names) and postpone sale and division of the proceeds until a future date.

Sale and division of proceeds

If you sell the house and split the proceeds within three years of one or other of you ceasing to reside there, you will be entitled to claim PPR exemption provided the home was your only, or main, residence throughout the period that you owned it.

If at any time you have two or more homes, either of them is potentially eligible for the PPR exemption. If, therefore, you have bought another home and the old home has not been sold, you may make a choice, usually within two years of divorce or separation, as to which one you wish to have treated as your PPR. (If you do not, your tax inspector will.) It may make sense to claim the exemption in respect of the house that is being sold, if this is at a gain.

Where the sale takes place more than three years after one of you has left, the person who ceased to reside there may not be fully exempt. Only a portion of the gain will be exempt: namely, the period of his or her actual occupation plus the last three years of ownership. (The last three years of ownership are always exempt.) Thus, the longer you wait beyond three years after separation before selling your old home, the greater the possibility of CGT having to be paid by the person who left. (The person who remains will not be liable for CGT provided he or she has remained permanently in residence.) However, do remember that indexation relief will be available as well as an annual personal exemption. On top of these exemptions, Extra Statutory Concession Form D6 may be applicable, and is available from the tax office. This is designed to cover the situation where a home (occupied by one spouse) is sold as part of a settlement and the other spouse has not elected to treat another property as his main residence. Although these rules are complex, the net effect is that CGT can very often be avoided.

Transfer of the home to your spouse outright

Although no money changes hands, the transfer would in theory be a 'disposal', based on the market value at the date of disposal. Quite apart from the fact that there may well not be a capital gain anyway (after taking inflation into account and the current year's exemption), the transaction would qualify for PPR exemption if made within three years of the transfer or of the spouse leaving the home.

House in joint names sold much later

Transferring the house into joint names will not attract CGT liability.

When the house is sold many years later and the proceeds divided, the spouse who has remained in the home will not have to pay tax on his or her share because that will be fully covered by the PPR exemption. But the one who moved out might be liable to some CGT. The same applies if the house is not in joint names but the one who moves out has a charge on the property. On realisation of the charge, that spouse will be liable for CGT on the rise in the value of the charge after taking into account the increase in the RPI and his annual exemption. The extra statutory concession mentioned above may, however, cover this.

Second home

Selling a second home to raise money may render you liable to CGT if there is a sufficient gain. (By 'second home' in this context is meant a property for which PPR did not apply while you were living together.)

It could make more sense to transfer it to the spouse who is moving out of the matrimonial home for him or her to live in it as his or her PPR. When it is eventually sold, it will be possible for him or her to claim PPR exemption on the whole of any gains from the date when the property had first been acquired – provided that the transfer between the spouses took place before the end of the tax year in which they separated.

Seeking advice

You may feel that you need specialist advice about CGT, perhaps from an accountant. For someone in receipt of legal aid, it might be better for the solicitor to instruct the accountant since he or she can then pay the accountant's fee if it will be recoverable from the Legal Aid Board as an expense reasonably incurred; prior authority of the Legal Aid Board to incur the accountant's fees would be needed. If the accountant were instructed directly, the client would have to find the money more or less straight away (whereas a legal aid statutory charge may not be payable until considerably later).

Chapter 10

Money in divorce

Money and the Child Support Agency

Since the Child Support Agency (CSA)* has in the main taken over responsibility for child support, there have been radical changes in the way money in divorce is dealt with – unless of course there are no children, in which case the courts' powers remain the same.

Where there are children, the most important change is the approach to the way that money will be divided up. Because the CSA's formula provides, in theory at least, a clear and precise answer to the question of how much child support should be paid, child support is usually the place to start (see Chapter 5).

You can then see how the remainder of the income and assets (if there are any) should be divided. Because of the likely increase in overall support payments to be made by the absent parent, there may be less money to go around to be able to afford capital divisions. Many lawyers have predicted a decrease in the numbers of clean-break orders being made, for example, because an absent parent may not be able to afford to buy a new property and thus will need to keep his share in the old one.

The Child Support Agency is still in its relative infancy. The formula for working out child support may not be particularly easy to apply where the parent who has left the home (or even just plans to leave sometime) has not yet bought or rented a new home, as the actual housing costs will still be a question mark. However, it is still worthwhile doing an estimated calculation – often the courts too require a child support calculation, even if based on guestimates, to give them an idea of how much maintenance might be payable. (Most solicitors' offices have computer software packages enabling them to do the calculation fairly speedily.) Having explored child support in Chapter 5, we now look at what the courts' approach is in relation to money matters overall.

Money and the courts

It is perfectly possible under current law to obtain a divorce without dealing with the question of finances, but it would be unwise to leave this unresolved and uncertain. (Once the Family Law Act 1996 is fully implemented, arrangements over children and finances must be approved as satisfactory by the court before a divorce or separation order is granted.)

If you have reached an agreement with your spouse on financial matters, your agreement should be drawn up in the form of a consent order (see Chapter 2) to ensure that it is as watertight as possible. If you are unable to reach a satisfactory agreement, you will need to start off financial proceedings (often known as 'ancillary proceedings') at the divorce court.

A further warning about costs is appropriate here. Many couples have found themselves engaged in time-consuming and costly legal battles over money. Money swallowed up in legal fees will not be available for distribution from the family's 'pot' of resources at the end of the day. Even if you are legally aided, the likelihood is that through the statutory charge you will have to meet the legal fees incurred by your solicitor during the course of the financial proceedings.

If, however, you are faced with a recalcitrant spouse who demonstrates a refusal to cooperate and who is likely to delay deliberately a financial settlement, your best bet may be to follow the practice of some solicitors, who, from a very early stage, prepare the evidence for as much of their client's case as possible. Some solicitors make it their practice to submit to the court right at the start, in difficult cases, an application for financial relief supported by an affidavit, with valuations of any relevant property and a list of the documents to be relied on. This has the immediate effect of placing the ball firmly in the court of the uncooperative spouse. It also means that future endeavours by the solicitors can be concentrated on extracting information from the unwilling party.

As a financially healthy alternative, an increasing number of couples are turning to mediation as offering a cost-effective means of resolving their disputes – see Chapter 4 for more information.

A legal aid certificate in matrimonial cases covers work in connection with financial applications, including representation at the hearing, although the work covered will generally exclude child maintenance, which is now usually dealt with by the CSA.

Applying for financial relief

The formal claim for financial relief is usually included within the prayer in the petition and/or, where the case is defended, in the prayer in the answer. To trigger off these claims, the petitioner or the respondent will have to file another application (form M13 or form M11), supported by an affidavit, giving notice to the court that he or she wishes the financial issues to be dealt with. Since 15 January 1997 a fee of £50 is payable on making this application.

If for any reason the prayer in the petition did not include a claim for financial relief, the court must be asked for permission to make such a claim before an application can be made by the petitioner, or by a respondent who is defending. (A court fee of £50 is payable for amending a petition.) Maintenance applications for an ex-spouse can be made only if the applicant has not remarried.

After divorce in another country

A court in England or Wales can make orders for financial provision in cases where a marriage has been dissolved or annulled, or the couple have been legally separated by judicial or other recognised proceedings, outside England and Wales. However, permission to pursue such an application has first to be obtained from the High Court, which has to decide whether, bearing in mind the domicile and other circumstances of the applicant, England or Wales would be an appropriate jurisdiction to hear the application.

An affidavit explaining all the circumstances must be filed with the request for leave to apply. It would be foolish not to consult a solicitor before embarking on this.

After separation

Where a divorce is based on the fact that the parties have lived separately for a period of two years and each agreed to the divorce, or have lived apart for five years, the respondent can indicate on the acknowl-edgement of service form that he or she intends to apply to the court to consider what his (or, more usually, her) financial position will be after the divorce. This is known as a section 10 application (because the matter is dealt with in section 10 of the Matrimonial Causes Act 1973).

A special form for a section 10 application (form M12) can be obtained from the court office and must be filed at court. The decree absolute cannot then be granted until the district judge is satisfied that the petitioner is going to make fair and reasonable financial provision for the respondent, or the best that can be made in the circumstances.

A section 10 application is advisable where the respondent wife is in her mid-forties upwards and is particularly concerned about the loss of her pension rights (for more details about pensions see pages 213, 223 and Chapter 11). Although the law changed in 1996 enabling a spouse to claim for a future share of her spouse's pension, pension-sharing (until recently termed 'pension-splitting') is still not available, and therefore the law is still comparatively restrictive. When a section 10 application is made, the marriage continues for the time being and thus the pension rights are preserved pro tem. (Pension rights are usually lost to divorced ex-spouses unless the divorce court makes an order in their favour or a binding agreement is arrived at.) Solicitors acting for spouses (usually wives) who stand to lose out financially by getting divorced and are in their mid-forties or older will usually advise submitting a section 10 application unless the wife specially asks them not to take this step.

As an alternative delaying tactic, a solicitor could file a section 5 application, which in essence says that the divorce should not, on the grounds of grave financial or other hardship, go ahead. It is rare for such an application to succeed – the courts tend to take a pragmatic approach that it takes two to make a go of a marriage and if one wants a divorce then ultimately the marriage should probably be ended. Although a section 5 application should not be made lightly, it will halt the divorce proceedings and give a person more time to negotiate over potential losses of a spouse's financial rights – particularly the pension.

The orders

An application can be made for all or any of the following:

- an order for maintenance pending suit (MPS), i.e. before decree absolute is granted

- a periodical payments order
- a lump sum order
- an order for secured provision
- a property adjustment order
- an order directing pension fund trustees to pay part or all of pension rights as they fall due.

If you make a claim for a lump sum order, the court can order only one lump sum, received wisdom being that there is no provision for the courts to order an interim payment of capital. Recent case law has challenged this, and in two cases the courts allowed, as an interim measure, a capital sum to be released to be invested in the home. Lawyers are continuing the fight for the right to ask for an interim lump sum, but the effect of these two cases will be minimal. Both of them involved fairly large sums of money and the decisions are unlikely to be applied in the average family case. However, once the Family Law Act 1996 is fully implemented, the courts will have power to make an interim lump sum order.

Preventing a spouse from disposing of assets

If a partner has assets in his or her sole name and is threatening or scheming to try to dispose of them in order to thwart the other partner's claims, the latter can apply to the court, without telling the other spouse if necessary, for an injunction preventing or restraining the former from so doing. If another person is involved, that person (for example, if a second home is being sold subject to a mortgage, the mortgagee of that property) must also be served with notice of the application.

An affidavit must be filed setting out full details of the need for such an order. But it is wise to obtain legal advice before applying for such an injunction.

Starting off your claim

The procedure set out below is the standard procedure in most courts. However, a pilot ancillary relief scheme is being tested in 30 courts (including London) which puts the courts more in control in ancillary matters, and aims to cut costs. See below for more information.

You should consider filing your application for financial provision at an early stage. Maintenance payments can be backdated only to the date of the application. For the petitioner the date of application is the date of the petition; for the respondent this is the date of the application itself. An application (other than for MPS) will not be considered by the court until the decree nisi. If you are still negotiating about financial matters with your spouse, make it plain to him or her, either directly or through a mediator or solicitors, that filing a formal application should not be interpreted as an unwillingness on your part to try to negotiate an agreement. On the contrary, by setting out your own financial position in the affidavit supporting the application, you are paving the way to productive negotiations.

If you are the petitioner, you apply by Notice of intention to proceed with application for ancillary relief made in petition (form M13); if you are the respondent, you apply by Notice of application for ancillary relief (form M11). Both forms are available free from divorce court offices. A court fee of £50 is payable on making the application.

Two copies of the notice of application have to be completed (and keep an extra one for yourself) and both have to be lodged at the court office. They must be accompanied by an affidavit of means in support of your application.

Do not fill in the space on the application form for the date of the hearing. This will be dealt with by the court office.

List the orders you are seeking, but do not state the amounts you wish to claim for the maintenance payments or lump sum. These will be decided during negotiations or at the hearing. It is usual to make a claim for all the available orders to enable the court to consider the financial position comprehensively.

Where the application includes a property adjustment claim, the address of the house or flat or description of any other property which you wish to be transferred should be given, with particulars, so far as you know, of any mortgage, whether the title to the property is registered or unregistered, the title number if it is registered, and the name and address of the mortgagee (building society or bank). If there is a mortgage, the mortgagees will have to be sent a copy of the application and, if they request it, of the affidavit in support of the application.

Once an application for property adjustment has been made, you can register a 'pending action' against the title to the property, which may be useful if the registration of your right to occupy the matrimonial (family) home is about to be overtaken by decree absolute or if the property in question is not jointly owned by you and is not the matrimonial home.

If a claim over a pension is being made, again a further copy of the application and affidavit will need to be served on the pension fund trustees or managers.

The affidavits

Standard blank forms of affidavit may be obtained from the divorce court office or from law stationers' shops. You do not have to use the standard form but it is a useful guide to the relevant information to be given in your own affidavit. Once the affidavit has been sworn, the original needs to be lodged at court, one copy is to be sent to your spouse with the application, and one is for you to keep. If a magistrates' court order for maintenance is already in existence, a copy should be sent to the divorce court with the affidavit. The application will be sealed (that is, officially stamped) at the court office and handed back to you. You must then send this copy of the application to your spouse (together with a copy of the affidavit you lodged with the application), within four days. If your spouse does not turn up at any subsequent hearing, you will have to satisfy the court that the application was sent.

The application form requires the other spouse to file an affidavit of his or her means within 28 days of receiving the notice of application. This requirement was rarely honoured before the Children Act came into force. However, under more recent Family Proceedings Rules, time limits under Children Act applications have become much stricter, which has had a slight knock-on effect on other applications. So do your utmost to comply with time limits.

Information in the affidavits

The foundation of the evidence set before the district judge is contained in the statements sworn by each spouse. It is therefore important to make sure the information given in your own affidavit is complete and accurate and contains all the information that the district judge is likely to require. It is equally important to ensure that your spouse discloses all relevant information. Affidavits are written in the first person and in concise numbered paragraphs.

It is not necessary to go into very detailed explanation, and summaries of your income and expenditure (for example) will often suffice. At the end of your affidavit put in the paragraph: 'Save as set out above, I have no other source of capital or income' – and this should be the truth. Remember that an affidavit is made on oath; false statements amount to perjury and can lead to your being penalised, probably by having to bear a greater share of the costs of the case if you are found to have misled the court.

Give clear and accurate details of your own capital and income, and liabilities, as well as what you know of the financial position of anyone you may be planning to marry or live with on a permanent basis. It will be helpful for the court if at this stage you set out a summary of your needs in the form of a budget, putting outgoings on either a weekly or a monthly basis and giving a total – but you may consider that, tactically, from the point of view of current negotiations with your spouse, this would be best left until later.

As much information as possible should be given about any property that you want to have transferred to you: its value, when it was bought and the price paid for it and by whom.

For a house or flat, whether or not you want to have it transferred to you, details should be given of any mortgages on it (including any insurance policy which is collateral security for a mortgage) and the amount still owing to the mortgagees.

Where several properties have been owned during the marriage, try to give details of each and the dates of purchase and sale (approximately), the prices paid and obtained for each property and the contributions made by each spouse to the purchase (including loans or gifts by in-laws) or to the improvement (particularly structural) of each home.

Also include any relevant information you have about your spouse's other property (if any).

Details of any other substantial assets should be included, for example, a car, insurance policies, and pension schemes.

If yours is the first affidavit, you can set out what you know of your spouse's finances, especially areas which you think might be 'forgotten', such as valuable personal belongings or fringe benefits. If your partner has already filed an affidavit, you can comment on any omissions or inaccuracies in it.

Note that very often you will be required to produce in evidence copies of bank statements – say, for the last three years. If those bank statements had been lost, banks have in the past made hefty charges for supplying duplicates – sometimes £5 per page. A useful tip is that under the Data Protection Act 1984, banks must not charge more than £10 per request, no matter how many pages are requested. (However, if the bank statements are some years old and have been transferred to a manual microfiche, or if the request relates to more than one area of registration – e.g. for a credit card and mortgage with the bank too – then the bank will be entitled to charge more.) If you have to get duplicate bank statements, ask the bank for them as a 'subject access request' and state specifically that you will pay only £10 under the Data Protection (Subject Access) Fees Regulations 1987.

If you are the applicant, you will have the opportunity later, once the recipient has filed an affidavit in reply, to lodge with the court a further affidavit which can cover and clarify matters which you feel may have been misrepresented by your spouse or on which it is necessary to give further evidence to the court.

What accompanies the affidavit

It is usual to attach to the affidavit copies of several recent pay slips (for example, for the last three to six months) and your P60 (a form issued to all employees at the end of each tax year, and giving details of gross pay and tax deducted). If you are self-employed, you should attach at least your most recent sets of accounts.

Attachments to the affidavit are described as 'exhibits' and should be numbered chronologically: for example, in the affidavit of John Smith, a self-employed bookseller, 'I produce and exhibit marked "JS1" copies of business accounts for the last three financial years'.

'Directions' and preliminary hearing

Usually there will first be an appointment for 'directions', at which the district judge gives directions about the steps that need to be taken so that all the required information will be available to the court at the eventual hearing. This 'directions hearing' is a preliminary hearing; the district judge will not make a decision about the application (but, in some courts, it may be coupled with a hearing of a claim for MPS or for an agreed order).

Certain courts will automatically fix a date for the hearing of directions. In other courts, you will have to apply for a specific date. Check with your local court for details.

Other courts issue standard directions automatically after the filing of a financial application (for example, as to when further affidavits must be filed or how an owner-occupied home should be valued).

You yourself can apply for a hearing for directions if one has not been fixed or if you want an interim order for maintenance. Notification of the date of the hearing is sent by the court to both parties.

At a directions hearing, the district judge can make orders for further affidavits (or order that there shall be no further affidavits without the court's permission), for information or documents to be supplied, for discovery of documents relevant to the applications, for either or both parties to give oral evidence, or for valuation. The courts are becoming increasingly concerned that such an exchange of information should not get out of hand (and thus run up huge legal bills). So two valuations would usually be regarded as unnecessary for a family business, for example, especially if that business could not be sold on the open market. The parties would be expected to try to agree an appointment of a valuer.

In 1995 a Practice Direction was issued by the courts to try to limit further the amount of evidence that each side could produce. In future it is likely that the courts will prefer most of the evidence to be in written form rather than in the form of oral examination and cross-examination of the parties, which is often time-consuming and thus costly.

Interim order

If your affidavit contains some reasonably up-to-date information about your spouse's financial position, this may enable the district judge to make at least an interim order at a preliminary hearing even if your spouse has failed to file an affidavit in time. You can apply for a hearing for your application for MPS or an interim order, although if the district judge feels that such a hearing was unnecessary, he or she may order you to pay your spouse's costs or expenses in attending.

Some district judges are willing to listen to an application for an interim order for spousal maintenance based on a wife's estimate of her husband's income and a general assessment of his likely liabilities. Others prefer the husband to file an affidavit even if he has shown himself unwilling to do so. The courts have a discretion in this respect.

If the husband is clearly not cooperating at all, a district judge might well make an interim order for high MPS, with the deliberate aim of forcing the husband to disclose his means if he wants to obtain a reduction of the order. Otherwise, an MPS order may be pitched at a lower level than a later periodical payments order, as it is rare for district judges to have the opportunity of a full examination of the facts at a preliminary hearing. The courts will also take account of any child support application made to the CSA, and if assessment is already in place may reduce the spousal maintenance in the light of what the husband can afford to pay.

An interim order can be replaced later by a lower (or higher) order backdated to take effect from the date of the interim order.

Getting an affidavit from an unwilling spouse

If your spouse has failed to file an affidavit and you think that he or she is going to continue to be difficult about this, do not allow matters to drift on too long; delaying may be a deliberate tactic on his or her part. You can apply to the district judge for an order requiring that an affidavit be filed within a set period and to have what is known as a 'penal notice' endorsed on the order. If this is done and a copy of the order is served personally (by you or someone acting on your behalf) on your spouse, he or she will be in contempt of court in still failing to comply, and an application can be made to the judge to commit him or her to prison.

Finding out more about your spouse's financial position

When you receive a copy of your spouse's affidavit, go through it carefully to see whether he or she has omitted any major assets or sources of income.

You can respond to specific inaccuracies or points made by filing another affidavit, but do not let the number of affidavits spiral uncontrollably. As mentioned above, courts may give directions limiting the number that can be filed.

If your spouse in an affidavit 'puts you to proof' of information, you must provide this and may do so in an affidavit.

At the directions hearing, the district judge may provide for an exchange of information either by each party supplying a list of documents to the other side or, more likely, by means of 'Rule 2.63' questionnaires.

Information given in an affidavit can be checked, investigated or clarified by means of a written questionnaire sent to a spouse or his or her solicitor. Rule 2.63 of the Family Proceedings Rules 1991 states:

> Any party to an application for ancillary relief may by letter require any other party to give further information concerning any matter contained in any affidavit filed by or on behalf of that other party or any other relevant matter, or to furnish a list of relevant documents or to allow inspection of any such document....

It is quite usual to ask for this kind of supplementary information and documentation. What it is appropriate to ask for depends on how comprehensive the other person's affidavit is and how complicated his or her other finances are. Requests may be made, for example, for:

- copy of pay slips for, say, the past three to six months
- copy of form P60
- copy of forms P11d, tax returns and notices of assessment for the past three years
- copy of contract of employment or statement of terms of employment
- copy of bank and credit card statements for, say, the past 12 months, and building society passbooks
- statements of current surrender values of insurance policies
- statement of value (usually a cash equivalent transfer value, CETV: see page 214) of pension scheme and copy of pension rules
- valuations of antiques, jewellery, etc. (market value, not insurance value).

If the information or documentation is not supplied in response to your questionnaire, you can then apply to the district judge asking for an order that your spouse provide such information or documents. Whether or not you will be successful in obtaining such an order depends on the reasonableness of your request.

Just as it is usual to make an application to the court for financial relief even though you hope to negotiate an out-of-court settlement, it is also quite usual to make requests in the form of a 'questionnaire' in order to clarify the financial picture before proposals are made or agreed. If in the end you can reach no agreement and there has to be a court hearing, a spare copy of the questionnaire and answers should be made available for the court.

Property valuations

If you can include in your affidavit an estimate of the value of the property you or your spouse own, do so.

You may have asked a local estate agent to tell you what a reasonable asking price would be for your home, but your spouse may think the value is over- (or under-) optimistic. It is then generally best, if possible, to agree to instruct one valuer to carry out a formal valuation – for which you will then have to pay a fee – agreeing that you will both accept what that valuer says. Otherwise, if you each instruct a separate valuer, their reports may disagree; if there is then a contested hearing, each valuer may have to be called as a witness (adding to the cost) and the court will have to decide what value to attribute.

If there is delay before the final court hearing, it may be necessary to get the valuation updated, particularly in times of fluctuating property prices.

If your spouse has other assets, such as a business, it may be necessary to get his or her interest in the company valued. A direction on this point will usually be made by the district judge at the directions hearing.

Before you decide to ask for a direction for a valuation of a business in which your spouse is involved, consider carefully the question of costs. An investigation of a company's business, which will usually be carried out by an accountant, can be expensive, and is worthwhile only if:

- you have serious concerns that your partner is attempting to disguise its true worth; *and*
- the asset is important from the point of view of capital as well as providing income for living; *and*
- the business itself is valuable.

Warnings about excessive amounts of costs are constantly being made in the courts. One judge, Mrs Justice Booth, issued these guidelines to lawyers in 1990:

- affidavit evidence should be confined to relevant facts

- professional witnesses should avoid taking a partisan approach
- extra care should be taken to decide what evidence should be produced; non-material emotive evidence should be avoided
- care should be taken to avoid duplicating documents
- a chronology of material facts should be agreed by both parties' solicitors
- if a case looks to be substantial, a pre-trial review should be arranged to see if settlement can be reached.

Pension valuations

Pensions can often be the most valuable matrimonial asset, especially if the family home has minimal equity. (For information on the different types of pensions see Chapter 11.) However, there can be problems in working out exactly how valuable a pension is. The first revolves around the period of pension payments which should be valued. Although the new Pensions Act 1995 updated the law on pensions in divorce generally, it is silent about what period of the pension should be valued. In Scotland the law is clear – a husband or wife is entitled to a share of the contributions made by a spouse only during marriage. In England and Wales a younger spouse will potentially be able to claim a share of the entire pension pot accumulated during a partner's whole career. It is possible that later on the courts may limit claims to pensions built up during marriage, but at present this is one of the uncertainties faced under the new legislation.

The next problem is how best to value a pension. Personal pension plans, in which regular amounts are paid in to the pension, are in some ways similar to a savings account and thus can be more easily valued. Occupational pensions are not so easy to determine. Take the example of employees of the Civil Service, whose pensions are 'unfunded': the government does not pay regular amounts in to the pension scheme but makes a commitment that when the employee retires it will pay a pension broadly based on his or her final salary and the length of employment. It can be difficult in these circumstances to work out how much the pension will be worth, because neither the final salary – which would depend on promotion – nor the length of time the employee will work for the Civil Service is known.

Regulations issued in 1996 to implement the Pensions Act 1995, which, among other things, allows for a share of a pension to be 'earmarked', laid down that the value of a pension would be the 'cash equivalent transfer value' (CETV). This is the equivalent of how much a pension scheme holder would be paid if he or she were to take out the money from the current pension fund and transfer it to another. Pensions experts advise that this valuation method can under-shoot the real value especially of occupational pensions, but it is more realistic for personal pensions.

Most computerised pension schemes can produce a CETV fairly simply. A fee for preparing the valuation by the pension trustees or managers will have to be paid by the pension scheme holder (or some-times the spouse); the amount is likely to be set by each individual plan.

Once the basic information about the pension is available, if the pension is potentially valuable, solicitors will often advise their client to instruct an actuary to prepare a valuation. Pension valuations can be prepared from instructions given jointly by the husband's and wife's solicitors. The Divorce Corporation* for example charges £125 plus VAT for an actuarial calculation of pension rights, which it prepares on an even-handed basis. It states that the same valuation will be pro-vided whether instructions are given by the husband or wife. The advantage of joint instructions are that later arguments over pension value will be minimised.

The Divorce Corporation will accept instructions only from other professionals such as solicitors. Other firms which offer pensions valuations could be contacted for example, via the Society of Pension Consultants* or the Association of Consulting Actuaries.* Again fees will be charged – check how much before asking a pensions specialist to prepare a report.

Coming to an agreement

Once affidavits have been filed, it is wise to send to the other side an offer setting out the terms on which you would be willing to settle the case. The letter, which should be marked 'without prejudice' so that it cannot be used in evidence against you (except on the point of costs), is known as a Calderbank letter (from the name of the case which decided this principle). Briefly, it is a 'without prejudice' offer of financial settlement which, if not accepted and the case goes ahead, will be made known to the court at the end of the financial hearing. If the court awards an amount similar to the offer that was refused, the person to whom the offer was made will usually have to bear the offeror's legal costs. (Even if the amount awarded by the court to a spouse is quite a bit higher than the offer turned down, the court may make him or her pay his or her own legal bill; see example below.) Merely sending a Calderbank letter can bring issues to a head because if your offer is fair your partner is running the risk (if he or she decides to continue the case) that the costs incurred after the making of your offer will be awarded against him or her. The courts have indicated that each spouse is under a *duty* to try to settle financial disputes by making a Calderbank offer. Either side can made an offer, or counter-offer, although the initiative usually lies with the wealthier spouse (in most cases the husband).

Making a Calderbank offer can be viewed as a gamble, but an experienced solicitor can help reduce the odds. In some cases the gamble pays off even if the offer is slightly on the low side, especially if the other party refuses to negotiate or make a counter-offer.

Example   The husband made a Calderbank offer of £400,000 which the wife rejected. After a contested hearing the wife was awarded £435,000. But the judge refused to award the wife her costs because of her refusal to negotiate over the original offer, so she had to pay her own legal bill instead of this being awarded against the husband. [*S v S*, 1990]

Fewer than one in ten financial applications ever reaches a full hearing. Many are settled well before couples get to court, although a number are settled on the steps leading up to the court on the date of the hearing. The earlier that you can settle your case, on reasonable terms for you, the greater will be the savings you achieve in terms of legal costs, time and hassle.

Getting a hearing date

When you are satisfied that you have obtained as much information as is necessary to enable the court to make a realistic judgment, you, jointly with your spouse, can apply for a hearing date. If you have instructed a solicitor, he or she (or a barrister if one will be representing you at the hearing) will prepare a 'certificate of readiness for trial and time estimate' and lodge this with the clerk to the district judge, with a request for a hearing date. How quickly your case will be heard depends on the relative pressure of work on the court which will hear your application, and on how long it is likely to take. The date you will be given is likely to be more than three months away.

Preparing for the hearing

Before a contested hearing, you or your solicitor should prepare a summary of the financial position of you and your spouse in both income and capital terms, together with details of any debts and liabilities. If the marriage has been long or the financial dealings are otherwise complex, a chronological listing of events can help. Such information will help to present the case clearly to the district judge, and many solicitors now prepare and agree with the other side a financial schedule to summarise the facts.

Both parties should attend the hearing, together with any witnesses, whether or not they are legally represented. Your solicitor may have instructed a barrister (counsel) to represent your case to the district judge. You may well have had a meeting (known as a conference) to discuss your case with the barrister before the hearing. Make sure you take to court all the relevant documents, including copies of all affidavits and any questionnaires, and check with your solicitor whether any updated financial information is required.

Because of the potentially profound effects of costs on a case, both parties should prepare for the district judge a summary of their legal costs up to hearing, and an estimate of costs (including those of the hearing itself). If you are legally represented, these will include the solicitor's fees and VAT, disbursements (which can include estate agents' fees for valuing your house) and counsel's fees and VAT.

The hearing

The hearing is 'in chambers' – that is, not open to the public. Each spouse has an opportunity to state his or her case, either in person and/or through a solicitor. A spouse may have to give oral evidence on oath, if only to bring his or her affidavit up-to-date. Where there is oral evidence, the applicant gives evidence first and can be cross-examined by the other party, who can similarly be cross-examined on his or her evidence, if appropriate.

If you have to give oral evidence, here are some tips:

- always listen carefully to any questions put to you

- answer the questions clearly and simply and do not ramble or mumble
- remember that the person who you need to convince is the district judge (or judge), not the lawyers. It can be helpful to turn slightly towards the judge and answer him or her directly after a question has been put to you by a lawyer
- take a deep breath before answering any questions and try to speak slowly: often the other party's solicitor and the district judge (as well as your solicitor, if instructed) will be taking notes of what you are saying
- avoid becoming heated or emotional in response to the other party's questions; the district judge will want to confine his or her enquiry to the facts.

If any witnesses are called, they will not be able to come into the district judge's room until they give evidence – sometimes this may entail a long wait. Witnesses should give evidence only about matters that have been raised before the court hearing. You should not try to spring something on the other side (although where a new piece of evidence has only just come to light and is relevant in the proceedings, the district judge will usually use his or her discretion to hear it).

When oral evidence is not asked for, neither side is subject to cross-examination, but both sides can make submissions or comments after the affidavits are read.

The ancillary relief pilot scheme

A new ancillary relief rule has been piloted in specified courts (see box) since 1 October 1996. The main thrust of the scheme is to put the courts more in charge of the financial applications, so that they can define what money issues are disputed between the parties early on and see if financial issues can be resolved before heavy costs have been built up. The new rule provides for an early 'directions' appointment (when the court will give directions about how the case will be run), which is to be fixed between 10 and 14 weeks after forms M11 or M13 have been submitted to court. Strict time limits will apply, so 35 days before this first appointment both parties must file at court and supply to their spouse's solicitor a sworn statement of information about the marriage and finances – the particular issues to be covered are laid down in the rule. Your solicitor will have more details about the issues.

Courts piloting the ancillary relief scheme

The courts in which the new ancillary relief rule is being piloted are the Principal Registry of the Family Division in London and the county courts in Barnsley, Bath, Blackwood, Bolton, Boston, Bow, Bristol, Bury, Crewe, Guildford, Harrogate, Hertford, Kingston, Maidstone, Northampton, Salford, Southampton, Southport, Stafford, Staines, Stoke-on-Trent, Taunton, Teesside, Trowbridge, Tunbridge Wells, Willesden and Wrexham.

A week before the first appointment, each party must again serve on their spouse's solicitor and with the court:

- a questionnaire setting out the further information sought from their spouse
- a schedule asking for documents sought from their spouse
- a concise statement of the issues between the parties
- confirmation that everyone required to be served with the application (for example, a mortgagee and trustees of a pension scheme) has been served.

At the first appointment the court can give directions about, for example, how far each questionnaire should be answered, valuations and other evidence, whether the case could be transferred for mediation and whether it should be referred to a financial dispute resolution (FDR) appointment.

This FDR appointment is a key change under the new scheme – what will happen might appear a bit like quasi-mediation, except that the district judges (at least at an initial stage) are unlikely to have been trained as mediators and so may well use the opportunity metaphorically to bang the parties' heads together to see if any settlement can be reached. All proposals and offers to settle must be disclosed before the FDR appointment. Whatever negotiations take place at the appointment will be made 'without prejudice' so they cannot be mentioned to the court later if the case is not settled but proceeds to a full court hearing.

If the FDR appointment is successful in helping the parties reach agreement, a consent order can be applied for to translate the agreement into a court order (a court fee of £20 is payable). If unsuccessful, the case will proceed to a full court hearing. The only difference under this rule is that two weeks before the final hearing, open proposals for settlement (what orders are being sought from the court) must be exchanged by the parties and filed at court. Making such open offers may increase the likelihood of a settlement being achieved before the court hearing or even on the steps of the court as the hearing is about to begin.

One of the main effects of the new scheme is that there will be constant pressure on both parties to settle the case, which might force otherwise reluctant spouses to come to terms. Thus costs savings could well be made, although some critics have pointed out that it will be more difficult for proper voluntary mediation to take place in the hothouse atmosphere created by the new rule.

How the court decides

The courts no longer have a wholly free rein in deciding how the family income can be divided, as the CSA usually has jurisdiction over child support (where there are children covered by its jurisdiction). After that has been worked out, the lawyers (and ultimately the courts, if the case proceeds to a full hearing) will examine how much is left for division and will apply the court-based guidelines given below.

The other important question to be decided is with whom (in cases involving children) the children should live and whether the family home needs to be kept on. From these decisions, all other matters will flow.

Before deciding on the amount of maintenance to order, the district judge will look first at the shortfall between the child support and the needs of the parent looking after the children. Factors particularly relevant to maintenance are:

- the gross income of the husband and any necessary expenses of his work that can properly be set against his gross income together with any future earning capacity
- the gross income of the wife and any necessary expenses of her work that can properly be set against her gross income, together with any future earning capacity
- the needs of the children, now and in the foreseeable future
- the needs and outgoings of husband and of wife

- the possibility of each being financially self-sufficient (a 'clean break')
- the effect of tax on any proposed order
- the effect of any order on welfare benefits entitlements.

When dealing with a request for a property adjustment or a lump sum order the district judge will consider:

- the full extent of each party's capital and details of any other assets
- the value of the family home and of any other properties owned by either the husband or the wife or by both
- the amount owing on any mortgages
- the needs of each for accommodation
- whom the children live with
- the financial contributions or other contributions made by each towards the purchase or improvement of the family home and any previous homes
- if husband or wife is legally aided, the effect of the Legal Aid Board's statutory charge on a property adjustment or lump sum order.

In all cases, the overall question of costs must be considered.

In deciding whether to make financial orders on a divorce and if so what orders, statutory guidelines require a court to take account of:

- the income, earning capacity, property and other financial resources of both spouses, both now and in the foreseeable future, including any increased earning capacity which the court could reasonably expect either person to try to acquire
- the financial needs, obligations and responsibilities of both spouses, both now and in the foreseeable future
- the standard of living before the breakdown of the marriage
- the ages of both spouses
- the length of the marriage
- any physical or mental disabilities
- the contributions of each spouse to the welfare of the family including any contribution in caring for the family or looking after the home, both in the past and in the foreseeable future
- in some circumstances, the conduct of either spouse

- the value of any benefit, such as a pension, which either spouse would lose the chance of acquiring as a result of the divorce.

These guidelines are set out in section 25 of the Matrimonial Causes Act 1973, as amended by the Matrimonial and Family Proceedings Act 1984. The 1984 Act altered the previous guidelines in various ways and specifically directed that the court must give first consideration to the welfare of any child of the family under 18 when considering all the circumstances of a case. In practice, the needs of dependent children have long determined what course the court could reasonably follow in making appropriate orders, but the specific endorsement of this principle gives recognition to the role of the parent with whom the children make their main base, while also discouraging any assumption that that parent is automatically entitled to life-long support without further question, purely as a result of having looked after the children.

The 1984 Act abolished an old and quite unrealistic objective, namely that the court should try to place both spouses in the financial position they would have been in if the marriage had not broken down, insofar as was practical and just. The thrust of the guidelines is now more clearly forward-looking – but only after careful note is taken of the circumstances relating to the marriage and the family. The court must still consider the standard of living enjoyed before the breakdown when considering appropriate provision for the future.

Part of the emphasis of the 1984 Act was that the guidelines specifically mention contributions that will be made to the family's welfare in the foreseeable future (as well as those made in the past).

If the new pilot scheme applies in a case, the court will also doubtless consider the open offers that must be made before the hearing by both parties.

Earning capacity

The court is specifically directed to consider whether either spouse could reasonably increase his or her earning capacity. The 1984 Act reflected the desirability of a husband and wife aiming at financial independence from each other after divorce, to the extent that this may be realistic. Courts recognise, however, that women who have long been out of the job market may not be able to return straight away and, even if a job is found, it may well turn out to be with low earnings, little job security and few career prospects. A 1997 case called *Flavell v Flavell* held that it would not usually be appropriate for the courts to order an end to maintenance for a wife in her mid-fifties or so who has not worked for a long time.

Generally speaking, if there are very young children at home, a court would not expect a mother to go out to work unless she had been working before the breakdown of the marriage, in which case she would be expected to go on earning if practicable. This is also true of a father if the children live with him, except that it may be more realistic for him to go out to work, particularly if his level of earnings would mean that he could afford a housekeeper or childminder.

As the children grow older, the courts expect mothers to be able to return to work, at first perhaps part-time, or after a period of retraining (which the husband might need to finance).

A woman who has not worked outside the house throughout the marriage, who has grown-up children and is herself only a few years from retirement age, is recognised as having a very limited earning capacity, perhaps none. The extent to which it might be reasonable to expect her to find paid employment would depend very much on how realistic an option this is, set against the background of the marriage, the husband's earnings, her health, her tangible job prospects and all the other circumstances. Her need for a form of pension, to cover her maintenance needs after retirement age, will also very much need to be taken on board.

The court cannot order anyone to get a job but it can 'deem' a level of income which it considers either spouse could reasonably get. This can work both ways. If a wife is felt to be unreasonably refusing to work when there are job opportunities available, her maintenance order might be reduced. If a husband gives up his job simply to avoid paying maintenance, a bullish court might still make a maintenance order against him based on the amount that he should realistically be earning, in the hope that this will spur him back to work. The court will, however, take account of economic realities.

Conduct

The old provision was that the court had to take the conduct of each party into account 'so far as it was just to do so'. This was interpreted by the courts as meaning conduct which was 'gross and obvious' or such that it would 'offend one's sense of justice not to take it into account'. The courts are now directed to have regard to conduct if it is such that in the opinion of the court it would be inequitable to disregard it. Many lawyers and judges thought that the new wording would have no significant effect on the way courts considered the question of conduct, and this has been borne out by more recent cases decided since the passing of the 1984 Act. Bad conduct as a partner, for example having an affair, will usually be ignored.

In practice, only in exceptional cases will conduct be brought into account and then only where one party's conduct was 'gross and obvious' while the other party's conduct was comparatively blameless. Where both parties behaved extremely badly, the court is likely to disregard conduct. Even where conduct is relevant, it is only one of the factors that the court must look at.

Pension rights

There has been increasing concern about women being potential losers over pensions when their marriage breaks up. This is particularly the case if:

- the wife has spent her time largely looking after the children and home and has either no, or relatively low, earnings from which to make her own savings for retirement, *or*
- a more mature wife, who fully expected to share in the benefits of her husband's pension, and again has devoted herself to children and the home, finds she is divorced and will have insufficient time to build up a reasonable pension, even if she were able to get a job of her own.

Until June 1996, when a divorce case came to court, the court could take into account any pension rights when deciding how to allocate assets between the husband and wife, as part and parcel of the process termed the section 25 'balancing' exercise. Although the pension rights themselves could not be shared out, the wife for example could be compensated for the loss of the benefit of her husband's pension by being given a larger share of the family home, or even getting an outright transfer.

This, now old, law was not always satisfactory, because:

- although the courts had discretion, a ten-year foreseeability test came to be applied, so that pensions were taken into account only for wives who were looking at a loss of pension benefits in about ten years' time (i.e. typically wives in their fifties upwards, although occasionally wives in their late-forties were brought into the safety net too)

- there was no guidance to the courts about how to put a value on the pension assets
- where the non-pension assets of the couple were limited, it was not always possible to pay the compensation deemed to be just.

A further problem faced by the courts was that except in very limited cases, they were powerless against pension fund trustees, who vigorously maintained their absolute right to make their own discretionary decisions in the best interests of pension scheme members, not their spouses.

For petitions filed since 1 July 1996 the position has improved somewhat. Under the Pensions Act 1995, which covers petitions filed since 1 July 1996, courts must take pension rights into account. They have the power either to redistribute other assets as compensation, as described above, or to order pension trustees or managers to 'earmark' part of the pension to be paid at retirement to the ex-wife, in other words to allocate a share of the husband's pension to the wife for the future. (The courts can also order part of a lump sum payable on death to be paid to a non-pension member.) The first option – to compensate – is what courts will do by preference, but if other assets are not available, the courts do have new powers and are given teeth to use them.

The husband can also make parallel applications for his wife's pension to be, for example, earmarked in his favour, but as this situation is less common, in the rest of this section we assume that it is the husband who has the pension rights and the wife who wants to claim.

The part which is earmarked can either be a percentage of the whole pension or a fixed sum. Once it starts to be paid – namely when the husband retires or sometimes if he dies in service – the earmarked pension will be paid directly from the pension scheme itself to the ex-wife. The court has been able to make full earmarking orders (both for a lump sum and annual payments) since April 1997, and can specifically make the pension trustees pay up, overriding their discretion.

The earmarking approach is an improvement on the previous system, but it still suffers from a number of drawbacks:

- valuing the pension is still problematic, and the designated CETV (see *Pension valuations*, page 213) which the courts must now use in working out pension values undervalues occupational schemes, according to pensions experts. Moreover, current values cannot always predict a change in the fortunes of the pension fund – another Maxwell-type pensions fraud is unlikely but possible, and a stock market crash could depress the value of a fund

- the health (and remarriageability prospects) of each of the spouses will also have to be examined for a realistic appraisal of how earmarking might work in practice

- the earmarked pension will be payable only as long as the ex-wife does not remarry – on remarriage she would lose the maintenance-style pension previously and provisionally assigned to her (although probably not a lump sum)

- there are also tax considerations. The Inland Revenue has said that it will treat earmarked periodical payments orders as being taxable in the hands of the payee at the payer's marginal rates. So whilst other forms of maintenance are not taxable in the hands of the payee, earmarked periodical payments will be

- the wife cannot begin to draw her earmarked pension until the pension benefits are payable – usually when the husband retires. This would be a particular problem where the wife is older than the husband or if the husband decided to defer his pension beyond normal retirement age

- if the husband has already retired or is close to retirement, the system could work fairly equitably. But if the husband is many years from retirement, he could stop the pension plan or leave the pension scheme in which the rights are earmarked – if he changes job, for example. The wife would then have the right only to a share of an early leaver pension, which will be substantially lower than the retirement pension would have been if contributions or membership had continued. A new pension arrangement started by the husband after the divorce settlement would not be affected by the earmarking order

- if the husband dies before his planned retirement, the wife may receive nothing at all. Moreover, if he remarries and divorces, perhaps more than once, before retirement, what share the first ex-wife would be entitled to is not clear. If, for instance, she had been awarded 30 per cent of the pension payable to him, it is not yet known whether she would get 30 per cent of the whole pension or

30 per cent of what is left of the pension after his second ex-wife (if he remarries and re-divorces) claims an earmarked portion too. The law may become clearer once some test cases give enlightenment about the courts' approach

- earmarking flies in the face of the clean-break approach favoured by the courts; an earmarking order in effect keeps a couple tied together financially after their divorce even if they have no other on-going maintenance or other financial obligations
- the ingenuity of pension trustees (or that of their lawyers) should not be underestimated. Considerable legal fees are already being spent to see whether there are any loopholes in the new law that will allow trustees to hold on to their discretionary powers and pension scheme holders to keep their hands on their full pensions. As cases come up before the courts to test the limits of their powers, expect to see strong legal arguments testing any potential weaknesses.

It is not just the future retirement pension that an ex-wife or ex-husband may lose on divorce. Most pension schemes pay lump sums or pensions to widows and widowers. The tax rules still allow these payments to be made to the ex-spouse after a divorce, but the trustees or plan-providers generally have the power to decide who receives them and will tend to follow the wishes of the scheme-holder or plan-holder. If the ex-spouse can show that he or she was financially dependent on the deceased pension-scheme holder – say if he or she was receiving maintenance payments from the latter – he or she may qualify for some or all of the dependants' benefits, but that will also depend on who else is making a claim.

However, it is possible under the Pensions Act to apply for a lump sum order in respect of a lump sum payable on death. The courts can also require the spouse with pension rights to nominate the person to whom a lump sum payable on death is paid, if he or she has the power to do so.

Compensating

The various problems linked to earmarking have been explored above. Under the new law, compensating (i.e. giving one spouse a greater share of the family home or a larger lump sum payment in recognition of the loss of his or her pension rights) is to be preferred by the courts to earmarking, which will be used only if no assets are available to compensate. Two considerations are likely to reduce any payment made. The first is the fact that the receiving spouse will be getting a certain amount right away and will therefore not be subject to uncertainties about the performance of the funds invested or whether the pension member might die before retirement or soon after. Second, the lump sum is likely to be tax free (whereas maintenance-style pension payments will bear income tax on current rates of say between 20 and 40 per cent). Both compensation and earmarking, therefore, have pros and cons.

Pension-sharing

An alternative to earmarking is pension-sharing (formerly termed pension-splitting), whereby the wife would be awarded a share of the husband's pension as a form of lump sum which she could then keep as her own pension with the husband's pension scheme or transfer to a scheme of her own choice. The previous government had consistently blocked this approach arguing that administrative costs and the costs of paying transfer values from unfunded schemes would be too expensive. An amendment made to the Family Law Act 1996 – about the only amendment popular with the public – was to include a pension-sharing provision, and the previous government promised that it would change the law on pension-sharing. However, after the Act was passed by Parliament, the previous government announced that the amendment was unworkable, saying that necessary changes to computer software to deal with its implications could not be finalised until 'at least 2000'. The current government has confirmed that pension-sharing is high on its agenda, but it is still likely that the necessary practicalities to make it effective will not be in place until about 2000.

If pension-sharing were to be introduced, a successful claimant spouse would become a 'former spouse member' of the pension fund, but would receive any benefit probably only on her own retirement. How much she should then get would be calculated on actuarial advice, depending on how much is available in the pot and her life expectancy. Likely drawbacks of the new system are that pension-sharing may not be available for unfunded schemes (predominantly public service occupational schemes) nor for judicially separated couples, divorce settlements already reached or pension rights built up overseas.

227

Although it is currently not known what the final plans for pension-sharing will be, key features are likely to be as follows:

- the courts should have the power to share the second state pension – SERPS, the earnings-related state pension scheme – despite the fact that historically state benefits have been excluded from the jurisdiction of the divorce courts as they were not seen as matrimonial property. A new computer system will doubtless be required
- there will be no automatic 50:50 split – each case would be determined (or settled) on its merits – there are likely to be no minimum requirements, so in theory the court could order, say, a 10:90 split
- the valuation method will probably still be the cash equivalent transfer method – even though many pensions experts argue that it undershoots the true value especially of occupational schemes
- a key issue (as yet still debated) is when a pension-share pension could be able to be received by the non-member spouse – her retirement age will not necessarily be that of the member but quite what it will be is unclear – possibly it may be left to the simple choice of the claimant spouse.

Lobbying for pension-sharing to be introduced before 2000 will probably continue – the organisation Fairshares* has been particularly articulate – but for now, sharing a pension is not an option which the divorce courts can offer.

Another option: Brooks v Brooks

A case decided by the House of Lords in June 1995 (*Brooks v Brooks*), will probably help only a few ex-wives, but is still worth considering.

The *Brooks* case was decided on unusual facts. Mrs Brooks, who had no pension of her own, had worked for some years for her husband's company and Mr Brooks' pension scheme was set up individually for his company. In a complex decision, the House of Lords decided that the pension scheme could be seen as a type of marriage settlement and as such a court could order that the pension trustees use part of the scheme's funds to provide a pension for Mrs Brooks.

This decision may not help very many wives, first because of the narrow way that the Lords decided what could and could not be classed as a marriage settlement – the judgment is likely to affect only small self-administered pension schemes and not occupational schemes. Second, the Lords said that the case could not be used if it affected third parties adversely, thereby excluding the majority of schemes, which are likely to have a number of members. Finally, the fact that Mrs Brooks had worked for the company meant that the Inland Revenue would cooperate in allowing her to be paid a pension from the pension funds. In cases where a wife has not worked outside the home, the hurdle of getting tax approval for payment of a pension for an ex-wife is often insurmountable. However, if your family situation is similar to the *Brooks* case, you may benefit from the precedent set in that case.

New relationship

If either or both parties in a divorce have formed a new relationship, the break-up of the marriage may be less damaging financially. The fact that one of the parties is moving out to live with somebody else, although emotionally hurtful, may be the best thing that could happen as far as accommodation costs are concerned. It reduces the biggest financial strain of all – the cost of two homes from one income. Where an ex-spouse's living expenses and accommodation costs are substantially reduced because of a new partner's contribution, there is more of the ex-spouse's money to go around and be shared out. (See also Chapter 14 on Stepfamilies.)

Length of marriage

The question of whether the time of pre-marital cohabitation can be taken into account has caused some legal controversy. It is likely to be taken into account if children were born during that period, or if one party had made a substantial financial contribution to the shared home before marriage. It is likely to be considered under the provision dealing with 'all the circumstances of the case' rather than the factor relating to length of the marriage.

After a short marriage in which there are no children, the court may be inclined not to order maintenance, or perhaps only for a limited period. The question as to what constitutes a short marriage is not clear: a marriage of three years has been held by the court not to have been a short marriage, whereas a marriage of five years was considered 'of short duration'. A short marriage between a young couple who are both working or able to do so is likely to be treated very differently from a short marriage between two people in, say, their mid-fifties where the woman had given up secure accommodation and/or a career and/or maintenance from a former spouse when she married, or if she is/was suffering from some kind of disability.

No strict definition exists of what a long-lasting marriage is.

Secured payments

The courts have the power to order that periodical payments be 'secured' by a capital asset that the paying party possesses. A secured order is rare and is relevant only where there is a lot of available capital. It should not be contemplated without legal advice. A secured order can last for the life of the recipient because it survives the death of the payer; no other maintenance order does so.

Guidelines on maintenance levels

Maintenance for the children

Children covered by the CSA

The implementation of the Child Support Act 1991 in April 1993 has made the issue of how much maintenance should be paid paradoxically both more and less certain for parents with children. As long as the children come within the jurisdiction of the CSA (see Chapter 5) the amount of child support that should be paid can be worked out in most cases relatively precisely. If the necessary information is available to make the calculation, a 'right' answer can be arrived at, which leaves only the question of how much spousal maintenance should be paid.

The figures to be included in the calculation may not be easily available – say if one spouse plans eventually to leave the home but has not yet moved out, his (or her) future housing costs will not yet be known, so a vital element of the calculation is missing. Even so, it should be possible to guess how much rent will be paid approximately and thus make a good stab at the eventual figure. This will provide a starting point for working out how much maintenance should be paid for the wife (or, where the wife is comparatively wealthy and the husband has no income, for the husband). See Chapter 5 for further information.

Children not covered by the CSA

Some children of the family are not covered by the CSA's powers, and so an application must be made to court for their maintenance. Those *not* covered by the Agency include:

- stepchildren
- children who are, or whose parent(s) are habitually resident abroad
- children whose parents made a pre-existing agreement for maintenance.

If an application is made to the court for children's maintenance, the court may look at how much child support would be if the CSA formula were used, in addition to the factors it would have taken into consideration in the past. It may also look at other yardsticks – a report published by the Joseph Rowntree Foundation in autumn 1997, for example, noted that the 'average' yearly cost of bringing up a child was nearly £3,000. However, the courts take pride in being flexible in family cases and will be able to take other outgoings – like travel, childcare costs and debts – into account before deciding how much should be paid.

Having worked out child support, the court will then address the question of spousal maintenance.

Spousal maintenance

There are no set guidelines on how much should be paid for spouses. The old rule was that a wife might expect to receive something like one-third of the overall gross income. Now that way of dividing up incomes is out of date: families often have two incomes, and most of the tax advantages that used to exist in paying maintenance have been abolished. The court has instead adopted a more realistic approach, often dubbed the 'needs and resources' approach. It looks at how much each partner needs and then what the overall resources are to meet those needs. Producing a budget of how much each spouse needs to live on will be helpful.

As mentioned above, the courts first work out child support before looking at spousal maintenance. Their primary concern is to see that the needs of the children and those of the parent looking after the children are met. Where these are not met by the income of the parent looking after the children, the courts will where possible set a level of spousal maintenance to top up that income. If not enough money is available to do this, the courts will merely order the absent parent to pay what he (or she) can reasonably afford (if anything). Welfare benefits may be available to top up maintenance levels. Remember, however, that maintenance will be deducted pound for pound from income support, although there is a £15 disregard for maintenance when calculating family credit.

A court's overall task is to evaluate all the various factors, balance them one against each other, give what weight is considered appropriate to each factor and then try to arrive at an order which is fair and reasonable. Capital and income are looked at together. It may be appropriate for a wife to receive more capital and less maintenance even if there is not to be a clean break.

The Finance Act 1988 changed the tax treatment of maintenance orders on divorce. Before then, parties had been able to maximise the tax effectiveness of maintenance orders by utilising each child's single person's tax-free allowance through orders for maintenance payments to the children, to reduce the burden of tax upon the payer.

The changes in tax law mean that it is now easier to calculate the tax burden on the family; no skilful manipulation of maintenance figures can result in a decrease of the tax burden on the family after divorce. Divorcing families thus have to translate into reality a problematic equation: the division of (often) one income to support two households.

Maintenance payments and welfare benefits

For a recipient, maintenance payments have a direct effect on all means-tested welfare benefits, for example income support. The basic rule is that all the maintenance paid is taken into account when the amount of benefit is calculated by the Department of Social Security (DSS), so for each pound of maintenance paid income support goes down by a pound. This does not, however, apply to family credit or disability working allowance, nor to council tax benefit or housing benefit, where the recipient is *not* in receipt of income support. In such cases the first £15 of maintenance is disregarded: it is in effect an extra sum of income for the family on top of these welfare benefits.

Maintenance payments will not affect non-means-tested benefits, such as child benefit, disability benefits, non-contributory jobseeker's allowance, sickness and maternity benefits, or a retirement pension.

If in doubt about the impact of a claim for maintenance on your benefit claim, consult your solicitor or Citizens Advice Bureau

(CAB). Further information on maintenance payments via the CSA can be found in Chapter 5.

New maintenance credit system

As an incentive for lone parents to return to work, since April 1997 a maintenance credit system has been in operation. This is in effect like making notional savings while a person is in receipt of income support – the savings can be cashed in when he or she starts work. Thus parents with care who are on income support and are being paid maintenance build up a credit of £5 per week which they can receive in a lump sum (maximum £1,000) once they return to work. No benefits can be seen for as long as he or she receives income support, but on starting a job the cash sum could help out with extra expenses of going back to work – childcare costs and buying new clothes, for example.

The clean break

The courts have the explicit obligation, when making an order for financial relief, to consider whether it would be appropriate to make an order which would lead to each spouse becoming financially independent of the other 'as soon after the grant of the decree as the court considers just and reasonable'. They can (although this is rare) make a clean break even in the face of adamant opposition from a wife (or, very rarely, a husband).

The ability of the husband to finance a clean break may, however, have been adversely affected by his having to pay higher levels of child support under the CSA formula. Child support levels will usually have to be worked out first, and only then can the husband's ability to make a clean break be assessed. Remember that clean breaks can apply only in respect of spousal maintenance, never for maintenance for the children.

Where an order for periodical payments is to be made to a spouse and a clean break might be appropriate, the court should consider whether the payments should be for a specific period only and then cease. The specified period should be what, in the opinion of the court, would be sufficient to enable the recipient to adjust without undue hardship to the ending of his or her financial dependence on the other spouse. In practice, courts are reluctant to look more than two or three years into the future, and only if the future is pretty clearly foreseeable will a limited term order be appropriate. Time-limited periodical payments are much less likely to be appropriate where there are dependent children than, say, where there has been a short, childless marriage and what the wife requires is just one or two years of financial assistance while she re-establishes herself.

A clean-break settlement is sometimes fair and reasonable especially if one spouse buys out the other's maintenance claims with an additional capital payment. The availability (or more usually the non-availability) of funds is critical. The court will look at all the circumstances, including the wife's prospect of remarriage and any future earning capacity.

In cases involving wealthier couples, the amount of the lump sum which could buy out the wife's maintenance is worked out according to a 'Duxbury' calculation. In essence the idea is that a lump sum will be calculated which will be sufficient to meet the wife's needs for the rest of her life on the basis that she draws capital as well as income. The calculations are complex – they try to take account of foreseeable changes such as reductions in expenses when the children leave home (when a wife may move to a smaller house). In general Duxbury calculations tend to work only where there is a large amount of free capital available and where the wife is not too far off retirement age – the cost of buying out a young wife's claims with a Duxbury calculation is usually prohibitive. A wife of 42, for example, with a further life expectancy of 43 years would need to be paid £178,000 to give her an annual income of £10,000, whereas if she were ten years older, at 52, with a life expectancy of another 33 years, the lump sum Duxbury calculation would fall to £144,000. Of course, a wealthy wife may be ordered to pay a lump sum to her husband, perhaps to enable him to buy a house, just as a wealthy husband can be ordered to pay a lump sum to his wife.

Since July 1996, with the new law on pensions earmarking in place, even if a clean break is ordered, the court can still award a wife a share of her husband's pension, payable on retirement, thus eroding the 'pure' clean-break principle.

Advantages and disadvantages

The main advantage of a clean-break order is certainty, in terms of both the husband knowing that his maintenance obligations to his ex-wife will end and the wife knowing that she will receive a specific sum of money. It can also encourage both parties to create independent lives after the divorce. However, following the implementation of the Child Support Act 1991, even if a clean break and lower levels of child maintenance are agreed now, the Agency is likely to have the right to review child support in the future and can raise the levels in line with the formula.

Another disadvantage for the recipient is that the capital awarded is unlikely to produce as high an annual income if invested at standard rates as the maintenance provision that there might otherwise have been. Moreover, the lump sum cannot later be increased to keep pace with inflation or a husband's financial fortune. If something unexpected happens, such as the wife falling ill and being unable to work, she will not be able to look to her ex-husband for support. Similarly, the spouse making the payment must remember that it is possible that the recipient could get remarried a short while later.

Even if there is no capital other than the net equity of the family home, a couple may prefer the wife to receive all or a disproportionate part of the net equity and to have her maintenance claims dismissed. But this is not always a realistic solution and must be considered very carefully. The court will be unwilling to provide for a clean break in circumstances where the wife's only means of support is income support. Where the marriage has been long-standing and the wife is in, say, her mid-fifties without ever having worked outside the home during the marriage and without reasonable prospects of working in the future, it is highly unlikely that the court will willingly grant a clean-break order.

The court's power and duty under the 1984 Act

Before the 1984 Act the courts had in effect been able to order what amounted to clean-break settlements by refusing to order more than nominal periodical payments if circumstances so warranted, but a claim for maintenance could not finally be dismissed without the applicant's consent. The 1984 Act gave the courts more muscle: where a clean-break approach is appropriate, a spouse's maintenance claim can be dismissed either at once or by an order for maintenance for only a specific period.

A clean-break order should include a provision to prevent one spouse from having a claim on the estate of the other spouse after death under the Inheritance (Provision for Family and Dependants) Act 1975, as amended by the Law Reform (Succession) Act 1995.

The courts have a duty to investigate whether it is realistic to expect a husband and wife to be moving towards financial independence, but where there are dependent children, this may very well not be in their interests, and the courts have a specific duty to give first consideration to the welfare of children. It cannot be over-emphasised that the clean-break approach can extend only to the parties in the marriage, not to provision for children.

The district judge's decision

Once all the evidence and all the arguments have been heard, the dis-

---

The steps in financial proceedings

1 Include financial claims in 'prayer' of petition (or answer).

2 If divorce is based on two-year or five-year separation, the respondent can file 'section 10' application.

3 Lodge in duplicate form M11 or M13 (plus affidavit of means) and a fee of £50, and serve a copy ('sealed' by the court) of the form and the affidavit on the other spouse (keep photocopies for yourself).

4 If you are seeking a property adjustment order, it is wise to register a 'pending action' against the property in question at the Land Registry/Land Charges Department.

5 Apply for directions hearing (the function of this hearing will be to ensure that all documents and information are ready for the main hearing); some courts fix a date for the directions hearing automatically, some courts give directions right away.

6 At the first directions hearing the district judge can order:
• further affidavits • 'discovery' by exchange of lists of documents or 'Rule 2.63' • questionnaires • valuations • each party to attend final hearing to give evidence.
The district judge can also make a maintenance pending suit order.

7 Consider making now (if you have not already made) – or accepting – a Calderbank offer.

8 Exchange 'evidence' about means via lists of relevant documents and/or questionnaires (and replies) under Rule 2.63.

9 If spouse is uncooperative about supplying information, ask

---

trict judge can give judgment there and then. In a more complex case, he or she may reserve judgment until a later day.

If the district judge dismisses an application for periodical payments, it cannot later be revived. The applicant may have agreed to this in return for some other financial provision, such as a larger lump sum or transfer of the home.

If there is presently no scope for a lump sum order but there is a real possibility of capital arising in the foreseeable future, the application for a lump sum can be adjourned with 'liberty to apply' later.

Make a written note of the district judge's judgment in case there is an appeal. It may also be useful to have a record of why he or she

---

for penal notice to be endorsed on directions order and serve on your spouse.

10 You can go back to the court at any stage to apply for further directions that something should be done or supplied by your spouse.

Check both now and in future whether a Calderbank offer can be made or other moves can be taken to settle the case by consent: fully contested court cases are very costly.

11 When both you and your spouse are ready, apply to the court for a hearing date by lodging 'certificates of readiness for trial and time estimates'; hearing date is fixed by the court (likely to be at least three months later).

12 Each of you (or your solicitors) has to prepare 'bundles of documents' including Rule 2.63 questionnaires and replies.

13 Before the hearing, prepare brief schedule of financial position and cost estimates, and update valuations, if necessary.

14 The hearing: arrange in advance for witnesses where appropriate; speak up.

15 District judge considers all evidence and gives judgment and makes appropriate orders (but can 'reserve', i.e. postpone, judgment to a later date).

NB: If you wish to claim child support, this will usually be dealt with by the Child Support Agency, not the courts.

The above table does not apply in the same way if the ancillary relief pilot scheme is in operation.

---

arrived at the payments ordered – for example, a low maintenance payment may have been ordered because the wife is receiving a larger share in the family home. This may be taken into account on any subsequent application to vary a periodical payments order.

Costs

An order for payment of costs can be asked for at this stage, as soon as the district judge has given his or her decision. You will have to explain why you think an order for costs should be made (or why there should be no order) and produce the relevant figures of overall costs incurred. The district judge will ask whether any Calderbank offers have been made and whether the terms of the order coincide with, or approximate to, the terms of the offer. This is also the time to raise the question of any costs 'reserved' on a previous interim application which deferred the decision on the amount of costs until the final financial order.

The court can order costs against either party on two bases only: 'standard' and 'indemnity'. If you have been legally represented, the standard basis will only cover a proportionate amount of your costs – probably about 60 per cent. An order for indemnity costs (that is, total costs) is made only in exceptional circumstances where one party appears to have been really unreasonable, leading to an unnecessary increase in legal costs. Even more rarely, the court can order costs on what lawyers terms a *Leary* basis – which means that an overall fixed sum for costs can be ordered where (usually) the husband has been wholly unreasonable throughout and has tried to deceive the court and his spouse over his financial affairs.

Attachment of earnings

You can apply for an attachment of earnings order at the same time that a spousal maintenance order is made under the Enforcement of Maintenance Act 1991. Under the same Act, the court can order that the payer sets up a standing order from a bank account. Both these measures can be useful in reducing the risks of arrears building up.

The orders

After the hearing, the court office prepares the order(s) and sends a copy to both parties. Check the wording and figures carefully, in case there is a clerical error, and keep the documents in a safe place.

If any orders affect your tax position, a copy of the order should be sent to your inspector of taxes promptly.

Appeal

An appeal against an order or decision of the district judge can be made to a judge by filing a notice of appeal within five working days. The notice setting out the grounds is best prepared by a solicitor. From a judge's decision, an appeal proceeds to the Court of Appeal and thereafter to the House of Lords, although it is very rare (and expensive) for a case to get this far.

Tax, separation and divorce

When spouses separate and where the separation is likely to be permanent, the married couple's allowance is available (in full) for the year of separation but not in later years. This allowance will go to the husband, unless a claim has been made to transfer half or all of it to the wife. (This date of separation is a question of fact.) Note that the wife can claim half the married couple's allowance as of right – she can only get more than half with the husband's agreement.

Before 6 April 1990, when a husband and wife were taxed jointly, a husband could continue to get the married man's allowance (as it was then called) up to the year of divorce if he wholly maintained his separated wife by means of unenforceable payments. But this does not apply to the married couple's allowance. (Where, however, a couple separated before 6 April 1990 and the husband was entitled to the married man's allowance under the old provisions, he will continue to get the married couple's allowance so long as the conditions are satisfied.) Additional personal allowances may be claimed by both the husband and the wife in the year of separation if they each have a qualifying child resident with him or her for all or part of the remainder of the year. The definition of a qualifying child means under 16 years (or older, if in full-time education), at the beginning of the year of assessment. 'Resident' is taken to mean that the child is resident with you for all or part of the year – the Inland Revenue's view is that 'resident for part of the year' means more than just the occasional short visit. If the child has his or her own bedroom and belongings at the home and spends significant time there, that should be sufficient.

If the husband and the wife both claim in respect of the same child, the allowance is apportioned between them, but two allowances are available if each has a qualifying child resident with him or her for at least part of the year. But the available allowance is reduced by any married couple's allowance to which the husband or wife is entitled. The additional personal allowance will continue in later years as long as the conditions are satisfied. If, however, either of them lives with someone else as man and wife, note that only one additional personal allowance is available per household — so if each of the new partners has a qualifying child from a former marriage, only one additional personal allowance is available and it will be given for the youngest qualifying child.

Tax and maintenance payments

The tax treatment of maintenance payments depends on whether the payments are made to the spouse or to the children, and when the maintenance first became payable. All maintenance that qualifies for relief must be paid in full — i.e. without any deduction of tax — save for pension-type periodical payments earmarked under the new law, when 'net of tax' payments should be ordered. Any tax relief due will be given to the payer and any tax due is collected from the recipient by means of an adjustment to the PAYE coding for employees and otherwise in an individual's self-assessment.

Maintenance payments to a spouse

Where you pay maintenance to a separated or divorced spouse under a court order, written agreement or Child Support Agency assessment, you can claim a maintenance relief deduction from your tax bill for 1997/98 of 15 per cent of £1,830 (£1,790 in 1996/97) or 15 per cent of the amount paid if less. You cannot save tax on more than £1,830 worth of maintenance payments however much you pay or even if you are paying to two or more ex-spouses. Your spouse will not be taxed on the amount received. The full allowance is available in the year of separation as well as the married couple's allowance. Payments due after your spouse remarries, however, do not qualify for relief.

Special provisions apply to any payments made under agreements made before 15 March 1988 (or court orders made before 30 June 1988). For 1997/98, the first £1,830 of qualifying maintenance to your spouse and children (where relevant) saves you tax at 15 per cent.

The balance qualifies for relief at your top rate of tax. The payee spouse will be liable to tax on the maintenance, except for the first £1,830.

Where maintenance has been increased since the tax year 1988/89, the amount on which a taxpayer can qualify for relief will be limited to the maintenance paid in that year – again the payee spouse will pay tax only on that amount, less £1,830.

Maintenance payments to children

The only circumstances in which maintenance payments made directly to your children qualify for tax relief are where the payments are made under a pre-1988 agreement or court order as above. Even then, relief ceases once they reach age 21. The first £1,830 of the total qualifying maintenance to a payee spouse and children under 21 saves tax at 15 per cent. The balance saves tax at your top rate, but again the maximum qualifying amount will be limited to the maintenance payable in 1988/89. However, by ensuring that your maintenance payments will be made to your ex-spouse on behalf of your children (or under the CSA assessment), you can take advantage of the limited amount of tax relief which is available. You could ask your solicitor or accountant for more details.

Switch from the old to the current rules

Under certain transitional arrangements, it has been possible to choose to switch from being treated under the old rules to being treated under the current rules. You should check whether the rules under the Finance Act 1988 provide any real benefit to you, but in most circumstances it will be better to continue your tax treatment under the old rules.

Advising the Inland Revenue of the date of separation

You and your spouse should endeavour to agree the date on which you separated, for tax purposes. You may be able to choose a date between the date of your separation and decree absolute for the date of final separation. Although, given the Finance Act 1988, this is unlikely to have much effect on your maintenance position, it may affect your position with regard to Capital Gains Tax.

Enforcement of payments

Actually receiving maintenance following a court order or CSA assessment often depends on the continuing ability of the ex-spouse to make the payments.

Should the payer (usually the ex-husband) fall into arrears with maintenance payments, there are several channels for enforcement, none entirely satisfactory. If child support is paid through the CSA, you can ask it to use its collection and enforcement service. The Agency has now, in effect, taken over from the DSS's liable relative proceedings.

The main advantage of this service is that it is likely to be a lot cheaper than going to court. The CSA also has extra powers to trace a disappearing ex-husband, through access to Inland Revenue and DSS records, for example. It is still too early to judge how effective the service offered will prove to be. The CSA can make a deduction of earnings order, like an attachment of earnings order, which takes the maintenance due (plus a small administration fee) directly from the payer's salary. It can also apply for all of the enforcement procedures set out below: the ultimate sanction is committal to prison (although this is likely to be used only rarely). Since April 1996 the CSA has also been able to collect and enforce spousal maintenance.

The sooner steps are taken to enforce the arrears, the better. If arrears are allowed to accumulate, they may prove impossible to recover: courts will not enforce arrears that are more than a year old.

Enforcing a debt

A defaulting spouse getting away with not paying has traditionally been part of the wider problem of trying to enforce civil debts in general: your chances of success in enforcing a debt may not be particularly high.

An application for enforcement has to be made to the divorce court that made the order (unless the order has been registered at a magistrates' court). The divorce court will not automatically chase arrears and will make an order for enforcement only if asked to. But you can apply to the Family Proceedings Panel (FPP) to register an order in the magistrates' court. The burden is then on the court to chase the arrears.

Enforcement in the county court

The main methods of enforcement are:

- a warrant of execution
- an attachment of earnings order
- a judgment summons for committal to prison.

Warrant of execution

A warrant of execution is an order issued by the county court for the district where the defaulting payer lives for the court bailiff to seize sufficient of the person's goods as will, on sale by auction, discharge the debt shown on the warrant.

Secondhand goods seized and sold at auction rarely produce much money. It is worthwhile getting a warrant of execution only if the goods are in good condition, but, on the other hand, merely the threat of seizure and sale may produce payment.

To get a warrant issued, you must swear an affidavit showing the amount of the arrears, provide a copy of the order, complete the appropriate county court forms and pay the appropriate fee (ranging from £20 to £80 – the latter if a warrant is sought over property – from 15 January 1997, which is not returnable if there are no saleable goods).

Attachment of earnings order

Provided that the ex-husband is in regular employment, an attachment of earnings order may be a more effective way of collecting arrears. (Since the Maintenance Enforcement Act 1991, it can be applied for even before arrears build up, at the time the maintenance order is made.) It requires the employers to deduct regular weekly or monthly amounts from his wages and to send the money to the court which will then pay it to the former wife. The amount of deductions can include not only a regular sum off the arrears until they are discharged, but also the ongoing maintenance. (The employers can deduct £1 in addition each time for their pains.) The procedure is no use where the man is unemployed or self-employed.

The application usually has to be to the divorce county court which made the maintenance order. The appropriate application form (in duplicate), with a copy of the maintenance order, must be supported by an affidavit giving details of the arrears and, if possible, the name of the employers. The court fee for this is now £50.

A notice of the application is served on the ex-husband, together with a form asking for details of his income and financial commitments. The court can ask the employers to supply information about the man's earnings over the past few weeks. The applicant should attend the hearing to give up-to-date evidence about the arrears.

Any order the district judge makes will be on the basis that it must not reduce the man's net income below the protected earnings rate. This is the amount which would be allowed for him and his dependants for income support together with the amount of his rent (or mortgage payments) and rates, and other essential and reasonably long-term commitments, such as other court orders or a hire purchase agreement.

When making an attachment order, therefore, the court may well take the opportunity – after an adjournment, if needed, for a formal application to be made – to adjust the maintenance order to take account of the realities of the situation as disclosed at the time of enforcement proceedings.

Committal to prison

A judgment summons can be issued for maintenance arrears if it can be shown that the ex-husband has the means to pay maintenance and has failed to do so; in theory, he can be sent to prison. A judgment summons is a potentially effective means of enforcing payment of arrears where a man has capital or is self-employed and cannot be touched by an attachment of earnings order.

A request for a judgment summons can be made to any county court convenient to the applicant. Legal aid is not available for a judgment summons in the county court but it is in the High Court. (If the applicant would be financially eligible, the solicitor should consider whether it will be possible to have the case transferred to the High Court.) The county court fee is £50.

The former wife, or her solicitor, should attend the hearing of the judgment summons to question the ex-husband in an attempt to prove that he could have paid the maintenance but neglected to do so. If it is proved that he had the means, an order committing him to prison can be made. If an ex-wife is applying for the ex-husband's committal to prison it is essential that the application is drafted accurately. This is because the courts view committal as a remedy to be used only in extreme circumstances, so the documents that are drafted must be prepared correctly.

Sending an ex-husband to prison is unlikely to produce the money that an ex-wife needs, although the threat of imprisonment may do so. The order can be suspended if he undertakes to pay regular amounts off the arrears together with current maintenance; it can be reinstated if he fails to keep up the payments.

The court is likely to order the ex-husband to pay the costs of the application.

Disappearing ex-husband

If a woman does not know her ex-husband's address, it may be possible to get the DSS to disclose it to the court because his up-to-date address may be known to it through his National Insurance record. A form can be obtained from the court on which the ex-wife should give as much information as she can about his last known address and employer, his date of birth and National Insurance number. The CSA too has powers to trace a missing parent for child support purposes but it cannot reveal his or her whereabouts unless he or she authorises it to do so. The same duty to keep the address confidential applies to the court.

Enforcement of lump sum or property transfer order

An unpaid lump sum may be enforced either by bankruptcy proceedings (unwise, except as a powerful threat) or by a court order that any property belonging to the person ordered to pay be sold to raise the sum. An order for such a sale (for example, of a house or stocks and shares) can be made when the lump sum is ordered. If it is not made then, the usual procedure is to apply for a charging order and then for an order for sale of the asset.

If the transfer of property order is not complied with, the district judge at the court can execute the relevant conveyance in place of the person who is refusing to do so. Application has to be made to the court with the relevant documents prepared for the district judge and an affidavit in support.

It is advisable to have a solicitor's help in such proceedings.

Enforcement in or via a magistrates' court

If an order made in the divorce court is registered in the FPP (magistrates' court), the court staff will summons the payer to appear in court if he or she defaults. The procedure is quicker and simpler than that in the county court.

If the payer is in arrears, the magistrates can order that a disclosure of means be made, and can make one of the following orders:

- attachment of earnings
- distraint on goods (seizure and sale)
- committal to prison (for not more than six weeks).

Changes in circumstances: variations

Variations and the CSA

One potentially useful feature of child support worked out by the CSA's formula is that there is an automatic in-built review of the amount paid every two years, on the anniversary of the assessment. Fourteen days before the anniversary is due, the Agency will send out further forms asking the parents about any changes in circumstances. Once the forms are returned, it will recalculate the amount of maintenance.

As the formula is based on income support rates, which go up every year, there is an element of inflation-proofing built into the system, although usually the amount of child support actually paid will increase only where the paying parent's income has gone up too. In recent years, given the rises in National Insurance contributions, the amount an absent parent has had to pay may have gone down unless he received a pay rise.

As well as the automatic review every two years, parents can ask the Agency for a change of circumstances review. There is no definition of a change of circumstances, so potentially any life or monetary change will be covered. One parent may, for example, gain or lose a job or go on to part-time working or have a baby. The Child Support Officer will review the case once a review has been asked for (either parent can request one) but the amount paid will change only if certain trigger points are reached. These are where the changes result in a difference (up or down) of:

- in most cases, at least £10 per week, *or*

- in cases where the absent parent comes under the protection of the protected income formula, at least £5 per week, *or*
- in cases where a qualifying child has left or joined a household of the person with care, at least £1.

In cases where the absent parent is on income support or is otherwise liable to pay the minimum payment (or exempted from paying this), a fresh assessment will be made straight away.

Variations and the courts

With a periodical payments order, even if a spouse had merely a nominal order of, say, 5p per year, which has not expired because of either remarriage or time limit, it is possible to apply to the court to have the order varied – that is, for the amount payable to be increased or decreased, or even for the order to be brought to an end – if it can be shown that there has been a material change in the financial circumstances of either party. You can apply on your own behalf and/or on behalf of your children.

An application for a variation can be made at any time after the decree nisi, even many years later, provided that the recipient has not remarried. There is no limit on the number of variations that can be applied for. However, if the maintenance payable is only for a specified period – for five years for example, under the original order – a variation must be applied for well before the date the maintenance is due to expire.

The court can also vary any agreement that the couple made between themselves, even though they may have agreed not to refer the agreement to the court. In law, any term in an agreement that precludes one party from seeking the assistance of the courts is void.

What cannot be varied

A lump sum order or a property adjustment order cannot be varied, nor can someone go back to court to obtain another one, nor ask for one later if it had not been included in the original application. Although a lump sum order cannot be varied, if the lump sum is being paid in instalments, the size and frequency of instalments can be varied, but not so as to alter the total of the lump sum originally awarded.

An order which was expressed to be 'final' cannot be varied, and a separation agreement so expressed is likely to be upheld.

If an application for maintenance made previously was formally dismissed by the court, the application cannot be revived later.

Applying for a variation

An application can be made at the divorce court where the order you want to vary was made. If that original court is now inconvenient or if it has not been designated a Family Hearing Centre (FHC), you should ask for the case to be transferred to an FHC more convenient for you. (If the order was registered in a magistrates' court you must apply to the FPP there, not to the court which originally made the order.)

The application should be made on the standard form of notice of application, available from the court office. If circumstances have changed, lodge the application as soon as possible so that any variation of periodical payments can be backdated to the date of the application. You do not have to file an affidavit with the application but you may need to do so in order to spur your ex-spouse into responding to the application. He or she then has to file an affidavit in reply within 28 days. Your affidavit should give up-to-date details of your financial position and why you feel a variation is (or is not) appropriate. The court fee is £30.

Reasons for an application

Major factors that are likely to affect financial orders made in the divorce court are:

- a change in financial circumstances of the payer or payee, including retirement
- remarriage of the payee (periodical payments order ends)
- cohabitation of the payee
- remarriage or cohabitation of the payer
- death of either
- either becoming disabled
- children having got older
- length of time elapsed since the making of the last order.

If the court rejects the application for a variation, this does not preclude an application for a variation being made at some later stage if circumstances change again.

Variations made after the Finance Act 1988

If your former spouse pays maintenance under a court order made before 15 March 1988 or an order otherwise qualifying as an 'existing obligation', he or she will continue to receive tax relief by offsetting against his or her taxable income the maintenance payment. The maximum amount of relief that will be given, however, is the limit of the amount due and paid by means of maintenance payments in the tax year 1988/89. For increases over and above this amount, the payer will have to pay any extra maintenance out of the taxed income and will be ineligible for tax relief. (See also pages 240–1.)

The court's approach

The court must consider all the circumstances of the case anew, as well as any change in them, giving first consideration to the welfare of any child of the family under 18. Where child maintenance is concerned, there are likely to be arguments that the amounts paid should increase to similar levels produced by the child support formula. The court must also consider whether given the circumstances it would be appropriate to vary an order so that the payments are for only as long as would be sufficient to enable the recipient to adjust without undue hardship to the termination of the payments, or to terminate the payments altogether – a clean break.

Marriage of ex-spouse

If she marries again, a former wife's right to maintenance for herself ceases immediately and cannot be revived against the ex-husband even if she finds herself on her own again – divorced, separated or widowed. If her ex-spouse is paying maintenance payments to the children or maintenance payments via a Child Support Agency Assessment, his limited tax relief (see above) will cease after her remarriage.

There is no formal requirement to tell the previous husband that she has married again, but if she does not do so and he finds out, he can ask her to repay what he has paid her since her new marriage; if she does not pay up, he can sue her for the overpaid money as a debt.

Maintenance payments for children are not automatically affected by the mother's new marriage, but the remarriage of either parent may give rise to a situation in which a variation is justified.

An ex-wife's right to occupy what had been the matrimonial home may cease on remarriage. The terms of the court order may require the house or flat to be sold and the proceeds divided in the specified proportions.

If a person made a lump sum payment of, say, £20,000, to an ex-spouse and six months later heard that he or she had remarried, the person cannot usually apply for a variation. Where a lump sum has been ordered to be paid in instalments and the recipient ex-spouse marries again, instalments have to be continued until the full amount is paid. (Very rarely an application to have the order set aside on the grounds of fraudulent non-disclosure of the intention to remarry may succeed.)

Cohabitation

When a man is paying his ex-spouse maintenance and she cohabits with another man, he may have grounds to apply to the court for a variation of the order. The courts will normally expect it to be proved that there is some permanence to the cohabitation and that it is reasonable to infer that there is financial contribution from the cohabitant. However, the courts are less likely to allow a variation for cohabitation because they are often reluctant to 'absolve' a former husband of his obligations to his ex-wife. In any event, the only way in which a cohabitant's financial position should be taken is the extent to which it 'frees up' the ex-spouse's financial resources. So if a cohabitant takes over payment of the mortgage, for example, then the ex-spouse might have up to the amount of the mortgage more in terms of financial income – although deducted from that could be the extra costs of having someone else in the home (extra food shopping costs, etc.).

If you are paying maintenance to your ex-spouse and children and you set up home with someone who already has children, which involves you in additional expenses, this does not mean that your obligations to your former spouse and children cease. If you apply for a variation, the court will take into account your new obligations even though you are not married, but these will normally be expected to take second place to your obligations to the children of your marriage.

Since the Child Support Act 1991 came into force, any assumed obligations to children who are not your own will in some circumstances be overridden by your obligations to pay child support for your natural children (whether born within or outside marriage).

Retirement

In the case of either the recipient's or the payer's retirement, an application should be made to vary the order by the party who is feeling the pinch. Usually, the court will look at the actual needs and resources of the parties and will be concerned to try to share out the more limited finances fairly. There are, however, extra tax allowances available for those over 65 which could help financially.

Variation of a magistrates' court order

Magistrates' court orders also can be varied, either upwards or downwards, where there has been a change in circumstances. Applications will now be dealt with by the FPP of the magistrates' courts.

If the couple subsequently divorces, this will not necessarily bring a magistrates' court order to an end. An order made during the marriage will end automatically only if the divorce court substitutes its own order. If not, the magistrates' court order will continue, and also the right to apply for a variation. The order will cease automatically on the recipient's remarriage or death. If the payer remarries, this does not affect the order but may provide grounds for variation.

In the case of a lump sum, the position is different to that in divorce proceedings: there is apparently no restriction on when and how often a lump sum may be applied for (subject to a £1,000 limit each time).

Registered order

If a divorce court order has been registered in the magistrates' court, an application for a variation has to be made to the FPP. The FPP cannot discharge a divorce court order but it can vary the amount of the order on application. No affidavits are required and the magistrates will not have before them the information and calculations on which the district judge at the divorce court based the original order. So, unless they are provided with full up-to-date information about the parties' finances, they may reduce the order unrealistically. A 1990 survey by the DSS showed that magistrates' courts made, on average, weekly maintenance orders of £15, as opposed to £20 by county courts.

When on income support

Maintenance paid by a husband counts in full as income for income support calculations. Unless the maintenance that the husband could pay is more than the total income support payable, there is little point in a woman seeking an increase in her maintenance because she will still only be topped up to the same 'needs' level by the DSS; if maintenance increases, therefore, income support decreases. Occasional presents to an ex-wife or children are not counted as income, so it might be better for the wife to concentrate on getting these, where possible. However, the first £15 of maintenance will be disregarded in calculating entitlement for family credit, housing benefit and council tax benefit (as long as the claimant is not in receipt of income support). See page 233 for details of the new maintenance credit system.

Registration of a maintenance order in the FPP is useful when the amount of maintenance is equal to or less than the rate of any income support the recipient would be entitled to. When the order is registered, the payments due under the order can be assigned by the former wife to the DSS, which will then pay her the full amount of her income support entitlement, irrespective of whether any payments are made by the ex-husband or not. This saves anxiety and inconvenience if he does not pay up.

Where the amount of the order is greater than the income support entitlement, payments by the DSS will be limited to the amount of income support the woman is entitled to.

Death of a former spouse

When the recipient dies, the payer can immediately stop any maintenance payments. But any outstanding instalments of a lump sum become due to the deceased's estate, and an unfulfilled transfer of property order can be enforced by the estate.

If the person paying maintenance dies first, the maintenance order comes to an end (unless the order was for secured payments). The former spouse may be able to apply to the court under the Inheritance (Provision for Family and Dependants) Act 1975 (as amended by the Law Reform (Succession) Act 1995) for financial provision out of the deceased's estate (unless the court has previously ordered that such a claim shall not be made). An application can also be made by or on behalf of a child. The application must be made within six months of probate being granted – to be safe, make sure the application is lodged as soon as possible.

Other payment on death

Employers' schemes normally provide a lump sum death benefit (of up to four times the member's pay) when the member of the scheme dies before retirement. After the divorce, it is likely that the ex-husband will have changed the name of the person he wishes to receive the money on his death, so that his ex-wife may not benefit. The decision whether to pay any sum to her used ultimately to rest with the trustees for the pension scheme and some schemes prohibit ex-wives from benefiting in any event. Since the Pensions Act 1995 was brought into force, the divorce court can order the husband to nominate the wife as his beneficiary for the lump sum death in service benefit, and the trustees must accept this.

Changes under the Family Law Act 1996

If and when the new Family Law Act is fully implemented, in mirroring provisions to those on children, a married couple will not be able to get a divorce until their financial arrangements for the future have been satisfactorily worked out and are in place. At present, in many cases the decree absolute of divorce can be pronounced months or sometimes even years before finances are settled. If the new Act works as its drafters intended it should, that will no longer be the case. No financial arrangements settled, no divorce.

The ways in which a couple can show that their arrangements have been satisfactorily worked out and are in place are fourfold (under section 9 of the Act):

1 A court order – by consent or otherwise (very similar to the current workings of the law).
2 A negotiated agreement as to financial arrangements. The negotiated agreement means a written agreement between parties as to future arrangements that have been reached as a result of mediation or any other form of negotiation involving a third party, that satisfies such requirements as may be imposed by rules of the court. This is a pretty radical departure as on the face of it it looks as if Memoranda of Understanding, as worked out through mediation for

example, would suffice, without the necessity of getting the court to approve the terms.

3 A declaration by both parties that they have made their financial arrangements. This could potentially be even more radical if the courts do not have to sanction the terms, but it is as yet unclear whether the courts' powers would be so severely curtailed in this way.

4 A declaration by one party (to which no objection has been notified by the other) that: (a) he or she has no significant assets and does not intend to make an application for financial provision; (b) he or she believes the other party has no significant assets and does not intend to make an application for financial provision; and (c) there are therefore no financial arrangements to be made. Concerns are already being expressed that unscrupulous spouses will try to bend this section to serve their own purposes and escape from financial obligations.

In an endeavour to side-step problems that might be raised to hold up a divorce unreasonably, there are a few exemptions from having to fulfil one of the fourfold requirements under section 9, namely where there has been delay, ill health or injury, non-contact and/or domestic violence.

Chapter 11

Pensions and other money matters

Pensions

The issue of the courts' new powers to deal with pensions has already been looked at in the previous chapter. In this chapter the different types of pensions, including state pensions, are examined in a little more detail. *The Which? Guide to Pensions* will give you a fuller picture.

Pensions can broadly be divided into state and private pensions (all non-state pensions, such as occupational and personal pensions in the private and public sector).

State pensions

The state retirement pension consists of two main components – the basic pension and an additional pension paid under the State Earnings-Related Pension Scheme (SERPS) which began in 1978. The rate of the additional pension is based on earnings between the lower and upper earnings limits for National Insurance contributions paid by class 1 (employed earners). At state pension age, earnings are revalued in line with the growth in national average earnings.

The current state pension age for women is 60. However, women will be brought into line with men for a standard retirement age of 65 by the year 2020.

Since SERPS was introduced, employers have been able to contract out (i.e. provide a pension to their employees in place of SERPS), provided certain conditions have been met. Employees must either participate in SERPS or be fully contracted out. If they are contracted out in a defined benefit scheme, the pension payable must not be less than an amount known as the guaranteed minimum pension (GMP). This is roughly the equivalent to the SERPS provision which would have been earned had the employee not been contracted out. For benefits built up from 6 April 1997 onwards, there are no longer GMPs. Instead, the package of benefits from the scheme must, for at least nine members out of ten, be at least as good as the benefits from a 'reference scheme'. The chief problem with SERPS in family law terms is that according to both the previous government and the current Labour one the process involved in working out SERPS entitlements is so complex that it is unlikely that the divorce courts will be given powers to order pension-sharing until at least the year 2000.

The whole area of pensions is indeed very complex and is currently the subject of further review to see how much the burden of financially providing for people in their retirement can be shifted from the state to private individuals – hence the current discussion over 'stakeholder' pensions. We can only cover the basics here – you may well need to get further advice from a solicitor, accountant or financial adviser.

The payment of the basic state retirement pension to a divorced woman depends on her age when she got divorced and on whether it is based on her own or her former husband's National Insurance record (or a combination of both).

A woman divorced when under the state pension age can have her former husband's contribution record added to her own record if that helps her qualify for a retirement pension when the time comes, or gains her a larger pension. She has a choice of formulae to calculate her state retirement pension. Either her former husband's contribution years replace *all* her years up to the time of divorce, or the ex-husband's contribution years replace hers only for the years of the marriage. If, however, she marries again before she reaches the state pension age, she cannot make use of her previous husband's record: she has to rely on her new husband's record or on contributions she had made herself.

The accepted view is that if a woman who is approaching the state pension age can time the decree absolute to follow closely on her reaching that age, she may qualify for a retirement pension immediately, without having to have contributed at all herself. If, however, the decree is made absolute before that birthday, she may have to pay contributions for the intervening period in order to be eligible for a full pension.

A woman divorcing when she is over the state pension age may qualify for a retirement pension immediately after the divorce is made absolute, even if her former husband has not yet retired. If she was already receiving the married woman's lower rate of pension, she may be entitled to have her pension increased to the full rate. The amount of pension she gets depends on the ex-husband's contribution record: it is the amount she would have received had he died on the date of the decree absolute.

If a divorced woman marries again after the state pension age, any pension based on her previous husband's National Insurance contributions will continue to be paid, despite her second marriage. But if her new husband's record would give her a higher pension, that may be used instead.

The Department of Social Security (DSS) has a leaflet which deals with retirement pensions for women who are widowed or divorced, but the rules are complex, so ask for help from your local Benefits Agency.

The Pensions Act 1995 made changes in the way war widows are treated. Since October 1995 a war widow who has remarried and then later divorces (or is bereaved) will be entitled to claim the war widow's pension.

Private pensions

There are a number of different ways in which an employee or a self-employed person may choose to be pensioned. A spouse involved in a divorce may have a complex pension scheme history, and all of it may be relevant to the process of reallocation of pensions: a recent change of job, for example, may mean that there are substantial rights in past schemes but only small ones in the current one. The issue of pensions is too complex to explore at length here, but it is worthwhile knowing about the different types of arrangement available.

Funded tax-approved defined benefit schemes

This heading covers a number of different types of pensions, but the main feature of them is that the employee's pension is calculated according to a formula. The employer promises to pay the formula pension and must ensure that enough funds are in the scheme to meet the promise. The most common type of defined benefit scheme is the 'final pay scheme'. In such a scheme, the employee's pension is equal to his or her pay at or near retirement multiplied by the number of years in the scheme and a fraction (called the 'accrual rate'), which is often one-sixtieth or one-eightieth.

Unfunded public-sector schemes
In such a scheme, as with an unfunded defended benefit scheme, an employee is promised a given pension worked out according to a formula. However, instead of the pension being paid from a fund, it is paid out of whatever resources are available to the employer at the time the pension becomes due. In the UK, only the government and other public-sector bodies offer unfunded schemes. They are able to do this because, if need be, taxes can be raised to meet the bill.

Funded tax-approved defined contribution schemes
There are a number of variations of this type of pension, but broadly the contributions of the member and/or the employer are paid into the member's personal account and credited with interest at a rate depending on the investment return of the pension funds.

Additional voluntary contribution arrangements
A member of a pension scheme can pay at least 15 per cent of his or her salary into a pension scheme, but most members' ordinary contribution rates are less. There is thus scope for employees topping up their contributions voluntarily.

Small self-administered schemes and executive pension plans
Normally there are only a few members of such schemes, typically the owners and share-holding directors of a family company. This type of arrangement, particularly if it has only one or two members, could fall under the *Brooks* type of arrangement (see Chapter 10).

Funded and unfunded unapproved arrangements
For employees a limit is placed every year on the level of earnings which can be pensioned in a tax-approved scheme. If people want to put more into their pensions above this limit, this is termed an 'unapproved arrangement', and they will not get tax relief on their contributions.

Self-employed pensions
A personal pension contract (in technical terms a type of 'tax-

approved defined contribution arrangement') is now the normal vehicle for the self-employed. It has replaced the 'self-employed annuity' (more commonly known as the 'retirement annuity contract') but many of these remain in force.

Pensions – more safeguards?

The Pensions Act 1995 not only changed the law on pensions in divorce, it also introduced a new regime with the aim of making employer pension schemes safer (reducing the likelihood of another Maxwell-type pension fraud occurring) and better run. Pension scheme trustees and managers should have taken the changes on board since April 1997. One of the major changes is that for many there will be a switch from a defined benefit or final salary scheme to a defined contribution type of pension (although in general this will not apply to existing scheme members).

The key issue to remember in pensions on divorce is that a proper valuation needs to take place so that all parties know the figure placed on the value of either or both spouses' pensions. Valuing pensions is not an exact science – pensions experts argue over which basis is best in different cases. Government has laid down that the 'cash equivalent transfer value' or CETV (i.e. what a scheme would pay out to a member if he or she were leaving his or her employment or moving to another pension scheme) is the one to use in divorce. Some experts argue that this undershoots the true value of an occupational pension, particularly where there has been a long marriage, and that a better valuation would be one that is made on the basis that the employee is staying. However, the current position is that in dealing with pensions in divorce, the courts will look at the CETV to work out what the pension is worth. See Chapter 10 for more information about how to value the pension and how the courts deal with pensions on divorce under the new law.

Keeping tabs on an earmarked pension

If a spouse is awarded a share of a pension under an earmarking-type order, it is his or her responsibility – not the scheme's – to keep the scheme administrators up-to-date about changes of address. Ideally the spouse should write annually to the scheme with a note of his or her address. If the scheme's administrators cannot find the spouse, they can pay the earmarked share of the order to the member him- or herself.

Pensions mis-selling – the impact on divorce

If a spouse transferred pension funds out of a safe occupational scheme (for example) and into a personal pension scheme as a result of being 'mis-sold' a personal pension – i.e. not knowing that he or she was likely to lose out financially – what can be done? Since the Securities and Investment Board began a comprehensive review of the problem, some pension scheme members will already have been contacted, and may, if they are one of the lucky ones, even have received compensation. Other victims of the problem are, however, still waiting to learn what action will be taken, with a considerable number of pension companies dragging their feet. In September 1997, figures from the Personal Investments Authority showed that up until then the pensions industry had offered around £452 million of compensation to around 73,000 victims of mis-selling, averaging £6,000 per case. The number of priority cases overall has been estimated at 600,000. The government has, however, indicated that it thinks a further 1.5 million people may also have been mis-sold a personal pension.

The new government is continuing to put the heat on insurance companies that have failed to cough up. It is (conservatively) estimated that over £4 billion compensation should be paid to pension scheme holders who lost out in the mis-selling scandal. If compensation has been or is to be paid then this ought also to be considered at part of the matrimonial assests.

Since 1 January 1997, in place of or as well as compensation, people who were wrongly advised to take out a personal pension ought to be able to be reinstated in the occupational pension under the tax regime that originally applied to them. The government announced in November 1997 that this reinstatement should be extended to health service staff who were mis-sold pension plans (an estimated 42,000 in number) who will now be allowed to rejoin the NHS scheme.

Where compensation is received, it should not now be taxable. Lump sum compensation for losses incurred in mis-selling (but not annuities or other annual payments) should be exempt from both income tax and Capital Gains Tax, provided that it covers financial loss suffered by a person who took out a plan as a result of poor advice given between 29 April 1988 and 30 June 1994 (when new regulatory safeguards took effect). The compensation must either be paid into a tax-approved occupational pension scheme or a personal pension scheme, or paid in cash under a court award or out-of-court settlement.

Marriage contracts

The term 'marriage contracts' actually covers two different types of agreement – pre-nuptial agreements, made before a couple marry; and contracts made during marriage, which can include arrangements for division of the property on separation or divorce.

A primary purpose behind both types is to clarify who will get what in the event of marriage breakdown (whether by separation, death or divorce), often by side-stepping or trying to override the courts' powers. The formats can be flexible enough to cover agreements about other areas of concern for a couple (for example, the time they want to start trying to conceive a baby).

The Family Law Committee of the Law Society (which is broadly in favour of marriage contracts) recommends that areas covered should include:

- ownership of income and assets acquired before the marriage and the possibility of making claims against that property whether on death or divorce
- ownership of income or assets acquired in contemplation of or since the marriage
- the form of ownership of assets – as joint tenants or as tenants in common (and if the latter in what proportions)
- the exclusion, if required, of assets below a certain value
- treatment of gifts or inheritance
- ownership of items of personal use, such as jewellery
- liability for tax and debts
- provisions relating to duration, variation, review
- which country's law will govern the agreement
- liabilities for costs and expenses in relation to drawing up the agreement and any ancillary documentation
- methods of resolution of disputes arising from the document
- any other issues of importance to the individual couple.

(Extracted from *Maintenance on Capital Provision on Divorce: Recommendations for Reform of the Law and Procedure made by the Family Law Committee*, May 1991.)

In fact, despite their media popularity, marriage contracts (and even cohabitation contracts) are fairly rare: they tend to be entered into more often by the super-rich. It is doubtful whether a contract will actually achieve a couple's aim of circumventing the courts, especially, say, if one separating spouse later chooses to try to challenge a contract's validity. English courts are resistant to the notion that their powers can be overridden. The following case, sometimes cited in support of the effectiveness of marriage contracts, certainly does not give a surefire answer.

Example   A husband and wife had, as is usual in Brazil, entered into a marriage contract. Could the wife subsequently obtain a divorce and claim for financial relief in England? Held: yes, she could claim. The marriage contract would be included as one of the factors which the court would consider in accordance with section 25 of the Matrimonial Causes Act 1973. (*Sabbagh v Sabbagh*, 1975)

Although this case related to a Brazilian marriage, it still has persuasive effect in the courts here. However, all it really says is that a divorce court is likely to look at the terms of any marriage contract but may not necessarily feel itself bound by them. In subsequent cases, the courts have noted the existence of marriage contracts, but have often by and large ignored them, and have certainly not wished to be bound conclusively by them. In essence a marriage contract will be one of the factors considered by the court but will rarely be the decisive one. If a marriage contract is proved to have been entered into because of fraud, duress or without each party having properly received legal advice, it is unlikely to be worth the paper it is written on.

School fees

If your children are privately educated, the cost of funding their school fees adds to the overall juggling of finances on divorce. You may find that you can no longer afford to pay for private education and that the children will need to be moved to local state schools. Finding a new house in a catchment area for a good local state school may need to be a priority.

If, however, you want to keep your child at private school, it may be worth enquiring about the Assisted Places Scheme. If your total annual income is below £9,873 it may be possible to claim the full cost of the school fees if the school takes part in the scheme. Above that earnings level, there is a sliding scale up to £25,000, beyond which no assistance is available.

If you want to enquire about making provision by way of policies or investment schemes to fund the future cost of schooling, consider contacting an experienced broker. Alternatively you may find a local accountant who has experience of recommending tax-efficient funding schemes for parents (or even grandparents) to provide capital or income.

Other matters to consider

During the course of divorce proceedings, or once these are finally over, you need to consider protecting your overall financial position in the areas of insurance and wills.

Life insurance

Because maintenance payments will cease when the payer dies, it may be advisable, on divorce, for the spouse who is going to be dependent on payments from the other to take out a life insurance policy on the payer's life.

You have to have an insurable interest in the life of anybody on whose life you wish to take out an insurance. An individual has an unlimited insurable interest in his or her own life and also in the life of his or her spouse, and can insure it for any amount he or she chooses. Apart from yourself and your spouse, you have an insurable interest in somebody only if his or her death would cause you financial loss. You can insure for the amount of money you would lose if he or she dies to provide for your future upkeep. This would apply to an ex-spouse who is receiving maintenance or an earmarked share of pension payments.

The parent who is not looking after the children may want to take out an insurance policy on the life of the parent who is, so that if that parent were to die while the children were still dependent, some money would become available towards the extra cost to the other parent of taking on responsibility for the children.

The policy can be a whole life policy whereby the sum assured is paid out on the death of the insured person. Alternatively, it can be a 'term' insurance which pays out a set sum on death within so many years, taken out for the period of likely dependence. Premiums for term policies are generally lower than for other types of insurance. There are some term insurance policies, called 'family income benefit' policies, where instead of one lump sum on the insured person's death, regular sums are paid (say, every quarter) for the balance of the insured period.

Endowment policies

Endowment policies are insurance policies with a surrender value, usually used as security for paying off a mortgage. Such policies usually provide for the payment of a fixed sum on death to clear the mortgage and for a minimum sum, plus bonuses, to be paid to the policy-holder at the end of the term. Such policies can often be surrendered, but their surrender value is tiny in comparison with the amount payable once the policy matures, and typically amounts to only the monthly sums paid in, less administration costs, and occasionally a bit extra.

The most sensible financial action is to hold on to your endowment policy after divorce until it matures – the cost of taking out a loan for the equivalent of the surrender value will often be cheaper than losing the benefits of the policy. If you really cannot afford to keep it on, enquire about selling the policy via a broker who will auction the policy (if it has about ten years or fewer still to run) and thus raise extra funds, typically adding approximately 50 to 70 per cent to the basic surrender value.

National Insurance

Divorce does not affect a man's National Insurance contribution position. Nor does it affect that of a woman who is paying self-employed (class 2 and class 4) contributions or the standard rate of employed (class 1) contributions at the time. After divorce, each continues to pay as before.

It is not so straightforward for an employed woman who, before the divorce, had been paying the class 1 contributions at the married woman's reduced rate: she is treated as a single person from the date on which the decree is made absolute and therefore becomes liable to pay the full class 1 rate. She should get from her employer a 'certificate of reduced liability' or 'certificate of election' to send back to her local Benefits Agency. The full class 1 contributions will be deducted from her wages from then on.

Anyone whose earnings are below a specified minimum (£62 a week for the 1997/98 tax year), or anyone who is not earning at all, does not have to pay National Insurance contributions, but can pay class 3 contributions voluntarily; these give a woman the right to claim retirement pension. The DSS produces a leaflet which gives information about making voluntary contributions.

A woman over the age of 60 does not have to pay National Insurance contributions.

There are various free DSS leaflets explaining the position about contributions and benefits in specific circumstances. If you are at all unsure of your position, get advice from your local Benefits Agency in writing (and keep it safe), or a Citizens Advice Bureau may be able to help to clear up any queries. Detailed information about contributory benefits under the National Insurance scheme is given in the *Rights Guide to Non-Means-Tested Benefits*, produced by the Child Poverty Action Group.*

Other insurance

You should check that your insurance cover is adequate for the change in your personal circumstances. When your finances are tight, it is tempting to stop paying premiums in order to reduce outgoings. However, this may be a short-term benefit and a long-term loss.

Buildings insurance is insurance against the destruction or damage of your privately owned freehold property. If you have a mortgage on your home, buildings insurance will usually have been arranged by your mortgagee. If you own a leasehold property, your landlord will normally have arranged the insurance, but you pay the proportional cost for your property by means of a service charge.

Contents insurance, which protects against the loss of, theft of, or damage to your belongings, may need to be adjusted after divorce if now you own much more (or much less) of household goods and other property than before.

Car insurance, either 'third party, fire and theft' (the statutory minimum) or 'comprehensive' (providing you with full cover in the event of an accident, however it is caused), may have to be transferred from one spouse to the other, depending on who now has the family car.

Wills

Wills will need reviewing on divorce to ensure that they cover your new circumstances (if you have not already made a will, now is the time to do so). Check whether your will is a 'mutual will' – in which case you need to change it fast. A mutual will is a legal term used to describe wills made by a husband and wife which complement each other and which are made on the basis that the first spouse to die binds the second spouse to make a will in the original agreed format – no changes will be allowed. Mutual wills are rare – they are not the same as the more common 'mirror wills', whereby both spouses agree to make similar wills, which can be changed whenever a spouse wants. If a mutual will is to be changed, it must be changed before the other spouse's death.

When making a will, remember that if you own any foreign property you may need to take specialist advice about the effect of an English will on the foreign property – and you may even need to make a will abroad. If you own property in Spain, for example, you will have only limited freedom in deciding who your estate should go to. A spouse and children have priority rights which, if not reflected in the will, open up the way for a challenge to the will. Spanish law will recognise an English will, although if it is not drawn up in terms acceptable under Spanish law, you could still have a legal headache. It is best, therefore, to check the local law.

A will made by either a husband or a wife is not automatically revoked on divorce (or even an annulment of the marriage), but is interpreted as if the ex-spouse had died on the date of the divorce (or annulment). So if the ex-spouse was named as an executor, that appointment will be ineffective, and the same applies to an appointment of an ex-spouse as guardian of the children – unless there is any contrary intention expressed in the will.

The gift in a will of any property to an ex-spouse will fail as well.

As long as the will states that some other person should have the 'residue' – what is left after the payment of debts and expenses, and all the gifts – that person, known in legal jargon as the 'residuary beneficiary', will receive the ex-spouse's gift as well. If it was the ex-spouse who was the residuary beneficiary and there was no substitute beneficiary, the rest of the estate will be dealt with according to the intestacy rules – rules which apply to the sharing out of the estate of someone who died without making a will.

If there is no will and a divorced person's estate has to be dealt with under the intestacy rules, the former husband or wife will not be taken into account in the distribution of the estate. But any children remain eligible for their share of an inheritance.

Similarly, once all of the Family Law Act 1996 is brought into force, if a divorce order has been made, the former spouse will not be entitled to any of the estate under the intestacy provisions (although he or she may still be able to make a claim against the estate unless his or her right to do so had been dismissed by the court). If a separation order is in force, the surviving separated spouse will be treated as having died before his or her deceased spouse, and so will be entitled to nothing unless he or she makes a claim.

Green form advice for making a will is now limited. You can now ask for advice under the green form scheme for preparing your will (subject to financial eligibility) only if you are aged 70 or over, or are disabled, for example if you are blind or deaf, or if you have a child who is similarly disabled). A single parent looking after a child and who wants to appoint a guardian for the child to act after death is also eligible. But you no longer need to appoint a guardian for your child after your death via a will as this can be done by deed or in writing. Make sure you check first with the person you wish to act as a guardian that he or she is willing to take on this important responsibility.

Chapter 12

Domestic violence

Domestic violence most commonly occurs within the confines of the home, behind closed doors, with no outsider witnessing the event. That is not to say that it is rare. A campaign to challenge the acceptance of violence against women, Zero Tolerance (launched in February 1994), reported that domestic violence accounts for one in four of all reported crimes. Domestic violence cuts across all classes of society. It is more likely to occur where a pattern of violence has already been formed, in the relationship between the man and the woman, or even have its roots in the childhood of either one. Frequently, violence is linked to substance abuse of some kind, whether of alcohol or drugs. The crisis of a separation or divorce can, in a few cases, be itself sufficient to spark off an incident of violence. In the great majority of cases, violence is inflicted by men upon women, so the violent partner is here referred to as 'he' and the victim as 'she'.

If you are the subject of violence, you need to take steps quickly to protect yourself. If you are behaving violently towards your partner, you too need to take fast preventive action, for example by leaving the home or seeking help by, for example, contacting Alcoholics Anonymous.*

You can get legal advice about domestic violence matters under the green form scheme, if you are financially eligible. Legal aid is available (again subject to financial eligibility) for applications for an injunction (see below), and emergency certificates can be issued on the same day in extreme cases. (If you go to a solicitors' firm which has a legal franchise then they can make the decision as to whether an emergency certificate should be granted there and then.) In 1996 the Legal Aid Board* issued guidance that emergency legal aid would be granted only if the applicant 'is in imminent danger of significant harm'. If you are not eligible for legal aid, the cost of obtaining an injunction is likely to be some hundreds of pounds.

Contacting the police

In the past the police gained a reputation for failing to treat seriously incidents of domestic violence. The attitude is now changing. In London the Metropolitan Police have instructions to investigate and record every incident of domestic violence (which can provide useful corroborative evidence later in any proceedings). Some police authorities now have specific initiatives for tackling domestic violence, such as the Thames Valley Police, which not only monitors all domestic violence cases but offers help and support to victims too. It is wise to contact the police if violence is threatened. They can lower the heat of the situation by talking separately to each partner, or in certain circumstances by removing the threatening spouse from the home. If an assault has actually occurred, the police should consider whether criminal charges should be brought. Since June 1997, criminal prosecutions can also be taken to stop stalkers from harassing their victims (see page 276). Some police forces have a policy that if a crime has been committed, for example assault, they will prosecute. In other areas, prosecutions ensue only if the victim is prepared to give evidence. Studies abroad have shown that levels of violence can drop if police take a consistently strong line.

Leaving the home

In principle, and generally, it is tactically better to remain in the matrimonial home until either an agreement is reached or court proceedings have been finalised. But in an extreme emergency you may have no choice but to leave home.

If your physical and mental welfare are severely threatened, it may be safer to leave the home for a temporary period – but get legal advice as soon as possible about your rights in the situation. Take your children with you if at all possible. You may want to contact Women's Aid* for advice.

Finding somewhere to stay

As long as you have not made yourself 'intentionally homeless', your local authority is under an obligation to provide accommodation for you if you have priority needs (for example, you have young children living with you), and have nowhere else to stay. Contact – by telephone, or in person if you can – the housing department of your local authority or the social services department. The accommodation they are most likely to offer will be basic bed and breakfast.

There are a number of women's refuges across England and Wales which provide a roof to sleep under for female victims of domestic violence and their children. Women's Aid can advise you about where to go. The contact numbers for refuges are closely guarded to try to ensure that victims of violence in refuges and their families are not harassed further by their violent partners or ex-partners.

Changing the locks

If you jointly own or rent the home with your partner, you have no instant right to lock him out. Until divorce proceedings have been concluded, both spouses have a legal right to continue to occupy the matrimonial home. If you do change the locks, your partner may be able to get a court order restoring him to the home. If your partner has been extremely violent, you can apply to the court for an injunction to force him out of the house. After he has been ordered to leave, you will be in a position legally to change the locks.

Children and violence

In some cases where a spouse is behaving violently towards his partner, the children suffer violence as well. It is extremely important for you to protect your children's interests if they are being physically attacked by your spouse. If you have to leave home, take them with you if at all possible. However, if you have to leave them, get immediate legal advice on what action to take to get them back with you. Some solicitors in different areas have joined together to run a domestic violence hot-line to ensure that a victim of violence can get immediate access to a solicitor who specialises in dealing with these cases. The police or your local Citizens Advice Bureau should be able to give you more information.

Domestic violence and injunctions

The whole law covering domestic violence has changed since 1 October 1997 when a part of the new Family Law Act 1996, Part IV, was brought into force. This new law means that lots of confusing old laws have been scrapped and in their place one single statute, the Family Law Act, is now in force which covers all applications in all courts for domestic violence injunctions. The new law has opened up the categories of people who can apply to court for an injunction to protect them from domestic violence, so that cohabitants and ex-cohabitants, other family members and even people who have lived closely together in the same household can seek the courts' protection. As this book is written for people who are or were married, advice in this chapter will primarily be designed to cater for their needs.

There are now basically two types of court order which can be obtained, both of which are often termed 'injunction'. An injunction is an order by the court telling someone what he or she must or must not do; the penalty for disobedience can be imprisonment. The two types are:

- a non–molestation order
- an occupation order.

A non–molestation order orders the spouse not to assault, molest or otherwise interfere with you. Non–molestation orders can also be obtained for the protection of children. Molestation can include pestering, such as repeated telephone calls, or other forms of harassment.

An occupation order can require a violent spouse to leave the home and/or not come within a specified area around it (for example, 100 yards around the home). An occupation order can also allow a spouse back into the home if she has left it out of fear of violence and can require the violent spouse to let her back in (and possibly require him to leave too). Occasionally, the court may make an order confining one spouse to a defined part of the home, but this is rarely practicable.

When making an order, the courts have to weigh up the balance of harm as between the victim (and children if they are affected too) and the violent partner before deciding whether or not to make an occupation order. In some cases this will mean that the court will want to see whether the violent partner will have accommodation to go to if he is ousted from the family home.

Which court?

Before the new law came in, it had been thought that the government would restrict access to the courts for domestic violence injunctions to the family proceedings courts, but so far this has not been the case. All courts can make the orders: it will be up to you (after getting advice from your solicitor) to decide which. If you have already started off divorce proceedings, it is likely to be the court which is dealing with your divorce case which you will apply to – otherwise the local county court or possibly the family proceedings court.

If you are financially eligible and want to make an application in the county court or divorce court, you should apply for full legal aid. If your solicitors' firm has got a legal aid franchise, they should be able to make a decision as to whether an emergency application should be granted there and then. If it is not an extreme emergency, there may be a few days' wait before the decision is made. Sometimes you will need to comply with a requirement from the Legal Aid Board, that a letter should be sent to the violent partner asking him to stop harassing the victim, before court proceedings are taken.

Obtaining an injunction to protect the children

In the rarer cases where it is the children, rather than a spouse, who are at risk, the courts can make an order stopping contact between the violent (or abusive) adult and the children. This can be done either under the courts' inherent jurisdiction or by an order under the Children Act 1989. Since Part IV of the Family Law Act has been in force, social services departments can also take action under an emergency protection order or an interim care order and can seek an occupation order to oust an abuser (say a stepparent) from the family home.

Ex parte or on notice?

In the case of a real emergency, it is possible to apply for an injunction 'ex parte', which means that the other spouse is not told of the hearing before it takes place. Courts are more ready to listen to an ex parte application and grant an injunction if the application is for a non-molestation order. For occupation orders, the situation needs to be fairly desperate before a court will order a spouse out of the home without giving him the opportunity of presenting his case to the court. If an order is obtained ex parte, this will usually be limited to a temporary period (of a week), and the respondent (the person against whom the order is obtained) has to be told of the resumed hearing, which may be as early as one week later although it could be anything up to two months later, and be given the opportunity to put his case before the court. By this time, having received the papers from the court, he will have had the chance of obtaining legal advice.

In all other cases when an injunction is applied for, this application will be 'on notice', that is the respondent will be told in advance of the hearing date. The application with accompanying papers must be served on the respondent at least two clear working days before the hearing date.

The documents that must be filed at court to start off the application are:

- an application, in duplicate, together with the court fee of £30
- a sworn statement in support, giving particulars of any children, of the accommodation and alternative accommodation available to each party, and of the conduct complained of and why an injunction is necessary.

In turn, the respondent should produce a sworn statement dealing with the allegations and can suggest solutions, such as alternative accommodation, or explain the possibility of remaining in the same house.

Women who have been injured, or even just bruised, should go and see their doctor or the casualty department of the local hospital and make sure that a physical examination is carried out and the injuries noted on medical records. Such records can provide useful evidence in court proceedings. Indeed, a solicitor may ask the doctor concerned to prepare a report, for which a fee of about £40 will be charged. If anyone other than the two parties involved has witnessed the violence, that person should be asked if he or she would be willing to come forward to attend court, if need be, as a witness.

An application 'on notice' for an injunction is usually heard very quickly – normally within a few days. In ex parte proceedings, the application may be heard on the same day as long as there is sufficient time to file a sworn statement. Before making an occupation order, the judge or court will want to be satisfied both that the circumstances warrant such an order and that there is no satisfactory alternative in the light of the spouse's conduct, the children's needs and the available accommodation. In one case in 1993, an ouster order (the old equivalent of an occupation order) was granted because of very serious dissension caused by the husband's 'jealous, argumentative and unyielding nature': the wife found it impossible to live with him.

However, this case is very rare: usually the courts require evidence of fairly severe physical violence before an occupation order will be granted. An occupation order is seen as a 'draconian remedy'.

Injunctions can be limited to a specific period, for example three months, or in more severe cases they may have no time limit. If the parties are reconciled and resume cohabitation, the injunction can lapse.

Power of arrest

Where the court makes an occupation order or a non-molestation order and where the respondent (the violent partner) has 'used or threatened violence against the applicant or a relevant child' then the courts will nowadays attach a power of arrest to the order (unless the court is satisfied that the victim will be adequately protected without such a power of arrest). A power of arrest means that if, once the offending spouse has been served with the order, he breaches it, the police can be called to arrest the offender straight away without a warrant and take him before a magistrate. If a power of arrest is given, the applicant must take a copy of the order to the local police station straight after the court hearing, to put the police on notice. At the time when the power of arrest lapses, the police must also be notified.

A power of arrest normally lasts for a fixed period of three months. Under the new law it can last for the same length of time or a shorter period than the order itself. It is in practice the most effective preventive action that can be taken to curb future violent attacks. If, after violence has been threatened, the violent partner offers to give an undertaking at court not to be violent in the future, the court is likely to have to consider whether it is satisfied that the applicant (and/or relevant children) will be adequately protected – it looks as if the court cannot just accept an undertaking at face value. In any event, as a power of arrest cannot be attached to the undertaking, a victim should think carefully before accepting an undertaking rather than asking the court for a formal court injunction.

In the past, courts frequently accepted undertakings when offered, but when the new law was first introduced, many courts indicated that they would be likely to feel bound to make a preliminary legal finding as to whether or not violence or threats actually happened before accepting undertakings. This may mean in practice that the courts' time in dealing with domestic violence injunctions may have to rise significantly. One spectre which was raised by the changes under the new law was a potentially massive increase in the number of domestic violence cases that would have to have full hearings in court – thereby clogging up the court system to possibly unworkable proportions. This potential obstacle may have been overcome as the courts have become more familiar with the new systems and in any event this is not your problem but the courts' problem. Ask your solicitor for more advice if you need it.

A note of warning

Injunction proceedings should be considered carefully before being commenced.

Bear in mind the consequences of seeking and obtaining an occupation order in terms of your future relationship. If that is the way your divorce proceedings begin, the prospect of negotiating reasonably and reaching a sensible agreement recedes dramatically. If, however, you have no alternative, you must take the best steps to protect your and your family's safety.

What to do if you have been served with an injunction

If you know that you are at risk of being violent towards your spouse, whether because you have been violent in the past or because you feel the tension in the house is becoming unbearable, you need to take steps to minimise the risk. Take responsible action, such as leaving the house for a cooling-off period.

If you are served with an injunction or injunction application, read it carefully, together with any other documents given to you, for example the sworn statement. See a solicitor as soon as possible and make an appointment with him or her as much in advance of the hearing date as you can. If you are financially eligible, you can get advice under the green form scheme.

A few solicitors will not act for violent men, so check this in advance. The solicitor will take a statement from you and make this into a sworn statement to be lodged at the court. As an alternative to having an order made against you, you can offer the court an undertaking not to molest your partner. Breaking the terms of an undertaking can invoke just as serious a penalty as breaking the terms of a court order.

Unless you have real grounds to contest your partner's claim for a non-molestation order, you are unlikely to be able to obtain legal aid to be represented in court, even if you would otherwise qualify on financial grounds.

Stalking – new court powers

Sometimes the stresses of separation and divorce can surface in obsessional behaviour from an ex-spouse or others and stalking can be the result. Another new Act, the Protection from Harassment Act 1997, which creates a new criminal offence of what is effectively stalking, was brought in to the law in June 1997, and gives courts extra powers for serious persistent harassment. Although stalking is not defined in the Act, it is well known as having come to mean open or unmistakable harassment, of which the victim is aware. The new law says that:

> A person must not pursue a course of conduct
> (a) which amounts to harassment of another; and
> (b) which he knows or ought to know amounts to harassment of the other.

There are two criminal offences created by the new Act (see box). The police can now take action to stop stalking – several cases have been brought against ex-partners, including against a 78-year-old man who stalked his ex-partner and her new lover and against a woman who bombarded her former lower with up to four abusive letters a days after he ended their relationship; she moved to a home two doors away from him and broke into his home wielding two carving knives. They can arrest someone who is stalking a victim. When the case comes to court, prison sentences can be ordered in very severe cases and the courts usually will order the stalker to cease having any contact whatsoever with the victim.

Stalking has also become, in lawyers' terms, a 'statutory civil tort',

---

The new law creates two specific criminal offences:
- **the lesser:** causing harassment or distress (sections 1 and 2). A summary-only offence to be dealt with by the magistrates' court
- **the greater:** putting the victim in fear of violence (section 4). This is 'indictable' which means it is likely to be heard in the Crown Court

---

which means that a victim can claim money damages to compensate her (or him) for having been stalked, as long as a claim is made within six years of the conduct taking place. To try to avoid too much over-sophisticated legal argument about what the stalker intended, the new law says that these criminal offences are strict liability – i.e. that the victim's lawyer does not have to prove that the stalker himself or herself had criminal intent. The only defences are (a) prevention of crime; (b) legal authority (for example where bailiffs have to enforce a judgement) or (c) that in the particular circumstances the conduct was reasonable.

Chapter 13

Child abduction

Child abduction is one of the most fraught areas of separation and divorce. Reunite* (the National Council for Abducted Children), estimated in 1996 that about 1,000 children are abducted from the UK each year. Statistically this means that abduction happens only rarely, but when it does it tears the family apart as one parent faces the prospect of never seeing his or her child again.

Prevention is by far the most effective form of action. Many countries (including the UK) are signatories to the Hague Convention, under which they undertake to enforce other countries' custody orders about children (this will apply to residence orders under the Children Act 1989, too) and to return any abducted child to the country he or she was snatched from. However, many other countries have failed to sign the Convention, so in them it provides no recourse. Even if a child has been taken to one of the signatory states, the procedures for enforcement are at best time-consuming and at worst unsuccessful. In 1996 the Lord Chancellor's Department took the unusual step of naming the countries which were the worst offenders for harbouring children snatched by a parent – Germany came out worst (of the 17 cases in 1995 of children abducted from the UK and taken to Germany, none was handed over as a result of the legal process, although four were handed over voluntarily) and the USA, Greece and Spain also came out poorly.

There are two areas of law which have a bearing on child abduction. The first is the criminal law: the Child Abduction Act 1984 made kidnapping a child a crime. Under that Act, a parent who takes a child out of the country without the prior written consent of the other, or permission of the court, may be committing a criminal offence.

Second, there are civil laws which prevent children from being abducted, but the position now is different from that before the Children Act 1989 was brought into force on 14 October 1991. Thus it is important to see when (and if) a court order was made over the children.

Before 14 October 1991

Whenever there were children in families in divorce proceedings, the court made an order not only for custody and care and control, but also that the children should not be taken out of the country without the consent of the other parent or the court. If such an order has been made, it will remain effective and enforceable after 14 October 1991.

After 14 October 1991

After that date, in the majority of divorces involving children, no court orders will be made, so there will usually be no civil order stopping the other parent from removing the child abroad. (An abducting parent may, however, still be committing a criminal offence under the Child Abduction Act.) If a residence order is made, it prevents the other parent from removing the child without consent, but the parent in whose favour it was made is allowed to take the child abroad for periods of up to one month at a time.

The purpose behind these changes was to emphasise that it is the parents' responsibility to agree on arrangements for the children wherever possible and to allow the parent with whom the child lives to take him or her abroad for a holiday. Obviously, if there are real grounds for suspecting that the other parent intends to take the child abroad permanently and not just for a holiday, then the circumstances are different and court action can and should be taken fast.

Worries about abduction

If you have fears that your child may be abducted by the other parent (if, for example, the other parent is a foreign national and there are grounds for believing that he or she plans to return to his or her home country with the child), you could ask the court to make a prohibited steps order to state that the other parent cannot take the child abroad without your prior consent or the court's permission. Alternatively, it might be in the child's best interests for a residence order to be made either on decree nisi or later on: this will automatically include an order that the child may not be removed abroad without the consent of the other parent or the court. Talk to your solicitor about the best course of action.

If your child has been or could be abducted

If you believe that your child is about to be abducted by the other parent you need to take action fast. The need for immediacy cannot be overemphasised: as Reunite points out, 'the longer a dispute goes on, the more difficult it becomes to repatriate a child'.

Contact your solicitor immediately. He or she can act to obtain an emergency court order preventing the child from being taken abroad, either via a residence order and/or a prohibited steps order, or by using the old remedy of making a child a ward of court (whereby the court becomes in law the parent of the child and no step affecting the child can be taken without the court's consent). The courts can make such orders even outside court hours: a duty judge should always be available. The order should be served on the potential abductor if his or her whereabouts are known.

Emergency legal aid and advice under the green form are available, subject to financial eligibility.

In addition to taking legal action, either you or your solicitor should contact the police and ask for a port alert to be carried out. Under this, if there is a real and imminent danger of the child being abducted ('real and imminent' means within the next 24 hours), the police are obliged to notify all airports and seaports of the danger of the child being taken out of the country.

In practice, it is often difficult for officials to recognise and intercept children at ports where there is heavy traffic, and the effectiveness of this action has been lessened since the reduction or near-disappearance of border controls between European Union countries since 1993. To maximise the usefulness of a port alert, provide as many details as you can of the potential abductor and the child, such as full names, addresses and dates of birth, personal descriptions, photographs, and (best of all) details of the flight or sailing if you have them.

Once your child has been abducted and taken abroad, your remedies are fewer and harder to enforce, but you should still not give up hope. If the child has been taken to a country which is a signatory of the Hague Convention, you should be able to get the appropriate authority to act to get the child returned to you. Even if the child has been taken elsewhere, it may be possible to ask the court in England

and Wales to sequester (i.e. take away) the abducting parent's property if he or she has broken a court order. This can act as a lever to force the abducting parent to return the child (as in the 1993 Peter Malkin case). Ask your solicitor for more information.

Support for parents and families

For support and information for parents and families about child abduction, contact the parents' self-help group, Reunite.

A free booklet called *Child abduction* is available from the Child Abduction Unit.★

Chapter 14

Stepfamilies

Stepfathers and stepmothers often occupy a distinctive place within a new family, having taken on the burdens (and joys) of an actual parent but without being recognised by the law as such. However, the greater flexibility of the courts' new powers under section 8 of the Children Act 1989 can be helpful for stepfamilies.

Stepfamilies and children

Stepparents do not automatically have parental responsibility during a marriage (nor after divorce) for their stepchildren (for a further explanation of 'parental responsibility' see Chapter 8). Parental responsibility belongs automatically to both the natural father and mother of a child (if the parents were married at the time of the birth or later married each other) or to the mother alone if the parents were unmarried.

An unmarried father can acquire parental responsibility either by making a special formal Parental Responsibility Agreement with the mother and registering it at court or by successfully applying to court for a parental responsibility order or a residence order. If a residence order is granted to an unmarried father of a child, the court will also automatically order him to have parental responsibility too, under section 4 of the Children Act.

Stepparents cannot apply to the courts for a parental responsibility order on its own, although they can apply for a residence order (see below). A natural parent cannot agree to share parental responsibility with a stepparent by making a formal agreement. The only way that a stepparent can acquire parental responsibility is by successful application for a residence order (or by being appointed a guardian). So stepparents cannot in law make decisions about a stepchild's upbringing themselves, although they will usually be involved in decision-making via their partner.

To change this and to become recognised by the law as having the role of a parent, stepparents can apply for a residence order under section 8 of the Children Act jointly with their new partner if the children are living with them. This indirectly gives them parental responsibility and puts them on an equal footing with anyone else who has parental responsibility – usually the parents. In this case the stepparents' parental responsibility lasts only as long as the residence order lasts, rather than until the child reaches 18.

As long as the stepparent is married to the parent of the child, he or she will not need the court's permission to make an application for an order under the Children Act for residence or contact. Other people who can apply to the court as of right are those:

- with whom the child has lived for at least three years, *or*
- who have the permission of everyone who has a residence order in their favour, *or*
- who have the consent of everyone with parental responsibility for the child, *or*
- if the child is in care, who have the consent of the local authority.

Anyone else can apply too, but the court will first have to give its permission before giving the application the go-ahead. The factors the court then considers are the type of application being made, the connection between the applicant and the child, and any risk the application might have of harmfully disrupting the child's life.

When the court considers an application for a residence order, it will have to consider whether making an order is better for the child than making no order at all. Very often this 'no-order' principle means that in practice a court is reluctant to make a residence order. The court's first and paramount consideration is the welfare of the child (see Chapter 8 for a more detailed explanation of the welfare principle). The court may grant such an application in the joint favour of the parent and a concerned and involved stepparent, particularly if more certainty would benefit the new family (in particular the child) and if the absent natural parent takes little or no interest in the child. The court would want to be satisfied that the new family arrangement is stable.

Another option would be for the stepparent to apply jointly with his or her new spouse (i.e. the child's natural mother or father) for an adoption order. However, again the courts are not keen to grant this as they are unwilling to terminate all links with natural parents, which an adoption order necessarily does.

Stepfamilies and money

One situation which can generate considerable strain and even resentment for a new stepparent is the possibility of his or her partner's former spouse 'getting their hands on' the new couple's assets. Second wives or husbands can find it especially galling to feel that their own paypackets are being used to fund maintenance payments for their new partner's former spouse and family.

Since 1995 the formula used by the Child Support Agency (CSA)★ to calculate the amount that a parent or stepparent should pay as child support has taken into account the full housing costs for the second family but ignores debts and extra costs like childcare. However, low earners should find themselves and their second families being cushioned from the harsher effects of the formula by the protected income formulae. First there is a 'cap' of 30 per cent of the absent parent's net income, which ensures that he (or she) has to pay no more than this. Second, a further calculation is made, designed to ensure that an absent parent's income does not sink below income support rates. The CSA will need to know the amount of a new partner's income to work out the level of protected income (see Chapter 5).

The courts, on the other hand, will not approach the question of dividing up the family's assets by seeking to get their hands on the new partner's money. They will not formally take the individual income and assets of a new partner into account, but will look at them to the extent that the new partner's income and property increase the ex-spouse's ability to meet any financial order that may be made against him or her. So, if a man remarries and moves into his new wife's home, the bills for which are met out of her own earnings, the court will take into account the fact that his housing needs have been met without any great outlay, so he can possibly afford to make greater maintenance payments to an ex-wife. Conversely, if an ex-husband has to take on extra financial resposibility for a new family, the courts will also take that into account as limiting his ability to pay.

A new partner can refuse to disclose details of his or her income and assets. If the court feels that a new partner's means are relevant in the financial part of a divorce case, a 'production appointment' can be arranged. At this the spouse who wants information about the new partner's means can ask for some limited disclosure of financial evidence. The court will not necessarily need to know what a new partner earns, but will want to know the extent to which she or he relieves the ex-spouse from having to provide for living accommodation, for example. Usually a summary of the new partner's financial position will do.

The courts draw a distinction between a woman cohabiting and remarrying. On remarriage, her former husband's financial obligations to maintain her (although not the children) end. However, if she chooses to live with a new partner, although the ex-husband can apply for a reduction in her maintenance payments if her financial position has improved, the court will not transfer the ex-husband's duty to maintain her to her new live-in partner.

As a general rule, it is best to try to conclude arguments over money before remarriage (or even before permanent cohabitation) to ensure that problems of the earlier marriage do not become enmeshed in the creation of a new family relationship.

When the parent/partner dies

On the death of his or her partner, the stepparent has no automatic rights vis-à-vis the stepchildren. If the natural parents were married at the time of the birth, then the other parent (not the stepparent) should automatically take over responsibility for looking after the children and the stepparent would have no automatic legal rights. Moreover, the other parent may be unwilling to give access in the future to the stepparent: if there is any conflict the stepparent could apply for a contact order under section 8 of the Children Act. If the stepparent wants to continue looking after the children, then again he or she will have to apply for a residence order.

To protect against a legal shutting–out of the stepparent, especially where the absent parent was uninterested in the children, the parent/partner could make a will or written appointment nominating the stepparent as a guardian of the child on his or her death. This would suffice if the mother of the children had not been married to the father at the time of the birth or had married him later. Otherwise, to make the position watertight, the stepparent and parent should apply jointly to the court for a residence order as otherwise the appointment as a guardian would not take effect until the death of the surviving natural parent (which defeats the object of an appointment).

Another problem that can arise on death (or even if the remarriage breaks up) is that of securing a family home for the children. If, following divorce, a parent purchases a property jointly with a new partner, perhaps with the aid of a capital sum paid via the divorce courts, he or she should be careful how the joint ownership of the new home is expressed.

If the new partners buy as joint tenants, the share of one would pass automatically to the surviving partner whatever his or her will might state. This could mean that if there were relationship problems later between the stepparent and the children, the stepparent would be within his or her legal rights to ask the children to leave the home and they might have no financial security. If, however, a new property were purchased expressly under a tenancy in common, both partners' property interests would be clearly defined and the parent could ensure that his or her share passed to the children by will. A joint tenancy can easily be converted to a tenancy in common by 'severing' it. A letter from one joint owner to the other stating that the writer is thereby severing the property will suffice – ask a solicitor if you want to find out more.

A tenancy in common will be assumed to divide the ownership equally between the partners unless any other proportionate division is stated. So if the parent has provided most of the capital for the purchase and wants to ensure that the children are securely provided for in the event of death, the tenancy in common could be stated to be divided 75 per cent to the parent, 25 per cent to the stepparent. The parent should also execute a will leaving his or her share of the property to the children in trust until they reach the age of 18 (or some other later date). A deed of trust for the ownership of the property can also set out clearly what will happen if certain events occur: for example, if the parties split up, the agreements for one buying out the other.

A solicitor can advise further about ownership of the property, making a deed of trust and a will. Some of the costs may be offset by the green form, if you are financially eligible, although there are now restrictions on green form advice about wills (see Chapter 11). Otherwise, if you are paying privately, the extra costs of preparing a deed of trust are likely to be £200 (plus VAT) upwards.

Making a will

Remarriage (as with marriage) automatically revokes any earlier will unless that will was specifically stated to be made in contemplation of the marriage. In any event, if there are children, making a will after a remarriage should be a priority. Otherwise, the rules of intestacy will automatically operate after your death, which may not accord with what you actually want to happen. Although these rules differ depending on the circumstances, what they achieve in broad terms is to give an ex-spouse the first £125,000 (plus chattels and a life interest in one-half of the estate over and above this sum) following death if there are children, the first £200,000 (plus chattels and one-half of the remainder absolutely) where there are no children. The remaining balance will be divided among the children, where there are surviving children, or among other relatives if there are none.

Making a will is not a watertight guarantee that a person's wishes will be carried out after his or her death – claims can be made against a deceased person's estate by his or her widow(er) or other members of their family or dependants under the Inheritance (Provision for Family and Dependants) Act 1975. For example, since 1 January 1996, under changes made by the Law Reform (Succession) Act 1995, claims can be made against a deceased person's estate by an unmarried cohabitant as long as she (or he) lived with the deceased as husband and wife for at least two years.

There are significant advantages to making a will. As long as you have made a will at least the rest of the world will know what you wanted to happen after your death. If your priority is to ensure that the children are cared for after your death, by making a will you will be reasonably certain that your wishes will be carried out. You can also appoint a guardian to care for your children after your death: the appointment will be effective immediately after your death if you have a residence order in your favour; otherwise the appointment is not effective until your surviving ex-spouse has died too.

Stepfamilies and divorce

If the stepfamily itself breaks up, broadly the advice contained within this book will apply. However, the question also arises whether a step-parent (more commonly the stepfather) may face claims for financial support for the children of his or her ex-partner.

If the children have been treated as 'children of the family' (this term generally covers any child who has been brought up in the same household), their details must be included on the statement of arrangements form and in the divorce petition itself. The divorce court will consider the arrangements made for them as well as for any natural children of the parties. If the stepparent wants to look after the children in the future, he or she will probably have to make an application for a residence order even if this proposal is agreed to by the natural parent. Without such an order, the stepparent's responsibilities will not be recognised in law. Usually, however, the court will be predisposed to the natural parent continuing to care for the children.

Following the marriage of the stepparent to the natural parent, as the stepchildren would be 'children of the family', applications for maintenance (which could be secured), lump sums and transfers of settlement and of property could be made against the stepparent (although if the parties had never married and if the stepparent had not otherwise legally assumed financial responsibilities for the stepchildren, no such claims could be made). Applications will usually be limited to children aged up to 17, although they can be allowed after that age if the children are continuing in full-time education or training. Child support applications cannot be made against a stepparent via the CSA unless he or she had legally adopted the child(ren).

The CSA seeks to trace the natural (or adoptive) parents for them to pay maintenance for their children: financial duties to one's own natural (or adopted) children will specifically override assumed obligations for the previous children of a new partner.

The courts will also expect the natural parents to fulfil their financial obligations towards their children first, so before a financial order was made against a stepparent, the court would want to ensure that exhaustive steps had been taken to track down the absent natural parent to make an order against him (or her) for the children.

Which court? (England and Wales)

Before divorce

Applying for spousal maintenance or for maintenance for any children not covered by the Child Support Agency	Make application to: 1. Family Proceedings Panel (FPP) of local magistrates' court, or 2. Family Hearing Centre (FHC) (county court), or 3. If case is especially complex, the High Court
Applying for a Children Act order	
Applying for domestic violence injunction	Make application to: 1. FPP 2. County court or FHC

Starting divorce proceedings

	Make application to divorce county court (DCC) or FHC. DCC will deal with administrative paperwork of divorce only; contested applications (e.g. for finance, about the children) will be transferred to FHC.
	If divorce becomes defended or is especially complex, DCC or FHC will transfer case to the High Court.

Once divorce is under way

Applying for ancillary (financial) relief and/ or applying for a Children Act order and/or applying for domestic violence injunction	Make application to court dealing with divorce. If this is only a DCC, case will be transferred to FHC (see above).

Chapter 15

Divorce in Scotland

Scottish family and divorce law is significantly different from that in England and Wales. You can bring divorce proceedings in Scotland if you or your spouse are domiciled in Scotland (that is, if Scotland is regarded as your permanent home) or if either of you were habitually resident in Scotland for at least a year immediately before starting proceedings.

Grounds for divorce

There is no minimum period you have to wait after marriage before you can bring divorce proceedings. The sole ground for divorce is irretrievable breakdown of the marriage; this can be established only by proof of one of the following:

- adultery
- unreasonable behaviour
- desertion for two or more years
- non-cohabitation for two or more years and your spouse consents to the divorce
- non-cohabitation for five or more years.

If your spouse has committed adultery you do not have to show you find it intolerable to live with him or her. You cannot base your case on adultery which you have condoned or connived at. Condonation means that you forgave your spouse by resuming married life for more than three months after you knew about the adultery. Connivance means active encouragement, such as participation in wife-swapping or sex parties.

Unreasonable behaviour includes being violent, nagging persistently, abusing the children and being financially irresponsible, as well as negative conduct such as ignoring your spouse or his or her emotional or sexual needs.

Non-cohabitation means not living together as any normal married couple would. You and your spouse may have to continue sharing the home after your marriage breaks down because neither of you can get anywhere else to live. You would have to have been living separate lives to get a divorce on grounds of non-cohabitation.

Most divorces are dealt with in the sheriff courts. These are local courts situated in most towns throughout Scotland. You can bring proceedings in the court for the area in which you or your spouse have been living for the past 40 days; you would usually choose your own local court. Divorces are also heard in the Court of Session in Edinburgh. Legal aid is not available for a Court of Session divorce, unless the case is unusually complex or difficult.

There are no decrees nisi or absolute in Scotland. The court grants a single decree of divorce which is immediately effective, although a certain period (14 days in the sheriff court, 21 days in the Court of Session) is allowed for an appeal.

Getting a divorce

There are two types of procedure: the simplified procedure (usually called a d-i-y divorce), and the ordinary procedure.

D-i-y divorce can be used only where the ground for divorce is non-cohabitation for two or five years. In addition, there must be no children of the marriage under 16 years of age, no financial claims by you or your spouse and no other legal proceedings affecting your marriage waiting to be heard; the divorce must be uncontested, and you and your spouse must not be suffering from any mental disorder. As the name implies, you do not need a solicitor for a d-i-y divorce. Nevertheless, you should consider seeking legal advice before you start in order to make sure that you are fully aware of the consequences and are not giving up rights in ignorance.

Printed forms for the d-i-y procedure are available from the courts or Citizens Advice Bureaux (CABx). For a two-year non-cohabitation divorce, you fill out part 1 of the form, and send it to your spouse for completion of part 2 (for his or her consent to the divorce). On its return, you complete the affidavit in part 3, swearing it before a notary public or a justice of the peace. Most solicitors in Scotland are notaries public but they will charge for affidavits. Your local council will have a list of justices of the peace whose services are free. In the case of a five-year non-cohabitation divorce, your spouse's consent is unnecessary. Part 2 of this form is the affidavit which is sworn as before.

You send the completed form (parts 1, 2 and 3 or parts 1 and 2) to the court with your marriage certificate (the original or an official copy, but not a photocopy) and the court dues (currently £55). You may have to pay another £30 if the form has to be served on your spouse in a manner other than by post. If you are on income support or are seeing a solicitor under the legal advice and assistance scheme (the 'pink form scheme') you will not have to pay these dues. The court takes all remaining steps and will tell you and your spouse when the divorce has been granted. This usually takes about two months.

If you cannot get a d-i-y divorce, you will have to use the 'ordinary procedure' (see pages 294–8). This is more complex and you are strongly advised to get a Scottish solicitor to act for you. Most divorces are heard in the sheriff courts, so only that procedure will be described here. Court of Session procedure is slightly different.

Your friends may be able to recommend a solicitor if you do not already have one. Alternatively, your library or CAB should have lists showing which local solicitors undertake divorce work and whether they will act for clients on legal aid (most do). The Law Society of Scotland★ will also help you find a solicitor.

Divorce expenses and legal aid

In d-i-y divorces the pursuer (the spouse seeking the divorce) pays his or her own expenses (£55 plus more for service costs if necessary). The defender (the other spouse) usually has no expenses since the proceedings must be undefended and have no associated financial and other claims.

The procedure for an ordinary divorce, however, is not cheap. The expenses of an ordinary undefended divorce with financial and other claims will amount to about £700. Defended proceedings are much more expensive. It is sensible for couples to keep disputes and litigation to an absolute minimum. Your respective solicitors should be able to help you negotiate a fair settlement without having to fight it out in court. Mediation services are also available (see later in this chapter). You and your spouse should be flexible and not regard certain matters as points of principle. The more that goes in legal fees, the less there is for both of you and the children.

A negotiated settlement should deal with the divorce expenses. If there is no agreement as to expenses, the court will apportion them at the end of the proceedings. The main factors that influence the courts are which spouse won and whether each spouse conducted the proceedings in a responsible way. For example, if you make exaggerated claims or are uncooperative, thus forcing your spouse to litigate unnecessarily, you could end up paying most of your spouse's expenses as well as your own. Often no award is made, so each spouse is left to pay his or her own expenses. The courts are reluctant to order a legally aided spouse to pay the other's expenses. It is common for consent to be given to a two years' non-cohabitation divorce on condition that the consenting spouse will not be liable for the other's expenses, and this condition will be enforced.

For proceedings other than divorce proceedings the normal rule is that the loser pays the winner's expenses as well as his or her own.

Even if your spouse pays your expenses you will almost certainly be out of pocket. You will have to pay for consultations with your solicitor and other extras which your spouse is not required to pay for.

Legal advice and assistance is available to help you with preliminary advice and to find out whether grounds for divorce exist. It does not cover representation in court. Assistance by way of representation (ABWOR) is not available for family litigation in Scotland. Legal aid is available for court proceedings: divorce, financial claims and matters concerning the children or housing, whether with the divorce proceedings or separately. Your solicitor will help you apply for legal advice and assistance, or legal aid. The Scottish Legal Aid Board★ runs both schemes. Eligibility depends on your own income and savings (your spouse's income and savings are not considered together with yours where you are opponents or are living apart). For legal aid the Board has also to be satisfied that you have a reasonable case. The financial limits are the same as in England and Wales (see Chapter 1).

Legal aid does not mean you can indulge in expensive litigation without fear of the financial consequences. The Scottish Legal Aid Board deducts the amount of your expenses from money the court awards you, or property that the court orders to be transferred to you, if it cannot recover the sum in full from your contributions or from your opponent. However, no deduction is made from any aliment (money paid periodically for a person's support) or periodical allowance or the first £2,500 of any capital sum or transfer of property awarded.

Separation agreements

Instead of going to court a couple may enter into an agreement specifying aliment for the children, which parent they are going to live with, when the other parent can see them or have them to stay (contact), aliment for the wife (less commonly for the husband), and what is to happen to the family home for the period from separation to divorce. Separated couples may also enter into agreements as to how their property is to be divided. They can then rely on this agreement and need not apply to the divorce court for financial orders. An agreement may be an oral, written or formal one (i.e. one prepared after negotiations by the couple and their respective lawyers). The advantages of formal agreements are that they are clear, easily proven and readily enforceable.

An agreement cannot prevent later applications to the court relating to the residence of, and contact with, the children, or to the Child Support Agency (CSA)★ for maintenance for the children. You have to take into consideration the amount likely to be fixed by the Agency, as the amount could make it difficult or unfair for you to fulfil other terms of the agreement which you may not be able to alter. Terms which affect only the spouses, however, are generally binding so you ought to obtain legal advice beforehand. The court can set them aside only if satisfied they were not fair and reasonable at the time the agreement was made. A common term provides aliment for the wife at an agreed rate in return for which she gives up her right to apply to the court for aliment. The court can vary the amount in the agreement only if the circumstances have changed, and will take the agreed amount as the baseline.

Ordinary divorce procedure

Proceedings start with your solicitor lodging the initial writ in court. This document sets out briefly the facts of your case and details the orders you are asking the court to make. A copy of this writ is then served on your spouse. You are called the pursuer and he or she is the defender. A copy also has to be served on any person (a co-defender) with whom you aver your spouse has committed adultery. The children will be sent a notice telling them about the court proceeding unless the court considers it inappropriate because of the children's age and they will be invited to express their view either in person or in writing. In a divorce action based on either two or five years' non-cohabitation, your spouse is also sent a notice warning of the possible financial consequences of divorce (loss of pension or inheritance rights, for example). The notice alerts your spouse to the financial and other applications he or she can make to the court.

In your initial writ you can apply for various interim orders, or you can add them on later (which will incur extra court fees). Interim orders last until the divorce is granted, when the position is reviewed and fresh orders made. Examples of interim orders are:

- interim aliment for you. The CSA deals with maintenance for the children
- interim residence for and contact with the children
- an interim interdict (prohibition) against violent behaviour or disposal of assets
- an interdict against taking the children out of Scotland. Your application for this need not be intimated to your spouse so that he or she may get no warning at all
- an exclusion order excluding your spouse from the family home.

You can also apply for these remedies separately; they are not available only in divorce proceedings. If you cannot apply for a divorce as soon as you and your spouse split up, you may need to use separate proceedings.

Defences

A notice of intention to defend must be lodged within 21 days (42 if the defender is abroad). The court will then specify the date defences have to be lodged by and the date of the options hearing (see below). In your defences you can oppose your spouse's claims and/or make claims against your spouse. Each of you will then adjust your case to meet the other's. An options hearing will then be held during which the court will clarify the issues in dispute and decide how to proceed. You and your spouse and your respective solicitors are required to attend, but you or your spouse may be excused. Some courts involve the couple in the discussions, others listen only to the solicitors.

It is unusual for the divorce itself to be defended. More commonly your spouse will defend your application for financial orders or matters relating to the children or apply for similar orders. Where the divorce is defended, the case is heard in court with each side and their witnesses giving evidence. But where only financial aspects are at issue, the divorce itself is generally disposed of on the basis of sworn statements (affidavits) containing full information about your and your spouse's financial resources (income and capital) and needs.

Affidavits

An affidavit is accepted by the court as evidence of the facts contained in it. You, your spouse and others can give evidence by affidavits instead of attending court, but this is not advisable unless the action is undefended or the evidence is uncontroversial. Your solicitor will prepare your affidavit from the information you give, and you will then swear it before a notary public (who may be your own solicitor). The information must be up-to-date, complete and accurate; otherwise further affidavits or oral evidence will be called for. Deliberately concealing facts or making false statements is regarded as a very serious offence for which you could well be imprisoned.

Reconciliation

You and your spouse can still try to save your marriage even though divorce proceedings have started. The court will, if asked, stop proceedings for a reconciliation. If this does not work, you can ask the court to let the proceedings continue from where they were stopped.

The children

You have to show that satisfactory arrangements have been made for any children of the marriage who are under 16, before the court will grant your divorce. Most couples reach agreement about who is to look after the children. Your or your spouse's affidavit will state who is going to look after the children, how they are going to be looked after, and what accommodation will be available for them. In addition, the court requires an affidavit from a relative or a person (such as a neighbour) who knows the children well. If these affidavits are satisfactory, the court will accept the arrangements without interviewing the couple or the children.

If you or your spouse apply for an order in relation to the children, a child welfare hearing will be fixed. This hearing takes place on the first convenient date three weeks after lodging the notice of intention to defend. You and your spouse will be expected to attend; the children may attend and may be given an opportunity to make their views known. The court may decide the matter there and then, it may refer you both to mediation (see overleaf) or it may postpone the matter to a later date for more thorough consideration. If the outcome is the last of these, the court may ask an independent person to prepare a report. The reporter is usually an advocate, but sometimes a social worker is used. The court will consider this report along with all the evidence from witnesses and other sources before deciding what would be best for the children's welfare.

Joint minute

If you and your spouse can agree on the financial aspects and future arrangements for the children before proceedings start, you can ask the court simply to make the appropriate orders and your spouse need not defend. An alternative, which is sometimes adopted, is for a formal enforceable agreement to be prepared covering these matters (this is similar to a separation agreement, see page 294). Then the court is applied to only for the divorce; even a d-i-y divorce may be possible. In many cases, however, agreement is reached only after proceedings have started, as a result of negotiation or mediation. You and your spouse will then arrange for your respective solicitors to submit a joint minute to the court. This minute either sets out the orders that you and your spouse request the court to grant, or requests the court to make no orders because the matters are to be covered by a written agreement. The terms of the joint minute should be checked very carefully. Once it has been lodged in court it is normally impossible to change your mind and ask the court to do something different.

Where the proceedings are undefended or a joint minute is submitted, the court will normally grant the orders sought without further enquiry. The court may, however, demand further information in matters affecting the children.

Decree

A decree is a formal document containing the orders made by the court. The financial orders are usually granted at the same time as the divorce, although it is possible to have these left over for a later hearing if disagreement on this front is holding up the divorce.

The court will notify you that decree has been granted and also notify your spouse if his or her address is known. There is a 14-day period allowed for appeal (21 days in the Court of Session). After that, an extract (certified copy) of the decree can be obtained from the court which details the orders the court made. You will need an extract to show that you are divorced if you plan to marry again and to enforce the orders if your spouse refuses to pay.

Mediation

There are two kinds of mediation services for family breakdown problems. They can be used at any time: before, during or after legal proceedings. You can either contact the service directly or ask your solicitor to make the arrangements.

Local mediation services affiliated to Family Mediation Scotland★ help couples resolve disputes relating to the children. Mediation is free but donations are most welcome. Information about local services in your area can be obtained from a CAB or from Family Mediation Scotland. When you and your spouse are engaged in legal proceedings relating to the children the court may refer you to mediation if it thinks that might resolve the dispute. The court can refer couples to a local service affiliated to Family Mediation Scotland without their consent.

Members of Comprehensive Accredited Lawyer Mediators (CALM)★ deal with the financial aspects of splitting up as well as matters affecting the children. The mediators are all family lawyers accredited as mediators by the Law Society of Scotland. Mediation sessions are generally taken by two lawyers (one male and one female if possible). The fee charged to the couple is £80 per hour, and generally two to three sessions of about 1½ hours each are needed. If either of the spouses is legally aided, his or her share of these fees will be paid for. People entering into this type of mediation are encouraged to have their own solicitors because the outcome will be proposals which are worked up into a formal agreement by the spouses and their solicitors.

The home

Before divorce

Most couples now own their home together as co-owners. This means that both of them are equally entitled to live there and occupy it and are equally liable for the outgoings. Both have to consent to any sale or other disposal, although the court will order a sale against the wishes of one co-owner unless a sale is undesirable. A sale will not be ordered while the divorce proceedings are pending if the home is in issue. On sale, the proceeds of sale are divided equally between the couple unless the title deeds specify a different proportion. Each co-owner's share of the proceeds increases his or her capital which the court can reallocate on divorce.

The Matrimonial Homes (Family Protection) (Scotland) Act 1981 gives you certain rights if you do not own the home and your spouse is the sole owner. You are entitled to continue to occupy and live in the home. Moreover, your consent is required for any sale or other disposal, although the court can dispense with your consent if it is being withheld unreasonably. These rights are automatic: you do not have to register them in the Land Register for Scotland or the Register of Sasines (public registers of property and its owners).

Married co-tenants and spouses of sole tenants have similar protection against the tenancy of the home being given up.

You can renounce your occupancy rights but it is seldom in your interest to do so. A renunciation must be in writing and signed and declared before a notary public.

Exclusion orders

You can apply to the court for an order excluding your spouse from the family home and immediate vicinity if he or she behaves violently towards you or the children. This order is called an exclusion order and even a sole owner or tenant can be excluded. You can apply separately or as part of your divorce proceedings. An exclusion order will, if defended, take many weeks to obtain. You may apply for your spouse to be excluded during this period by means of an interim exclusion order. In many cases an interim order suffices, since it or an exclusion order lasts only until divorce.

The court has to be satisfied, first, that the (interim) exclusion order is necessary to protect you and/or the children from your spouse's violent behaviour or threats and, second, that it is reasonable for him or her to be excluded. Your spouse must be sent a copy of your application for an (interim) exclusion order and given an opportunity to oppose it. You will have to back up your claim with as much evidence as you can, such as affidavits from your doctor or neighbours about your health and past incidents of violence, reports by the police if they have been involved, and evidence of your need for the home and the unsuitable nature of your present temporary accommodation if you have been forced to leave home.

Interdicts

Another way of protecting yourself from violence or molestation by your spouse is to apply for a court order (called an interdict) prohibiting such conduct. Interdicts can be obtained extremely quickly, within a day if necessary. You can apply separately or as part of your divorce proceedings. Interdicts last until the court recalls them. Behaviour contrary to the interdict (a breach of interdict) is treated seriously. Your spouse can be fined or imprisoned, but is usually given a warning for the first breach.

It is possible to have a power of arrest added to your interdict. The advantage of this is that once you have sent a copy of the interdict and power of arrest to the police you can ask the police to arrest your spouse for breaching the interdict. Also, the police will generally respond more quickly to your call for assistance if you have a power of arrest. The drawback is that if you want a power of arrest added, your spouse has to be given notice of your application for the interdict and an opportunity to oppose it. Courts usually require evidence of one or more past violent incidents before a power of arrest is added. The power of arrest lapses on divorce.

On divorce

Orders regarding the home are part of the overall financial settlement (see *Financial orders*, page 303). The court on granting divorce may:

- make no order and allow the home to be sold; the proceeds will have been taken into account in any lump sum award made
- transfer the ownership (or tenancy) of the home or a share of it from one spouse to the other. The date of transfer can be deferred, but delays of more than a few months to allow time for the legal documents to be prepared are not common
- regulate who is to occupy the home after divorce. This is not often done, but it might be used to allow a wife and children to continue to occupy the home owned by her husband until she can get a job

and afford somewhere else. An express exclusion of her husband from the home might be necessary if he was likely to interfere with her occupation of the home. The wife's occupancy rights prevent the home being sold without her consent.

The children

You and your spouse have to decide what is to happen to the children after divorce. Talk things over with them, explain what is going on and what is going to happen to them and, if they are old enough, take account of their views as well as your own. You and your spouse should make every effort to reach agreement over the children. A mediation service is available to help divorcing couples resolve their disputes about the children (see page 298).

The Children Act 1989 does not apply to Scotland; the legislation applicable is the Children (Scotland) Act 1995. In Scotland parents have various legal responsibilities towards their children, such as safeguarding them, advising them and acting on their behalf in legal transactions; and various rights, such as deciding where they are to live, controlling their upbringing and having contact with them. These responsibilities and rights cease when the children reach 16. The children can then live where they like, look after their own money and generally make their own decisions. A child under 16 can consent to medical treatment if the doctor thinks that he or she can understand what the proposed treatment involves, and in such a case the parents cannot overrule the child.

While the parents live together they share the parental responsibilities and rights. Each can act alone, neither can veto the other's actions, and any irreconcilable disputes have to be resolved by the courts. On divorce the court may, on application, reallocate these responsibilities and rights. Orders may be unnecessary if the parents are going to cooperate or if the absent parent will not interfere with the day-to-day decisions of the parent looking after the children. Otherwise the parent who is going to be looking after the children may need to apply for a residence order, which will give him or her the right to have the children living with him or her in addition to the other responsibilities and rights. The other parent retains these except in relation to the children's residence.

If the parents cannot agree which of them the children are to live with, the court will decide on welfare grounds, taking any views expressed by the children into account. Children of 12 and over are presumed able to form a view, and courts rarely go against firm views of 14- or 15-year-olds. Children below 12 can also give the court their views, which will be taken into account.

Arrangements for contact are best worked out on the basis of what is mutually acceptable. The parent with the children should allow the other reasonable contact and, indeed, encourage the children to keep up links. If these informal arrangements break down, the court will regulate contact – for example, allow the other parent to see the children for a certain number of hours every weekend or to have them to stay for part of the school holidays. Only in exceptional circumstances will the court refuse contact to a parent who has been previously involved with the children.

A woman may want to change her children's surname to that of her new husband. She should think carefully about this because their father (and perhaps the children too) may resent a change. The court probably has no power to allow or prohibit changes of name.

Child abduction
The Scottish provisions of the Child Abduction Act 1984 are different from those for England and Wales. A parent commits a criminal offence by taking a child out of the United Kingdom only if:

- the other parent (or someone else) has been awarded custody or has a residence order and has not agreed to the child's removal, *or*
- the court has interdicted removal.

If your spouse is likely to take the children abroad you should apply for a residence order or an interdict at once. You can do so even without applying for divorce but if you have started divorce proceedings the application has to be made in the context of those proceedings. Children cannot be made wards of court in Scotland. In an emergency you can obtain an interdict at any hour of the day or night. Once you have an interdict or a residence order you can ask the police and sheriff officers to trace the children and prevent their removal from the country.

If your child is abducted abroad see your solicitor immediately. Most European and Commonwealth countries and states in the USA are in the Hague Convention, which obliges the foreign country to trace the children and secure their return.

Financial orders

Many couples negotiate a financial settlement instead of litigating. Such an agreement is binding and will be set aside only if the court is satisfied that it was not fair and reasonable at the time it was entered into. The court will not look at, still less vet, the agreement unless an application is made to set it aside. A bad bargain is not enough to make an agreement unfair, so you ought to get legal assistance in negotiating.

The negotiations will obviously be influenced by the financial orders the court is likely to make in the absence of any agreement. The principles in the Family Law (Scotland) Act 1985 make it fairly easy to predict what the court is likely to do. If negotiations lead to an agreement the couple can lodge a joint minute setting out the orders they wish or asking for no financial orders to be made at all, leaving the agreement to regulate matters.

The main financial orders the court can make on divorce are:

- ordering one spouse to pay a lump sum (a 'capital' sum) to the other; *and/or*
- ordering one spouse to pay the other a periodical allowance – a regular sum each week or month; *and/or*
- ordering a spouse to pay aliment for the children of the marriage but only if the CSA cannot assess maintenance (see page 305); *and/or*
- transferring the ownership of property from one spouse to the other.

It is possible, but unusual, for the court to grant a divorce and postpone the financial orders to a later date if disagreement is holding up the divorce.

The court can also order the house to be sold immediately or at a later date and/or say who is to occupy it and to have use of the contents. Where the house is rented, the court can transfer the tenancy from one spouse to the other.

Either the pursuer or the defender can apply for financial orders. You have to state in your initial writ or defences exactly what orders you seek from the court and give evidence of your and your spouse's needs and resources to demonstrate that they are reasonable claims. The court also needs to know the amount of aliment currently being paid. Making exaggerated claims is a bad tactic as it will merely get your spouse's back up. Almost inevitably a couple's living standards drop after divorce. A fair settlement should result in this drop being shared between the spouses.

A claim for a lump sum or transfer of property must be made before the divorce is granted. You can claim periodical allowance afterwards but you are very unlikely to get it then, because the principles required to justify an award (principles 3 to 5 below) generally speaking apply to your situation at the time of divorce. You cannot claim periodical allowance later if you and your spouse at the time of divorce made a formal agreement that you would not claim.

The Family Law (Scotland) Act 1985 sets out a series of principles to guide the court in making financial orders, as follows.

1. Sharing family assets

The home, its contents, savings, investments and other assets which you or your spouse own and which were acquired between the date of marriage and the date of final separation are family assets. The home and contents are also counted as family assets if they were acquired before marriage as a family home for the couple. Assets given to you or inherited by you are not regarded as family assets. Family assets are to be shared equally unless there is a good reason for unequal division, which might be ordered where, say, your parents helped you buy the home or where you run a business that cannot be divided. An important family asset, especially for older couples, is the lump sum and pension payable on retirement under a superannuation scheme. This cannot be divided between the spouses, but its value is taken into account in calculating each spouse's share of the total family assets.

2. Balancing economic advantages and disadvantages

The court has to take account of your financial and non-financial contributions to your spouse's wealth – and the other way round. Examples include helping with the running costs of the home, sacrificing a career to look after the children or working in your spouse's business at an artificially low wage. Courts tend not to use this principle to any great extent.

3. Sharing childcare

Future childcare costs are to be shared. These include your loss of earnings while looking after the children and the expense of keeping up a larger and more expensive house than you would need if you were living on your own. If maintenance for the children is assessed by the CSA it includes an amount for childcare costs; the court will then take account of this principle only for extra costs.

4. Financial dependency

Under this principle you are entitled to support for up to three years after divorce to enable you to become self-supporting if you were financially dependent upon your spouse during the marriage.

5. Severe financial hardship

If you are unlikely to be self-supporting after divorce (too old or ill, for example), you may need support for many years (the rest of your life, perhaps) to avoid severe financial hardship.

Court orders

Principles 1 and 2 can be satisfied only by the award of a lump sum and/or a transfer of property. The lump sum may be payable all at once, shortly after divorce or at a specified later date, or by instalments. Principles 3 to 5 should be satisfied by a lump sum or transfer of property if possible, otherwise by a periodical allowance. Wives who are looking after young children ought to get a periodical allowance under principle 3 as compensation for loss of earnings or the childcare costs if they work. Women tend not to ask for a periodical allowance as they do not wish to have continued financial links with their ex-husbands.

If a periodical allowance at the time of divorce cannot be justified by principles 3, 4 or 5 a spouse will not be awarded one. The court will not award a nominal periodical allowance on divorce with the intention that it could be increased later if the recipient's financial circumstances get worse.

Aliment for the children

The CSA now assesses maintenance for children up to and including 18 years of age who are still in secondary education. The courts have no power to deal with claims for aliment made for these children.

Certain categories of children are not within the Agency's remit and can still be awarded aliment by the courts. The most important of these categories are:

- children aged 19 to 24 who are undergoing further educational training at a university, college, apprenticeship or so on. Children have to look after themselves once they reach 25 as the parental obligation of aliment ceases then
- a child who has been accepted by you or your spouse as a child of the family. The accepting spouse will have an obligation of aliment. The usual example is a stepfather accepting his wife's children by her former marriage. The CSA will assess the children's father for payment, but if this is not feasible (father dead, untraceable or no money) aliment can be claimed via the courts against the stepfather
- where the parent due to pay aliment is abroad.

The amount of aliment awarded depends on what the person paying it can afford and what the child needs. The previous level of support the child enjoyed is also important.

A child over 11 can apply to the CSA for an assessment of his or her own maintenance. Children over 18 who wish aliment via the courts must claim themselves. Below that age a parent may claim on their behalf.

Change in circumstances

After divorce your or your ex-spouse's financial circumstances may change. You may be able to go back to court to get your orders changed, depending on the type of order involved.

Lump sum order

You cannot apply for a lump sum order after divorce. If you were awarded a lump sum on divorce the court cannot generally change the amount payable. There are two rare exceptions. First, if the true facts were concealed from the court or lies were told to obtain the original order, the court will make a new order. Second, if your ex-spouse became bankrupt within five years and the order resulted in his or her debts exceeding assets, then the court can order you to repay all or part of the lump sum. Apart from these two exceptional cases, all the court can do is to alter the way in which the lump sum is paid, perhaps by ordering payment by instalments or giving more time to pay.

Property transfer orders

You cannot apply for a transfer of property order after divorce. If you were awarded a transfer on divorce the court cannot alter the property to be transferred except in the two rare cases mentioned above. All it can do is to alter the date set for transfer.

Periodical allowance

You can apply for a periodical allowance after divorce but it would be awarded only in unusual circumstances. You cannot apply if you agreed not to do so as part of the divorce settlement.

You or your ex-spouse can apply to the court for the amount to be increased, decreased, terminated or made payable only for a certain number of years more. For example, if you lose your job or now work part-time your allowance could be increased. If your ex-spouse's business is not doing so well, your allowance could be decreased or even terminated. Your allowance, which was awarded on grounds of severe financial hardship, could have a time limit put on it if you were offered a re-training course with a job at the end. If you were awarded an allowance on financial dependency grounds (principle 4) it cannot be extended beyond three years after divorce.

You cannot expect your allowance to be increased simply because of inflation. After all, inflation may be affecting your ex-spouse just as much as you.

Your remarriage terminates your allowance automatically. A woman's allowance is usually terminated by the court if she lives with another man even if he is not supporting her, but not all courts take this attitude. Your ex-spouse's remarriage will result in your allowance being reduced or terminated if the court thinks his or her commitments have increased. Your allowance should not be reduced if your ex-spouse lives with another partner. But if they have children the court will take these new liabilities into account.

When you die, your allowance comes to an end automatically. But the death of your ex-spouse does not mean that your allowance comes to an end automatically. The executors have to apply to the court for it to be terminated. Occasionally the court will then order payment at a reduced rate or set a time limit on the allowance, rather than terminate it.

Any variation the court awards can be backdated to the date of the application, or to the date when the circumstances changed, as long as there was a good reason for the delay in applying for the variation.

Another variation the court can be asked to make is to substitute a lump sum (payable by instalments perhaps) for a periodical allowance. You and your ex-spouse should weigh up the advantages and disadvantages carefully because once the substitution order is made it cannot be reversed.

Old orders

There are some special rules for periodical allowance awarded in divorce proceedings started before 1 September 1986 (when the Family Law (Scotland) Act 1985 came into force). First, the court cannot substitute a lump sum for your allowance. You or your ex-spouse could, of course, agree to do this without going to court. Second, the court cannot backdate a variation of the allowance.

Aliment for the children

The CSA now deals with the assessment of most children's maintenance. The assessed amount depends on the financial circumstances of each parent and also on the age of the child. Application may be made to the Agency for variation of the assessment.

In exceptional cases (see page 306) the courts may still award aliment and can vary the amount awarded subsequently. Apart from these cases, if aliment is payable under a court order which was made in proceedings commenced, or a written agreement entered into, before April 1993, the courts retain power to vary the amount. A variation of aliment can be applied for if the circumstances of the child or the paying parent change. The amount of aliment is not reduced merely because the paying parent or the parent looking after the children remarries or cohabits. Aliment ceases automatically when either the paying parent or the child dies.

Enforcing maintenance

A great number of people who have a court order for their own aliment or periodical allowance or for aliment for the children never get paid regularly. The longer the time the arrears have built up, the less likely it is that you will be paid.

If informal demands for regular payments do not produce the required results, you will have to use legal enforcement methods (called diligence). You do not have to go back to the court but you will need a solicitor's help. The legal aid certificate for your divorce covers the cost of diligence for up to 12 months later. After a year, or if you are applying for your ex-spouse to be imprisoned for failure to pay, you will have to apply for legal aid or legal advice and assistance.

Where your ex-spouse is employed, the best diligence to use is a *current maintenance arrestment*. You (or your solicitor) send a copy of the court order to your ex-spouse, and if, not less than four weeks later, three or more instalments are in arrears, a current maintenance arrestment can be served by a sheriff officer on your ex-spouse's employer. The employer thereafter automatically deducts every pay-day the maintenance due to you for the period since the last pay-day and sends it to you or your solicitor. A current maintenance arrestment does not enforce arrears but you can use an earnings arrestment or another diligence at the same time to recover the arrears.

The following diligences enforce arrears only, although the threat of repeating them may make your ex-spouse keep up regular payments in future:

- *Earnings arrestment*: a sheriff officer serves a notice on your ex-spouse's employer who deducts every pay-day an amount which varies with the earnings payable then. The deductions are sent to you or your solicitor and stop when the arrears are paid off.
- *Arrestment of a bank or building society account*: a sheriff officer serves a notice which freezes the money in your ex-spouse's account. You then have to apply to the court for an order requiring the bank or building society to pay you, unless your ex-spouse agrees to release the money.
- *Poinding and sale of goods*: a sheriff officer goes to your ex-spouse's home or business premises and makes a list of his or her goods and their value. The court can then order these 'poinded' goods to be auctioned to pay the arrears.
- *Imprisonment*: if the court is satisfied that your ex-spouse's failure to pay was wilful, he or she can be imprisoned for up to six weeks. Only a handful of people are actually sent to prison each year, but

the threat usually works wonders. Imprisonment is available only for failure to pay aliment; you cannot use it to enforce your periodical allowance.

The CSA will collect and if necessary enforce child maintenance on request and will always do so if the parent looking after the children is on benefit. If your ex-spouse is employed, the CSA will use a deduction from earnings order (very like an earnings arrestment). If not it will have to go to court to get a liability order for the arrears and then use the diligences of bank arrestment, poinding or imprisonment.

Effect of divorce on your inheritance rights

After divorce, you have no rights to your ex-spouse's estate if he or she dies without a will or leaves you nothing. The Inheritance (Provision for Family and Dependants) Act 1975 does not apply to Scotland.

Legacies or other provisions for you in your ex-spouse's will are not cancelled by divorce after the date of the will. Generally speaking, you are entitled to take them unless the will makes it clear that you are not. Your ex-spouse's will is not cancelled by his or her subsequent remarriage.

After divorce, you and your ex-spouse should review any existing will. You will probably want to cancel any bequest to your ex-spouse, but other changes may also be desirable. Most married couples who own their home together have in the title deeds that the property will go to the survivor when one of them dies. This is another thing that ought to be changed after divorce. A solicitor's help will be needed to change the title deeds.

Judicial separation

Instead of a divorce, you can apply for a judicial separation. The grounds are the same as for divorce. The court granting a judicial separation has no power to award a capital sum or order a transfer of property: it can only award aliment for you. You and your spouse remain married to each other so neither of you can remarry. There is limited legal point in getting a judicial separation because now you can get aliment from the court without asking for separation, but a few couples still opt for a judicial separation for religious reasons.

A husband does not inherit any of the property the wife acquired after separation if she dies without having made a will. There is no equivalent rule disinheriting a separated wife.

Stepfamilies

A stepparent has, despite being married to the child's parent, few legal rights and responsibilities towards the child. He or she cannot act as the child's legal representative and does not have the right to say where the child is to live, unless the court grants such rights or appoints the stepparent as guardian.

A stepparent can obtain all the rights of a parent by adopting the child. The child then becomes in law a child of the marriage of the stepparent and the natural parent (the stepparent's spouse). Adoption by a stepparent is becoming less common because many consider that the legal relationship with the other natural parent (and his or her relatives) should not be terminated. Some stepparents apply instead for some of the parental responsibilities and rights, or for guardianship, which confers them all. The welfare of the child is the paramount consideration and the court will not grant an adoption application unless satisfied that to do so would be in the long-term interests of the child and that there is no better practicable alternative.

A stepparent becomes liable to aliment a stepchild if he or she accepts the child as a child of his or her family. This liability can be enforced by an application to the court by, or on behalf of, the child either in connection with the divorce proceedings between the stepparent and the child's parent or in separate proceedings. While the child's father is alive and able to afford aliment he is regarded as primarily liable to pay. The CSA will make a maintenance assessment against the child's absent father. It will not deal with aliment due by stepparents.

On the breakdown of the marriage between a child's stepparent and parent the court hearing the divorce must be satisfied that the future arrangements for the children of both the parties' first and second marriages are suitable.

As mentioned before, a person's will is not revoked by his or her subsequent marriage or divorce. If the stepparent is not mentioned in his or her spouse's will, a claim for legal rights could be made. Legal rights amount to one-half or one-third of the spouse's property other than land or buildings. The higher fraction applies if the spouse leaves no surviving children.

The title to the 'stepfamily home' may be taken simply in the name of the spouse and the stepparent. Each person then owns an equal share (unless the title deeds specify a different proportion) and on his or her death that share is dealt with by his or her will (or the rules of intestacy). Where the title is taken in the name of the spouse, the step-parent and the survivor of them, the home will belong entirely to the survivor. If you are remarrying you should think carefully about your will and whether to use a survivorship title.

The child's parent may by will appoint the stepparent to be the child's guardian after his or her death. The stepparent will then share parental responsibilities and rights with the other parent if he or she is still alive. Any disputes between them would have to be resolved by the court.

Chapter 16

Divorce in Northern Ireland

To a large extent divorce in Northern Ireland mirrors divorce in England and Wales. This chapter should not, therefore, be read in isolation. Much of what has been written in the preceding chapters regarding children, the Child Support Agency (CSA),★ financial issues and child abduction is relevant to readers contemplating divorce in Northern Ireland. However, the process in Northern Ireland is different in some ways from that in England and Wales. The most important differences – although not all – are highlighted in this chapter.

The High Court and county courts in Northern Ireland have jurisdiction to hear a petition for divorce or judicial separation if either of the parties is domiciled in Northern Ireland when the proceedings are begun. Divorce proceedings cannot be brought within the first two years of marriage.

A petition can be brought for judicial separation instead of divorce where one or both of the parties have religious objections to divorce. The main difference between divorce and judicial separation is that a decree of judicial separation does not formally end the marriage but simply brings to an end the couple's duty to live together. Neither of the parties is free to remarry following a decree of judicial separation. However, each party is still free to petition for divorce at a future date. The most obvious difference to a petitioner (i.e. the spouse initiating the divorce) in Northern Ireland is that he or she is required to give oral evidence in court regardless of the ground for divorce upon which he or she seeks to rely. The 'special procedure', which deals with undefended divorces, does not apply to Northern Ireland. There is provision under the Family Law (Northern Ireland) Order 1993 to dispense with oral testimony in cases where a petitioner alleges two years' separation and the respondent (i.e. the other spouse) consents to a decree being granted, or in cases where a petitioner is alleging five years' separation, but this has still not come into force.

A petitioner will be required to appear in person before a judge and formally prove the ground upon which the petition is based, whether it be in the county court or the High Court. The judge will hear the petitioner's evidence in private (known as 'in chambers'), and most undefended divorce hearings are relatively brief (about ten minutes).

After hearing the petitioner's evidence, the judge, if satisfied that the marriage has broken down irretrievably and that one of the five facts outlined below has been proved, will grant a decree nisi. Six weeks from that date the petitioner can apply to have the decree made absolute, thereby ending the marriage and leaving each party free to remarry. Divorce, judicial separation, or even the drawing up of a separation agreement may affect inheritance rights and it is advisable for the parties involved to discuss this with a solicitor at the earliest opportunity.

Which court?

In Northern Ireland divorces can be brought in either a county court or the High Court. There is at least one county court for each of the six counties in Northern Ireland, including Recorder's Courts in Londonderry and Belfast. The High Court is situated in Belfast. Whether the divorce petition is to be heard in a county court or the High Court is a decision for the petitioner's solicitor. By and large, for petitions that are likely to be defended or in which there are sizeable assets to be taken into account the High Court is considered the more appropriate venue. However, as more and more divorces are being heard in county courts, it is likely that fewer divorces will be heard in the High Court. In any event at present most financial matters are still transferred from the county courts to the High Court.

Stamp duty payable on a divorce petition is £115 in a county court and £135 in the High Court.

The petitioner must complete and include with the petition a form entitled 'Statement as to Arrangements for Children' outlining the proposed future arrangements for the children. The petitioner should try to agree the arrangements with the respondent in advance of lodging the form with the court, and should obtain the latter's signature on the form to show his or her consent to the arrangements.

Obviously this depends on the cooperation and goodwill of the respondent, and given the animosity which often surrounds divorce, this may not always be forthcoming. In such a case it would be sufficient for a petitioner to show that he or she had done everything possible to obtain the respondent's consent. The petitioner can sign the form him- or herself and lodge it with the divorce petition. The respondent still has the option of filing a statement of his or her own. When the statement as to arrangements for children is lodged in the court office it is then sent to the relevant health trust which will provide in every case, contested or otherwise, a welfare report where children are involved.

A social worker interviews both parents and completes a form provided by the court which gives details of income, living conditions and proposed arrangements for the children. Occasionally the social worker may be asked to provide further details, but normally a standard report is completed and forwarded to the court, where it is read by the judge before any order in relation to the children is made.

Proceedings can be adjourned by the court at any stage if there appears to be a reasonable prospect of a reconciliation between the parties. Counselling is offered to married, divorcing or divorced couples by RELATE.*

Legal aid

Full legal aid can be applied for to bring divorce proceedings in either the county court or the High Court. A solicitor should be able to give advice about legal aid eligibility at the initial interview if the petitioner outlines his or her earnings and savings. Only those on income support or very low incomes will be entitled to full legal aid, but a contribution system is still in operation in Northern Ireland whereby the petitioner makes a financial contribution to the costs of obtaining the divorce by paying 12 monthly instalments of an amount set by the Legal Aid Department.* The amount set will depend on the means of the applicant.

Divorce petitions – irretrievable breakdown

The Family Law Act 1996, which has led to extensive changes to divorce law being debated in England and Wales, does not extend to Northern Ireland. However, consultation is ongoing to see whether any of the provisions in the Act should be enacted in Northern Ireland. To date no consultation paper seems to have been drawn up by the Office of Law Reform, but it is likely that there will be some movement in this regard in the future. That means that one or more of the 'five facts' set out in the Matrimonial Causes (Northern Ireland) Order 1978 must be proved by the petitioner so that the court can find that the marriage has 'irretrievably broken down'. Put very simply the five facts are:

- the respondent has committed adultery
- the respondent has behaved unreasonably
- the respondent has deserted the petitioner for a continuous period of at least two years
- that the parties have lived apart for a period of two years and that the respondent consents to a decree being granted
- that the parties have lived apart for a continuous period of at least five years, provided that this will not result in grave financial or other hardship to the respondent.

The first three facts – adultery, unreasonable behaviour and desertion – are immediate grounds for bringing divorce proceedings. As mentioned above, it is intended at present that these grounds, known as 'fault' grounds, will remain in Northern Ireland.

However, there can often be difficulties in proving any of the three fault-based grounds. Obtaining evidence of adultery by the respondent, which the court will need, can be expensive. As regards behaviour, the court will not only look at the behaviour of the respondent that has been complained of, but also the character and personality of the petitioner. The courts are mindful that because fault grounds are immediate grounds for bringing divorce proceedings they are open to abuse. The judge will therefore study closely the type of behaviour being complained about. Desertion, while perhaps easier to prove on the facts, may be problematical if the respondent shows that a reasonable offer to return was made but was not accepted by the petitioner.

It is open to the respondent to defend any of the fault-based grounds. Defended petitions, although few in number, can be very costly, so a petitioner who wishes to allege the fault grounds for the sake of convenience and time should be extremely wary.

The most common ground for divorce is where the petitioner and respondent have lived apart for a continuous period of at least two years and the respondent consents to a decree being granted. This is quite rightly viewed as the most amicable basis for obtaining a divorce. It usually allows the matter of finances to be dealt with before the petition is issued (see below). An initial refusal by the respondent to consent to a divorce being granted on this ground can very often be reversed by the petitioner agreeing to bear the costs of obtaining the divorce.

Separation agreements

Unfortunately legal aid is not available for people wishing to enter into a separation agreement with their spouse. Separation agreements are, however, the preferred route for parties wishing to end their marriage as amicably as possible. This is particularly relevant where there are children, as a petition based on one of the fault grounds inevitably leaves a bad after-taste and often bitterness on the part of at least one of the spouses.

In essence, by entering into a separation agreement, the parties decide to deal with the financial matters relating to their separation before divorce proceedings are issued. The parties agree in advance that they will live apart for a period of two years and the respondent will consent to a decree being granted after the two-year period has passed. Both parties are under a duty to make full disclosure of their assets; they should, with their legal advisers, attempt to agree the financial separation. The terms of the separation agreement can be as simple or complex as the case requires and can include a clean break by way of a lump sum, ongoing maintenance, or the transfer of the matrimonial home or the realisation of part or all of the house's equity. The separation agreement should state the date upon which either party can issue the divorce petition on the two-years' ground and that the other party consents. It should also deal with the costs of bringing the divorce petition. Should the parties wish to make the agreement an order of court, they can do so when the divorce petition is issued.

Although a court will be mindful of the terms of the separation agreement when dealing with the divorce petition, it will not allow an agreement to tie its hands. It is not necessarily bound by the agreement, particularly if one of the parties has attempted to conceal relevant information.

Money matters – ancillary relief

Ancillary relief is the legal term for applications to the courts for financial relief, and includes maintenance pending suit (i.e. maintenance from the date the petition is issued to the granting of the decree absolute), financial provision (maintenance) and property adjustment. In cases other than the ones involving a separation agreement, when a decree nisi has been granted the court will deal with the financial position between the parties. As with the separation agreement, full disclosure of assets and liabilities will be required by both parties. What type of financial settlement the court orders will very much depend on the circumstances of the parties. Clearly most cases will involve some sort of financial provision to be paid by one party to the other. This can very often take the form of a lump sum payment to one party so as to attempt what is still termed a clean break. It is intended that this one-off payment will end any financial responsibility the paying party has to the other. However, since the creation of the CSA and in the light of the new legislation regarding pensions (see page 320) this has not always been the case. The courts may now prefer to order that one party make periodical payments (normally monthly) for the benefit of the other party or the children, for a term of years specified by them.

It is often the case that the only real asset the parties have is the former matrimonial home. This poses difficulties for the courts as clearly the parent with care and the children must have a roof over their heads, but also the other parent must have some means to access his (or, rarely, her) contribution to the home's worth. With this in mind the courts can alter the legal ownership of the matrimonial home (or other properties) by way of a property adjustment order.

Just because a spouse's name is not on the title deeds does not mean that he or she has no rights with respect to what is done about the house. The court may decide that the spouse has an 'equitable' interest in the property if it can be proved that he or she contributed to the family home by either direct or indirect financial contributions.

The Department of Social Security (DSS) may be able to help a divorcing spouse by providing information concerning financial help with housing and welfare benefit, and Benefits Agencies should have details of benefits which can be claimed. Information about help with rent and/or rates can also be obtained from the Northern Ireland Housing Executive.★

The Child Support Agency

The workings of the CSA in Northern Ireland mirror that in England and Wales. Under the Child Support (Northern Ireland) Order 1991 a child 'qualifies' under the scheme if either parent is an 'absent parent'. Article 5 (1) of the order states that each parent is responsible for maintaining a qualifying child and the duty to maintain shall be deemed to have been met where an absent parent makes the payments of maintenance determined by the CSA.

The CSA will be responsible for child maintenance in all cases where there is no existing court order. It is also intended that it will gradually be responsible for cases where there is an existing court order. The Agency will be automatically involved in cases where the parent who is looking after the child is in receipt of state benefits.

The 1991 order provides for considerable powers of enforcement and the Agency may use DSS or Inland Revenue records to trace absent parents. Also if a parent with care refuses to cooperate by naming the child's father, she may incur a deduction in benefit.

The Children (Northern Ireland) Order 1995

Until 4 November 1996 Northern Ireland did not have any legislation in place equivalent to the Children's Act 1989. However, the 1995 order brings legislation relating to children in line with the rest of the UK and creates a new concept of 'parental responsibility'. Where parents are divorcing and there are children of the marriage the courts in Northern Ireland will no longer make custody or access orders but will make what are termed 'article 8' orders, most important of which are residence and contact orders.

A residence order, as the name suggests, settles the issue of which parent the children of the family are to live with. Normally the other parent will be given a contact order, which will allow the children to visit or stay with him or her. Residence and contact orders will usually remain in force until the child reaches the age of 16 and parents will continue to have parental responsibility for their children even when they are no longer living with them.

It is important to note that the 1995 Children Order explicitly states, as does its counterpart in England and Wales, that when deciding where a child should live and who should have contact with the child the courts will consider the child's welfare to be of paramount importance.

Pensions

The Pensions Act 1995 which applies to England and Wales and which affects petitions lodged from 1 July 1996 also by virtue of section 166, inserts new sections into the Matrimonial Causes (Northern Ireland) Order 1978. As a result the courts must now consider pension benefits – both personal and occupational – when considering the divorce settlement.

As explained in Chapter 10 the courts will award one spouse a percentage of the capital value of the other's pension fund from the date of the divorce by making an 'attachment order' earmarking that percentage for the benefit of that spouse. Each case will be considered individually and a 50:50 split is by no means inevitable. As has been highlighted in Chapter 10 there are drawbacks to the legislation, the most obvious ones of which are that the benefiting ex-spouse has no control over the pension fund or the date when the pension holder chooses to retire, and most importantly that the pension itself may cease whenever the pension holder dies. This should be carefully considered by the spouse to whom the award is made as clearly it is a severe disadvantage in obtaining an attachment order. It may therefore be more prudent to consider a lump sum instead of a percentage of the ex-spouse's pension.

Domestic violence

In Northern Ireland a spouse or cohabitant who suffers from domestic violence can apply under the Domestic Proceedings (Northern Ireland) Order 1980 to the magistrate's court for protection. Articles 18 and 19 of the order provide for a personal protection order and exclusion order. The orders can also be applied for to safeguard any children of the family.

Article 18 of the 1980 order sets out the grounds for obtaining a personal protection order. These are that the other party has used or threatened to use violence against the party applying for the order or child of the family, and that such an order is necessary for the protection of either or both of them.

Article 19 sets out the grounds for obtaining an exclusion order. They are that the other party has used or threatened to use violence against the applicant or child of the family or that the other party is in breach of a personal protection order and that an exclusion order is necessary for the protection of the other parties. An exclusion order excludes the violent party from the matrimonial home or the area in which the home is situated. It can also include other properties such as a women's refuge.

Parties suffering from domestic violence can, after seeing a solicitor, apply to the magistrates' court for immediate relief. Some magistrates' courts may require an affidavit, although very often oral evidence from the party suffering the violence will suffice. Once satisfied that there is evidence of domestic violence the magistrate will issue an interim personal protection order and/or exclusion order and set a date for a full hearing (usually within a month) which the other violent party can attend. If the magistrate is satisfied that there has been domestic violence at the second hearing he or she may issue a personal protection order for which there is no time limited by legislation and/ or an exclusion order for a maximum of six months, which may be extended.

Breaching either order is a criminal offence and the police have powers to arrest the person doing so.

Glossary

absent parent   A term laid down by the Child Support Act 1991 to mean the parent not living in the same household with the qualifying child (q.v.)

access   See contact

acknowledgement of service   Form sent by the court to the respondent (and co-respondent, if any) with the petition, with questions about his or her intentions and wishes in response to the petition; its return to the court establishes service of the petition

adultery   Sexual intercourse by a husband or wife with a third party at any time before a decree absolute

affidavit   A statement in writing containing a person's evidence, on oath or by affirmation. The evidence in the affidavit need not be expressed in any formal way but should be set out in numbered paragraphs in the first person. If the person making the affidavit wishes to refer to any document, this document should be attached ('exhibited') to the affidavit

ancillary relief   General term for the financial or property adjustment orders that the court can be asked to make 'ancillary' to a petition for divorce or judicial separation

annuity   Money investment designed to produce regular fixed amounts of income, either for a fixed period or until death

answer   The defence to a divorce petition, denying the allegations in the petition or cross-petition; strict time limits apply for filing an answer

application   A document giving details, in broad terms, of the order sought from the court. All applications within divorce proceedings are started by filing a notice of application. Standard forms are available at divorce court offices; they include a space for the place, date and time of the hearing of the application, to be completed by the court office

Calderbank letter   Where a husband knows he will be ordered to make payment if the case goes to hearing, his solicitor can write a 'without preju- dice' letter making an offer of settlement; if the wife rejects the offer and at the hearing is awarded the same or less, she risks having to pay the husband's costs incurred after the date of the offer as well as her own; a wife can, similarly, make a Calderbank offer

care and attention   A term used to describe an uplift (increase) in a solicitor's legal bill which some solicitors apply if a case has been complex or has had to be dealt with especially quickly

care and control   An old order pre-dating the Children Act 1989 – care and control orders are no longer made. It means the responsibility for looking after and making everyday decisions about a child and providing the child's main home base

in chambers   When the district judge or judge considers an application in private rather than in open court; the proceedings tend to be less formal than normal court hearings and members of the public are not admitted

charge (on property)   Security entitling the holder of the charge to be paid out of the proceeds of sale when the house (or other property) is eventually sold

chattels   A legal term used for personal effects, usually of a house, like furniture, paintings, jewellery and ornaments

child of the family   Any child of both the parties and any child who has at any time been treated by both the parties as if a child of their own (but not foster-children); has to be listed in the petition irrespective of age

clean break   A once-and-for-all order that deals with all financial issues between spouses, provides for the dismissal of maintenance claims and is not capable of subsequent variations even if circumstances change

conciliation   A process of non-partisan mediation to help a couple reach agreement on issues flowing from divorce; more usually about the arrangements for children than about comprehensive financial issues. Conciliation can be 'in-court' as part of the court process to try to help parties settle their differences over the children, or 'voluntary' i.e. provided by an independent service, for which fees may be payable (see Mediation)

conflict of interest(s)   Where a solicitor cannot act for a potential client because he or she would be unable to discharge his or her duty to the client because of a pre-existing professional relationship to another client or a duty owed to another

consent order   Order made by a court in terms agreed by both parties

contact (formerly termed access)   An order under the Children Act for the child to visit or stay with the parent with whom the child is not living or exchange letters, cards or telephone calls; contact orders may also be made in favour of non-parents, e.g. grandparents (the obligation to provide contact is on the parent with whom the child lives)

co-respondent   The person with whom the respondent has committed adultery

counsel   Barrister

cross-decrees When a petitioner is granted a decree on the basis of the petition and the respondent on the basis of the answer

cross-petition When the respondent puts forward different reasons for the breakdown of the marriage from the petitioner's, and seeks a divorce on those facts

custody The right formerly granted by a court for one parent (or both) to make major decisions for a child, such as education and upbringing, change of religion (subject to the non-custodial parent's right to ask the court to review any such decision). An old order pre-dating the Children Act 1989: custody orders are no longer made

decree absolute At present the order dissolving the marriage

decree nisi Document issued once the court is satisfied that the grounds for divorce are established, allowing the petitioner to apply to have the decree made absolute after a further six weeks and one day. It does not end the marriage

directions for trial The stage of divorce proceedings when the district judge considers the petition and affidavit in support, and requests further information if required, before giving his or her certificate for a decree nisi to be pronounced by the judge; financial proceedings and applications about the children also have a directions for trial stage, when the district judge considers what further evidence will be required and makes orders accordingly

disclosure Full information about all matters relevant to any financial application; each spouse has a duty to give full and frank disclosure which if they fail to abide by may render a later court order invalid

discovery Procedure by which each party supplies to the other a list of documents relevant to an application and permits the other to inspect them

district judge Judicial officer appointed by the Lord Chancellor; responsible for dealing with most applications to a divorce court (used to be called a registrar)

divorce court Any county court designated by the Lord Chancellor as a court where divorce proceedings can be heard; the Divorce Registry in London serves as a divorce court. Divorce county courts not designated Family Hearing Centres (FHCs; q.v.) can deal only with the administrative process of divorces; any contested applications will be referred to an FHC

divorce order To be introduced under the Family Law Act 1996, the order dissolving the marriage

domicile Legal concept, not necessarily related to residence: domicile of origin is normally determined by the place where a person was born and is retained unless a new domicile – a domicile of choice – is adopted by a conscious decision to take up permanent residence in, and actually moving to, another country

equity (of a property)   The net value of house or flat after mortgage debts are discharged and expenses of sale met

exhibit   Document referred to in, sworn with, and attached to an affidavit; usually identified by initials and number

ex parte   An application made directly to the court without prior notification to the party or parties

Family Hearing Centre   A county court with the power to deal with the administrative process of divorce and any contested applications under the Children Act or for financial relief

filing   Leaving documents – petition and accompanying documents, affidavits, notices of application, for example – with the court office for sealing, and subsequent service

green form   Popular term for legal aid scheme under which a limited amount of legal advice and assistance is given

hearsay evidence   A fact reported to a witness, as opposed to being known by the witness; secondhand knowledge; hearsay evidence can be accepted by a court in family proceedings

injunction   Order by the court telling someone what he or she must do or must refrain from doing; the penalty for disobedience can be imprisonment

intestacy   Dying without a valid will

legal aid   Government-funded scheme administered by the Legal Aid Board based on financial eligibility and merits of case

liable relative proceedings   Proceedings taken by the Department of Social Security against person legally responsible for maintaining wife or husband and/or children who has failed to do so; usually predate Child Support Act 1991

Maintenance Application Form and Maintenance Enquiry Form   Standard forms sent out by the Child Support Agency to parents with care and absent parents respectively asking them about their means and circumstances

matrimonial home rights   Rights of occupation of a family home (or a home intended to be occupied as a family home) which last until decree absolute – to be introduced by the new Family Law Act 1996

mediation   An alternative form of dispute resolution over issues arising in the wake of separation or divorce. Comprehensive (or 'all issues') mediation covers problems over both the children and finances; other mediation (or conciliation, the terms are sometimes used interchangeably) services may deal with child-related disputes alone. Mediation may be offered by lawyer mediators or family mediators alone or both together

minutes of order   Draft terms of agreement placed before the court with a request that a consent order be made in those terms

mortgagee   The building society, bank or other corporate lender, or individual lending money on the security of a house or flat

mortgagor   The person who borrows money on mortgage usually to enable him or her to buy a house or flat

nominal order   An order for a nominal amount of maintenance (for example, 5p a year) made if, at the time an order for maintenance was made, payment could not be made or was not needed. This is done so that if circumstances change, there is an order on the court's file which can be reviewed and increased

non-molestation   Order to prohibit one person from assaulting, harassing or interfering with another

notice of application   Form on which applications to the court are made, beginning with the words 'Take notice that . . .' and containing full details of what is applied for

ouster   Order excluding one spouse from the matrimonial home (or from a part of it)

parental responsibility   The bundle of rights and duties that parents have towards their children; mothers and married fathers have parental responsibility automatically, while non-married fathers may acquire it by formal Parental Responsibility agreement or court order; others (e.g. guardians, a person with a residence order in his or her favour, a local authority) can acquire parental responsibility too

parent with care   A term laid down by the Child Support Act 1991 to mean the parent with whom the child has his or her home and who usually provides day-to-day care for the child

penal notice   A warning endorsed on a court order, notifying the recipient that he or she is liable to committal to prison for breach of the order

pending suit   While the divorce is still continuing (i.e. before decree absolute)

petitioner   The person who initiates divorce proceedings by filing the petition

pleadings   Formal statements or documents containing a summary of the issues in a case

prayer   Formal request in the petition, or answer, for the court orders which the petitioner or respondent seeks; for example, dissolution of the marriage, orders under the Children Act, costs, ancillary relief

prohibited steps order   Court order under the Children Act restricting a person's exercise of parental responsibility (e.g. preventing a parent from removing a child from the country without the other parent's consent or court permission)

qualifying child   A term laid down by the Child Support Act 1991 to mean a child under 16 or under 19 and in full-time non-advanced education – one of his or her parents must be an 'absent parent' (q.v.)

questionnaire   List of questions delivered by one spouse to the other requiring further information and/or documentation about finances, in accordance with that person's duty of disclosure; also referred to as 'request under Rule 2.63', the rule of court permitting such a questionnaire

recovered or preserved   Gained or retained (money or property) in the course of legal proceedings

relevant child   Child of the family under 16 years of age at the date of the decree nisi or between 16 and 18 years of age receiving instruction at an educational establishment or undergoing training for a trade, profession or vocation (or up to any age, if disabled and dependent)

reply   Document filed by the petitioner in response to an answer and/or a cross-petition from the respondent, containing the petitioner's defence

reserved costs   When decision on amount of costs to be awarded is deferred until later hearing

residence order   An order under the Children Act which settles the arrangements about with whom a child will live; residence orders can be split between parents (or others) or shared, e.g. in favour of a parent and stepparent

respondent   The spouse who is not the petitioner

Rule 2.63   The rule of court relating to the statement of information which has to be supplied to the court for a financial consent order to be made

sealing by the court   The court's stamping of a document when it is filed at the court office or for an order or decree when it is issued

Section 41 appointment   Or 'children's appointment' – this was a short hearing before a judge for certificate of satisfaction in respect of arrangements for any relevant children before decree nisi could be pronounced. Section 41 appointments are no longer made since the Children Act came into force

secured provision   When some income-producing asset of the payer is put under the control of trustees and, if necessary, the income diverted to the payee to provide the maintenance

separation order   A new order to be introduced by the Family Law Act 1996 which will provide for the formal legal separation of the spouses

SERPS   The earnings part of state retirement pension based on National Insurance contributions paid by an employee on earnings between the lower and upper earnings limits

service   The method by which the petition, notices of application, orders and decrees are supplied to the parties concerned; certain documents need to be served personally, others are served through the post, some by or on behalf of the person issuing them and some by the court

special procedure   In an undefended divorce, the decree can be issued without either petitioner or respondent having to appear (or be represented) at the court: the facts submitted by the petitioner in the petition and verified on affidavit are considered by the district judge. When he or she is satisfied that the facts in the petition are proved and that the ground for a divorce exists, he or she issues a certificate to that effect and fixes a date for the formal pronouncement of the decree nisi by the judge. A copy of the decree is sent through the post to both husband and wife by the court office

specific issue order   An order under the Children Act resolving some particular dispute (e.g. schooling) about the children's upbringing

statement of arrangements   Form which has to be filed with petition if there are relevant children of the family, setting out arrangements proposed for them in the future; this should be agreed with the respondent and countersigned if possible before the divorce is started

statutory charge   The amount payable by legally aided person out of any property or cash that was recovered or preserved in the proceedings, where contributions to legal aid fund not sufficient to meet the legal costs of the case (in matrimonial proceedings, maintenance and a lump sum of £2,500 are currently exempt but this may change)

summons   Demand issued by a court for a person against whom a claim or complaint has been made to appear at the court at a specified time

undefended divorce   Where the dissolution of the marriage and how it is to be achieved are not disputed (even if there is dispute about ancillary matters such as the children or finances)

undertaking   Promise to the court to do or not do something which is outside the court's powers to order but is incorporated within a court order so that it is enforceable; the court has no power of its own to vary an undertaking

unfunded scheme   A pension scheme where the employee has a right or expectation to a pension benefit secured only by an undertaking from the employer, for example in a contract of employment; no advance financial provision is made via a trust fund or other insurance contract

without prejudice   Phrase used to prevent communications in the negotiation process being made known to the court if those negotiations fail to produce agreement; however, Calderbank offers and responses to them can be disclosed to the court in evidence over costs

Addresses

Alcoholics Anonymous
Head office, tel: (01904) 644026
London helpline, tel: 0171-352 3001

Asian Family Counselling Service
74 The Avenue
London W13 8LB
Tel: 0181-997 5749
Fax: 0181-998 1880

Association for Shared Parenting
PO Box 2000
Dudley
West Midlands DY1 1YZ
Tel: (01789) 751157
Promotes the need for estranged
parents to play an equal part in the
care and upbringing of their
children. Has a number of regional
branches, and offers help and
support to parents, grandparents
and other relatives of a child who,
as a result of separation or divorce,
is experiencing difficulties.

Association of Consulting Actuaries
1 Wardrobe Place
London EC4V 5AH
Tel: 0171-248 3163
Fax: 0171-236 1889
Email: acahelp@aca.org.uk
Web site: http://www.aca.org.uk

Bar Council
2/3 Cursitor Street
London EC4A 1NE
Tel: 0171-440 4000 (*for advice and a
complaints form*)
or
3 Bedford Row
London WC1R 4DB
Tel: 0171-242 0082 (*for advice and to
obtain publications/leaflets*)
Fax: 0171-831 9217

Bar Pro-Bono Unit
7 Grays Inn Square
London WC1R 5AZ
Tel: 0171-831 9711
Fax: 0171-831 9733
Office open only Mon, Tue and Thurs

Both Parents Forever
39 Cloonmore Avenue
Orpington
Kent BR6 9LE
Tel: (01689) 854343
Provides help and advice to all
parents and grandparents involved
in divorce, separation or care
proceedings.

British Association of Lawyer
Mediators (BALM)
The Shooting Lodge
Guildford Road
Sutton Green
Guildford
Surrey GU4 7PZ
Tel: (01483) 235000
Helpline, tel: (0700) 766422

Cambridge Family and Divorce
Centre
1 Brooklands Avenue
Cambridge CB2 2BB
Tel: (01223) 576308
Fax: (01223) 576309

Child Abduction Unit
Official Solicitor's Department
4th Floor
81 Chancery Lane
London WC2A 1DD
Tel: 0171-911 7047/7140
Fax: 0171-911 7248

Childline
Helpline, tel: (0800) 1111
A confidential listening and
advisory service.

The Child Poverty Action Group
1/5 Bath Street
London EC1V 9PY
Tel: 0171-253 3406
Produces *The National Welfare
Benefits Handbook*, which covers
income support and other means-
tested benefits, *The Rights Guide to
Non-Means-Tested Benefits*, which
covers other social security benefits,
and the *Child Support Handbook*,
which provides detailed
information on the Child Support
Agency. Those on welfare benefits
can obtain the publications at
reduced prices.

Children's Legal Centre
University of Essex
Wivenhoe Park
Colchester
Essex CO4 3SQ
Helpline, tel: (01206) 873820
(weekdays 10–12, 2–5)
Fax: (01206) 874026
National organisation aiming to
improve the law and policy
affecting children in England and
Wales. Advice by telephone or
letter for children with legal
problems, service also available for
adults.

Child Support Agency
Enquiry line, tel: (0345) 133133

Child Support Practitioners' Group
c/o James Pirrie
Russell Jones & Walker
Swinton House
324 Grays Inn Road
London WC1X 8DH
Tel: 0171-837 2808
A group of about 200 solicitors
with experience in legal problems
relating to the Child Support
Agency. Will supply, where
possible (not fully nationwide),
names and addresses of local
solicitor members.

**Comprehensive Accredited Lawyer
Mediators (CALM)**
Caroline Graham
MacLeod & MacCallum
PO Box 4
28 Queens Gate
Inverness
Tel: (01463) 239393
Fax: (01463) 222879
Members are available to mediate all
issues arising from breakdown of
relationships.

Council of Mortgage Lenders
3 Savile Row
London W1X 1AF
Tel: 0171-437 0075 (*ask for the
information line*)
Provides a useful free leaflet called
Assistance with Mortgage Payments.

**Disability Working Allowance
Unit**
2 The Pavilions
Portway
Preston PR2 2GN
Tel: (01772) 883300
Fax: (01772) 898293

The Divorce Corporation
187 Baslow Road
Totley
Sheffield S17 4DG
Tel: 0114-262 0616
Fax: 0114-235 0878
Provides pensions reports for
matrimonial lawyers.

**Divorce Mediation and Counselling
Service**
38 Ebury Street
London SW1W 0LU
Tel: 0171-730 2422

Divorce Registry
Somerset House
Strand
London WC2R 1LP
(*personal visits or letters only*)

Fairshares
Flat 2
Homer's House
Church Street
Rugby
Warwickshire CV21 3PT

Families Need Fathers
134 Curtain Road
London EC2A 3AR
Tel: 0171-613 5060
Information line, tel: 0181-886 0970
Represents non-residential parents
and their children, and is primarily
concerned with the problems of
keeping children and parents in
contact after family breakdown. A
national network of volunteers
provides advice and support on
children's issues to separated,
divorced or unmarried parents.
Publishes booklets and information
packs, and a quarterly journal.

Family Credit Unit
Tel: (01253) 500050

Family Law Consortium
2 Henrietta Street
London WC2E 8PS
Tel: 0171-420 5000
Fax: 0171-420 5005
Email: slc@tslc.co.uk
Web site: http://tslc.co.uk

Family Mediation Scotland
127 Rose Street
South Lane
Edinburgh EH2 4BB
Tel: 0131-220 1610
Fax: 0131-220 6895

Family Mediation Service
76 Dublin Road
Belfast BT2 7HP
Tel: (01232) 322914
Fax: (01232) 315298

Family Mediators Association
1 Wyvil Court
Wyvil Road
London SW8 2TG
Tel: 0171-720 3336
Fax: 0171-720 7999

Family Records Centre
Public Search Room
1 Myddelton Street
London EC1R 1UW
(*personal visits only*)
Certificate enquiries, tel: 0151-471
4800
General enquiries, tel: 0181-392 5300
Fax: 0181-392 5307
Web site:
http://www.open.gov.uk/pro/
prohome/htm

Family Welfare Association
501–505 Kingsland Road
London E8 4AU
Tel: 0171-254 6251
Provides social work and social care
services to families and individuals,
from NHS referrals only. Staff offer
a variety of services to people facing
social and emotional difficulties,
including family and relationship
problems, bereavement, loneliness,
poverty and unemployment.

Gingerbread
16–17 Clerkenwell Close
London EC1R 0AA
Tel: 0171-336 8183
National helpline, tel: 0171-336 8184
(11–4 Mon–Fri)
Fax: 0171-336 8185
Email:
ginger@lonepar.demon.co.uk
Web site:
http://www.lonepar.demon.co.uk
A support organisation for lone
parents and their families, with
around 200 groups in England and
Wales. Also publishes advice and
information leaflets.

Grandparents Federation
Moot House
The Stow
Harlow
Essex CM20 3AG
Tel & Fax: (01279) 444964
(weekdays)
Gives advice, information and
support to grandparents of children
affected by a divorce, separation or
loss of contact for any other reason.

Jewish Marriage Council
23 Ravenshurst Avenue
London NW4 4EE
Counselling line, tel: 0181-203 6311
Fax: 0181-203 8727
Get advisory service, tel: 0181-203 6314
Crisis helplines, tel: (0345) 581999, 0181-203 6211
Provides a counselling service for Jewish people who are single, married, divorced, separated or widowed.

Land Charges Department
Burrington Way
Plymouth PL5 3LP
Tel: (01752) 635600
Fax: (01752) 766666

HM Land Registry
32 Lincoln's Inn Fields
London WC2A 3PH
Tel: 0171-917 8888
Fax: 0171-955 0110
Web site:
http://www.open.gov.uk/landreg/home.htm

LawGroup UK
85 Croydon Road
Caterham
Surrey CR3 6PD
Tel: (01883) 341341

LawNet
Ince House
60 Kenilworth Road
Leamington Spa
Warwickshire CV32 6JY
Tel: (01926) 886990
Fax: (01926) 886553

Law Society of England and Wales
113 Chancery Lane
London WC2A 1PL
Tel: 0171-242 1222
Provides names and addresses of solicitors. Not an advisory service.

Law Society of Northern Ireland
Law Society House
98 Victoria Street
Belfast BT1 3JZ
Tel: (01232) 231614
Fax: (01232) 232606

Law Society of Scotland
26 Drumsheugh Gardens
Edinburgh EH3 7YR
Tel: 0131-226 7411
Fax: 0131-225 2934
Web site:
http://www.lawscot.org.uk

Legal Aid Board
85 Grays Inn Road
London WC1X 8AA
Tel: 0171-813 1000

Legal Aid Board for Scotland
see Scottish Legal Aid Board

Legal Aid Department
Bedford House
16/22 Bedford Street
Belfast BT2 7FL
Tel: (01232) 246441

Legal Services Ombudsman
22 Oxford Court
Oxford Street
Manchester M2 3WQ
Tel: 0161-236 9532
Fax: 0161-236 2651

London Lesbian and Gay Switchboard
Tel: 0171-837 7324 (24 hours)

London Women's Aid
PO Box 14041
London E1 6NY
Tel: 0171-392 2092
National helpline, tel: (0345) 023468
(weekdays 10–5)

Lord Chancellor's Department
Fax: 0171-210 8740
Email:
mwicksteed@lcdhq.btinternet.com
Web site: http://www.open.gov.uk/
lcd/index.htm

Marriage Care
Clitheroe House
1 Blythe Mews
Blythe Road
London W14 0NW
Tel: 0171-371 1341
Fax: 0171-371 4921
Email:
marriagecare@btinternet.com

Marriage Care (for Scotland)
see Scottish Marriage Care

Marriage Counselling Scotland
105 Hanover Street
Edinburgh EH2 1DJ
Tel: 0131-225 5006
Fax: 0131-220 0639

National Children's Bureau
8 Wakley Street
London EC1V 7QE
Tel: 0171-843 6000
Fax: 0171-278 9512
Web site: http://www.ncb.org.uk

National Council for the Divorced and Separated
PO Box 519
Leicester LE2 3ZE
National helpline, tel: 0116-270 0595
Has around 100 branches
throughout the UK which provide
a venue where people with similar
experiences and problems can meet
and develop new interests.

National Council for One Parent Families
255 Kentish Town Road
London NW5 2LX
Tel: 0171-267 1361
Fax: 0171-482 4851
Works to help parents who are
looking after children on their own,
and produces a range of books,
reports, pamphlets and leaflets on
issues that a lone parent may have to
deal with, including taxation,
housing, social security benefits,
divorce, children and employment.
Most publications are free to lone
parents.

National Debtline
The Birmingham Settlement
318 Summer Lane
Birmingham B19 3RL
Tel: 0121-359 8501 (Mon, Thur
10–4; Tue, Wed 10–7; Fri 10–12)
Advice line, tel: (0645) 500511
Offers free confidential and
independent advice for those with
debt problems; also two free
information packs, on rent and on
mortgage problems.

National Family Mediation
9 Tavistock Place
London WC1H 9SN
Tel: 0171-383 5993

National Housing Federation
175 Grays Inn Road
London WC1X 8UP
Tel: 0171-278 6571
Advises housing associations on
local resources for rented housing,
including special needs.

National Stepfamily Association
Chapel House
18 Hatton Place
London EC1N 8RU
Tel: 0171-209 2460
Fax: 0171-209 2461
Email: tnsa@ukonline.co.uk
Web sites:
http://www.webcreations.co.uk/
stepfamily
http://www.ukonline.co.uk/
national.stepfamily
Counselling line, tel: (0990) 168388
Provides support and information
to stepfamilies, a confidential
telephone counselling service,
books, information sheets and
membership.

**Northern Ireland Housing
Executive**
32–36 Great Victoria Street
Belfast BT2 7BA
Tel: (01232) 317000
Fax: (01232) 248464

**Northern Ireland Women's Aid
Federation**
129 University Street
Belfast BT7 1HP
Tel: (01232) 249358
Helpline, tel: (01232) 331818
(24 hours)

Office of Fair Trading
PO Box 366
Hayes UB3 1XB
Tel: (0870) 606 0321
Produces a number of free
publications about personal finance,
e.g. *Debt – A Survival Guide* and *No
Credit*.

Office for National Statistics
General Register Office
PO Box 2
Southport
Merseyside PR8 2JD
Certificate enquiries, tel: 0151-471
4800
Web site: http://www.ons.gov.uk

**Office for the Supervision of
Solicitors**
Victoria Court
8 Dormer Place
Leamington Spa
Warwickshire CV32 5AE
Helplines, tel: (01926) 822007/8/9
(weekdays 9.30–4.30)
Enquiry desk, tel: (01926) 820082

One Parent Families Scotland
13 Gayfield Square
Edinburgh EH1 3NX
Tel: 0131-556 3899/4563
Fax: 0131-557 9650
Helps all parents bringing up children alone by providing information, publishing leaflets and booklets, offering counselling and establishing local support groups and services.

RELATE National Marriage Guidance Council
Herbert Gray College
Little Church Street
Rugby
Warwickshire CV21 3AP
Tel: (01788) 573241
Local telephone numbers are listed in the telephone directory under RELATE.

RELATE
76 Dublin Road
Belfast BT2 7HP
Tel: (01232) 323454
Fax: (01232) 375298

Resolve
83 Aylestone Road
Leicester LE2 7LL
Tel: 0116-255 2404

Reunite (National Council for Abducted Children)
PO Box 4
London WC1X 3DX
Tel: 0171-404 8356 (Mon, Fri 11–3; Tue, Thur 2–5; Wed 1–8)
Fax: 0171-242 1512
Email: reunite@bircom.co.uk
A self-help network for parents whose children have been abducted.

Scottish Legal Aid Board
44 Drumsheugh Gardens
Edinburgh EH3 7SW
Tel: 0131-226 7061

Scottish Marriage Care
196 Clyde Street
Glasgow G1 4JY
Tel: 0141-204 1239

Scottish Women's Aid
12 Torphichen Street
Edinburgh EH3 8JQ
Tel: 0131-221 0401
Runs refuges for abused women and their children. Also gives information and advice about legal rights and housing. Has network of local branches.

Shelter London
229/231 High Holborn
London WC1V 7DA
Tel: 0171-404 7447

Shelter National Campaign for the Homeless
88 Old Street
London EC1V 9HU
Helpline, tel: (0800) 446441 (24 hours)
If you live outside London, Shelter can give you the telephone number of a Shelter Housing Aid centre near you for help with problems to do with mortgages, occupation of the home, rates, rent and other payments.

Shelter Scottish Campaign for Homeless People
4th floor
Scotiabank House
6 South Charlotte Street
Edinburgh EH2 4AW
Tel: 0131–473 7170

Society of Pension Consultants
St Bartholomew House
92 Fleet Street
London EC4Y 1DH
(*letters only*)

Solicitors Family Law Association
PO Box 302
Orpington
Kent BR6 8QX
Tel: (01689) 850227
Fax: (01689) 855833
Offers a leaflet giving '10 good reasons' why to choose a family solicitor from the association, tel: (0345) 585671. SFLA members subscribe to a Code of Practice, available on request.

Women's Aid (for London)
see London Women's Aid

Women's Aid Federation for England
PO Box 391
Bristol BS99 7WS
National helpline, tel: (0345) 023468 (weekdays 10–5)

Women's Aid (for Northern Ireland)
see Northern Ireland Women's Aid Federation

Women's Aid (for Scotland)
see Scottish Women's Aid

Index

Rent Act 1977 186, 187
rented accommodation 28, 43, 50,
    186–7
request for directions for trial 139–
    40
residence order 119, 122, 161, 165,
    166, 170, 171, 175, 177, 178,
    278, 279, 280, 282, 283, 285,
    295, 301, 302, 319
    costs 34–5
Resolve 89
respondent 124
retirement, and maintenance
    payments 251
Reunite (National Council for
    Abducted Children) 278, 280,
    281
Rule 2.63 questionnaire 211

school fees 262–3
Scotland, divorce in 122, 290–312
Scottish Legal Aid Board 293
section 5 application 203
section 8 orders 161–3, 163, 164,
    165, 166, 175, 176, 177–8, 283,
    285
section 10 application 203
secured payments 230
secured provision 204
self-employment 44, 105, 208, 243,
    244, 258–9
separation
    affidavit 141, 147
    as grounds for divorce 123, 130–1
    attempted reconciliation after 132
    with consent 130–1, 137, 151
    date of 38, 131, 241
    judicial separation 123, 124, 126,
        310–11, 313
    in Northern Ireland 313, 317
    in Scotland 294, 309–11
    without consent 130–1
separation agreements or deeds 60,
    61–2, 114, 122, 124

separation order 123–4, 153
sexual intercourse, refusal to have
    129
sheriff courts 291, 292
social fund loans 59
Society of Pension Consultants 214
solicitors
    advice and assistance 51, 67, 68,
        69–71, 124–5, 147
    contract to provide legal aid
        services 14
    charge on money or property
        'recovered or preserved' 17
    choosing 71–3, 292
    Client Care Code 76
    complaints against 76–7
    conflict of interests 51, 68, 71
    costs 15, 30–2, 76, 125
    CSA, advice about the 101
    disbursements 31, 125
    domestic violence hot-line 270
    franchised firms 13, 14, 15, 21,
        268
    hourly charging rate 15, 30–1
    interim billing 31
    joint appointments 51, 67
    low-priced interview 30, 73–4
    and mediation services 67, 82, 83,
        85, 86, 88–9, 90
    payment for pre-certificate work
        22
    payments on account 31
    personal attendance at court 26
    proposed accreditation scheme
        73
    suing for his/her bill 31
    taxation of costs 31–2, 33–4
    using efficiently 74–6
    work under green form scheme
        13, 14–15
    work under legal aid scheme 13
Solicitors Family Law Association
    (SFLA) 72, 80, 89, 179
special procedure list 147, 148